Praise for
THE POWER OF SELF-ADVOCACY FOR GIFTED LEARNERS

"Self-advocacy is the keystone that has been missing from the arch of gifted education. Deb Douglas offers a solid down-to-earth guide for gifted students to take charge of their education and development. The tools she provides will become lifelong skills. Throughout the text, one hears the voices of students she counseled. One could not ask for a better guide."

—**Michael M. Piechowski**, author of *"Mellow Out," They Say. If I Only Could: Intensities and Sensitivities of the Young and Bright*

"*The Power of Self-Advocacy for Gifted Learners* is a valuable resource for helping gifted teens advocate for their needs in the constantly shifting world of education. Taking into account the risks of leaving students to the winds of chance and changing politics behind programs that often leave much to be desired for gifted needs, this book creates a plan for educating students about their own characteristics and providing them with bridges to reach mentors and others in their lives who can help them reach even further."

—**Kathleen Casper, J.D.,** president of Florida Association for the Gifted, former SENG board member, gifted education consultant, and national speaker and author

"As educators and scholars, we spend enormous amounts of time attempting to design and deliver optimal learning experiences for gifted learners from all backgrounds. Seldom, however, do we actively engage gifted learners in this process by asking what they truly need from us. To do this, the learners must be in the mode of self-discovery and have optional strategies in mind as they advocate for themselves. In this groundbreaking book, Deb Douglas has created a multilayered tool that will help educators working with gifted learners discover the power of self-advocacy. This book has potential to be a game changer in the field of gifted education, making learning a truly valuable experience with lifelong intellectual, academic, and psychosocial benefits."

—**Dr. Joy Lawson Davis**, associate professor of education at Virginia Union University, author of *Bright, Talented & Black: A Guide for Families of African American Gifted Learners*, and former at-large member of Board of Directors, NAGC

"This book provides educators, parents, and health-care providers valuable background information and tools to guide bright children in becoming happy, autonomous, lifelong learners. The author speaks from the heart and shares inspiring, real-life stories of young people who, with direct, systematic instruction in caring relationships, transitioned through the four steps of taking charge of their own learning and their own lives."

—**Rosina M. Gallagher**, Ph.D., NCSP, former president of SENG, the Illinois Association for Gifted Children, and the Illinois School Psychologists Association

"Replete with clear extrapolations of theory and research to practice, *The Power of Self-Advocacy for Gifted Learners* provides explicit guidelines and materials that have been field-tested for use with students. The foundations for self-advocacy are delivered in a style that students will quickly integrate into their personal repertoires for negotiating life. I commend Deb Douglas not only for encapsulating her years of expertise but also for her willingness to share her skillful techniques with others. Ultimately, gifted and talented children are likely to become better prepared for finessing day-to-day challenges thanks to this outstanding book."

—**F. Richard "Rick" Olenchak, Ph.D.,** professor of educational psychology, research methodology, and gifted education, and department head of educational studies at Purdue University

the POWER of SELF-ADVOCACY for GIFTED LEARNERS

TEACHING THE 4 ESSENTIAL STEPS TO SUCCESS

DEB DOUGLAS

free spirit
PUBLISHING®

Library of Congress Cataloging-in-Publication Data

Names: Douglas, Deb, 1950–
Title: The power of self-advocacy for gifted learners : teaching the 4 essential steps to success / by Deb Douglas.
Description: Minneapolis, MN : Free Spirit Publishing Inc., 2017. | Includes bibliographical references and index.
Identifiers: LCCN 2017020786 (print) | LCCN 2017040440 (ebook) | ISBN 9781631982040 (Web PDF) | ISBN 9781631982057 (ePub) | ISBN 9781631982033 (paperback) | ISBN 1631982036 (paperback)
Subjects: LCSH: Gifted children—Education—United States. | Self-culture. | BISAC: EDUCATION / Special Education / Gifted.
Classification: LCC LC3993.9 (ebook) | LCC LC3993.9 .D68 2017 (print) | DDC 371.950973—dc23
LC record available at https://lccn.loc.gov/2017020786

Free Spirit Publishing does not have control over or assume responsibility for author or third-party websites and their content. At the time of this book's publication, all facts and figures cited within are the most current available. All telephone numbers, addresses, and website URLs are accurate and active; all publications, organizations, websites, and other resources exist as described in this book; and all have been verified as of July 2017. If you find an error or believe that a resource listed here is not as described, please contact Free Spirit Publishing. Parents, teachers, and other adults: We strongly urge you to monitor children's use of the Internet.

All names of students and parents used within have been changed to protect the privacy of the individuals.

Cover and book design by Shannon Pourciau
Edited by Meg Bratsch

10 9 8 7 6 5 4 3 2 1
Printed in the United States of America

Free Spirit Publishing Inc.
6325 Sandburg Road, Suite 100
Minneapolis, MN 55427-3674
(612) 338-2068
help4kids@freespirit.com
www.freespirit.com

FSC
www.fsc.org
MIX
Paper from
responsible sources
FSC® C005010

Free Spirit offers competitive pricing.
Contact edsales@freespirit.com for pricing information on multiple quantity purchases.

Dedication

This book is dedicated to my sons, Drew and Wyn, who from their earliest days made me curious about this thing called giftedness and all it entails; and to my husband, Ray Aldag, whose sage advice and gentle encouragement keep me going.

Acknowledgments

My gratitude goes out to many who made this book possible: To all the students who have shared their experiences of struggle and success with me; without them the pages in this book would be blank. To Jim Delisle, whose work led me to believe students must be our partners in their education. To George Betts, Maureen Neihart, and Karen Rogers, whose insights and research gave structure to my process and practice. To Tom Zigan, my colleague, encourager, grammarian, punctuation guru, and friend. To my former colleagues in the Manitowoc Public School District EXCEL program, especially Lori Williams (my left brain) and Jody Ackley, who worked valiantly to keep the lights on. To my late husband, David Douglas, who encouraged me to follow my professional passions. To Susanne Skubal, who for oh-so-many years has been that one true friend every introvert needs. To my parents, Eleanor and Ralph Oltman, who gave me the start in life that I would wish for every child. To my husband, Ray, who read every word, caught every typo, and added much wisdom and insight. And finally, to my editor Meg Bratsch, who believed in my message and infused it with clarity and precision.

CONTENTS

LIST OF FIGURES

LIST OF REPRODUCIBLE FORMS

See page 194 for instructions on how to download customizable digital versions of the reproducible forms. Forms marked with an asterisk (*) are available only in the digital content.

FOREWORD

When I was in first grade, my teacher, Sister Patricia Ann, realized that I knew how to tell time. "It's 10:16 a.m. and 20 seconds," I'd remind her when she forgot to release us for our scheduled 10:15 recess. I'm sure I was a thorn in her side at times, yet Sister Patricia Ann did something for me that began my lifelong journey as an educator: she asked me to help her teach my classmates how to tell time. Armed with an analog clock made out of cardboard, I taught my lessons with relish and aplomb. I'm not sure how well the other kids learned what I already knew, but I certainly appreciated the chance to show them.

In my combined fourth/fifth-grade classroom, Sister Elizabeth pulled me, a fourth grader, aside one October day and told me she was going to change my seat. "I think you should sit in the row nearest the fifth graders," she said. "You're ready for the lessons I'll be teaching them."

These two examples, and others like them that occurred in subsequent years, showed me that my advanced academic skills were appreciated and accommodated by the people who taught me. Not every teacher was as observant or flexible, but I remember most fondly the ones who were. At the time, I don't recall being especially cognizant of the difference these teachers made in my life, but now, nearly forty years into my profession as an educator, I realize the incredible opportunities that opened up for me as a result of their caring and advocacy.

I didn't realize that it was within my power to ask for such changes, yet I was lucky enough to have some teachers who understood the importance of making my education as relevant as possible. From afar, I thank these educators for their commitment to my learning. And today, thanks to this book, all teachers have access to information that will help students like me advocate for their own challenging educational experiences.

The Power of Self-Advocacy for Gifted Learners is a unique book that will change the lives of the students in your care and in your classrooms. Unlike any volume before, this book describes, through both personal examples and detailed techniques, methods for helping gifted students take charge of their educations. The processes described for student self-advocacy are respectful, professional, and goal-focused, empowering gifted kids to make the most of their learning by asking for assistance, direction, and flexible options.

Perhaps the biggest reason that the ideas presented in this book are so valid is that they are given to you by Deb Douglas, an educator who has advocated for her gifted students over several decades. I have known Deb for over twenty years, and I have seen firsthand the ways she has helped her gifted students by giving them the tools to be their own best advocates. Each chapter in this book has stories of kids whose educations—indeed, whose *lives*—were changed forever thanks to Deb's guidance and experience. And now Deb provides you with all the tools you will need to be a transformative educator.

Near the end of her book, Deb writes, "Failing to plan is planning to fail." In too many instances, gifted kids are left on the sidelines of learning because they don't know how to advocate for their own educational interests. All that stops now. *The Power of Self-Advocacy for Gifted Learners* provides the instructional and emotional guidance you and your students will need to help them be successful, challenged, and happy. Enjoy the journey.

Jim Delisle, Ph.D.

Coauthor (with Judy Galbraith) of *The Gifted Teen Survival Guide* and author of *Dumbing Down America: The War on Our Nation's Brightest Young Minds (and What We Can Do to Fight Back)*

INTRODUCTION

"What do you need?" I asked a gifted student more than a decade ago. "What do you want to do differently?"

Ryan, a highly creative eighth grader, was acting out in class and his grades were dropping. I was pretty sure the traditional path through high school to graduation wasn't going to work for him. But I was stumped about what was going to work. I'd been working in gifted education for some time, but the obvious hadn't occurred to me until that moment: "Ryan is a bright kid. I should just ask him what he needs."

But Ryan was caught off guard by my question. He stared at me quizzically, shrugged his shoulders, and replied, "Nothing. Really, everything's fine."

But I couldn't let it go. I was sure Ryan knew what he wanted to change; he just needed to speak up. Ryan, however, was confused for good reason. The adults in his life, including myself, had never prepared him for that question. He didn't know why he was struggling. He didn't know he had options. He didn't know he had the right to seek alternatives that would better address his specific needs. He didn't feel comfortable asking us for help.

In short, he didn't know how to be his own advocate.

And truthfully, I didn't know much about self-advocacy in education either, so I turned to the internet. My search returned over 9 million results; virtually all of them about helping students with learning difficulties rather than advanced abilities. Perhaps the strongest definition of self-advocacy came from Loring Brinckerhoff, director of the Office of Disability Policy at Educational Testing Service, who described it as "the process of recognizing and meeting the needs specific to one's learning ability without compromising the dignity of oneself or others."[1] Since struggling *and* gifted learners fall outside the norm, it made sense that each group should be empowered to self-advocate.

So, Ryan and I spent many hours together in the next few months. We talked about what giftedness is (and isn't) and assessed his learning strengths as well as areas for improvement. We looked at what options would be available to him in high school and which were best for him. We listed his rights and responsibilities as a student and those of the district. Gradually, Ryan began to understand what I had meant when I asked him what he needed and why it was important to advocate for himself. And then, with Ryan leading the way, we created a step-by-step plan for his success. We also toured the high school and I introduced him to the adults who would be there to help him: his future school counselor, teachers, department heads, and principal. With a renewed sense of self-efficacy, Ryan's grades and behavior improved and his teachers began to see him as the smart, creative, and humorous person that he was rather than as a disruption.

My quest to help gifted students speak up for themselves is quite personal to me. And I'm guessing that it is personal for you as well. Who among us hasn't felt heartbroken for someone we care about who has experienced the challenge of being gifted? The loneliness, anxiety, humiliation, shame, frustration, despair. We are all at times insensitive to the challenges our students face, even though we work hard to stay tuned in.

I remember all too well the sixth-grade girl I knew who was partnered all day, every day, all year with a slower learner so the girl could learn humility and the "joy" of helping others.

And the brilliant little boy living in poverty whose well-worn pants split during the spelling bee. He misspelled an easy word so he could sit down and hide his shame.

And the talented teen painter who, after overhearing her mother claim her brother was their "family artist," never again lifted a paintbrush.

And the young boy in music class who wept with joy at hearing Rachmaninoff for the first time and then endured taunts on the playground for weeks.

And the precocious but bored middle school student whose math teacher announced loudly as she handed back his test, "I expected more from someone who thinks he's so smart."

And the young gifted writer who stayed up all night to write a five-paragraph essay because her teacher told the class to "turn in your best work."

We see our own experiences reflected in those of our students. We want to save them and let them know "It can be better tomorrow and I'll work with you to make sure it is."

This is not a book about helping students get into a selective college or preparing them for a lucrative career. It's not about teaching kids to wait until that ephemeral, magical moment down the road—advanced high school classes or electives or graduate school—when education suddenly makes sense. Rather, this book is about helping gifted middle school and high school students satisfy their love of learning right now. It's about making them feel excited, motivated, and challenged to use their innate abilities and passion for understanding every day.

How This Book Is Unique: Jump-Starting Students' Self-Advocacy

As a parent or an educator, you may already believe that all children—especially those with learning exceptionalities—should take a leading role in their educations. And you may already be familiar with much of the literature on gifted learners and their academic, social, and emotional needs. So, what does this book offer that's new? It provides you with a means to jump-start middle school and high school students' self-advocacy. It details much of the information and support that they need to create their personal paths to graduation and beyond.

Over the years I've experimented with various ways to encourage self-advocacy. One of the best methods I've found is a one-day introductory workshop to ignite students' interest and involvement. This book will walk you through how to create one of these workshops, an experience that unites students, parents, and educators in the common goal of advancing education through self-advocacy.

Included are real-life stories of students in grades five through twelve who have struggled to find their

way through "the system." To the best of my knowledge, these students continue to explore life, learning to solve problems, make good decisions, and connect with those who support their efforts. Many of these students I worked with during my years in gifted education. Others I met during the GT Carpe Diem self-advocacy workshops I conduct. These students' stories, as well as their responses to my workshop surveys included throughout the book, shed light on our role as advocates.

About This Book

I wrote this book specifically for the educators and school counselors who work with secondary gifted students and who may want to facilitate student self-advocacy workshops. However, the information and resources presented are also vital for parents, guardians, and other supporters of gifted children who are not in the school setting or who have no in-school advocate.

The first two chapters lay the groundwork for teaching students to self-advocate. These chapters provide evidence supporting the key assumptions regarding gifted learners and their ability and willingness to speak up for themselves. The meaning of self-advocacy is clarified and its benefits for all stakeholders are described. These chapters also examine why gifted students may not be advocating for themselves and the importance of talking with them about their wants and needs.

The middle chapters focus on the four steps that help students begin their own advocacy:

1. Students understand their rights and responsibilities as gifted individuals.
2. Students develop their learner profiles by assessing their abilities and interests, strengths and weaknesses, learning preferences, and personal characteristics.
3. Students investigate available options and opportunities and match them to their learner profiles.
4. Students connect with advocates who can help them accomplish what needs to be done.

The final chapters provide concrete examples of students' action plans and describe the GT Carpe Diem Workshop and accompanying survey that I've been conducting with students for many years to help them take charge of their own educations. These chapters also review the four steps to self-advocacy as they relate to the story of Ryan, the gifted student discussed at the beginning of this introduction. The workshop materials (facilitator's guide, handouts, and surveys) also are included. Here are more detailed descriptions of each chapter.

Chapter 1 begins with a look at six diverse profiles of gifted learners, the way each type of learner relates to the education system, and the needs of each learner in navigating the system and growing toward greater autonomy. It lays out the following integral assumptions about the needs of gifted students:

- Gifted students need to understand themselves as unique individuals.
- Gifted students need programming matched to their learner profiles.
- Gifted students need to grow toward autonomy.
- Gifted students need specific, direct instruction in self-advocacy.

Also included are students' survey responses, which encourage us to talk with students about their giftedness and counter the winds of chance and change that impact their lives.

Chapter 2 focuses on the basic information and beliefs that support teaching gifted learners to advocate for themselves. It discusses the key benefits of self-advocacy for students:

- More appropriate academic challenge
- Increased motivation
- Greater independence and self-direction
- Improved academic performance
- Greater equanimity and less frustration

The chapter also describes benefits to stakeholders, including benefits to other students, parents, classroom teachers, gifted education coordinators, school counselors, and the school district in general. Survey responses provided confirm that without encouragement, gifted learners are unlikely to ask for what they need.

Chapter 3 features the first step in self-advocacy: *understanding one's rights and responsibilities*. It explores gifted students' two important rights:

- The right to understand giftedness and how it relates to their unique selves
- The right to an appropriately challenging education

It also delves into the students' responsibilities to take charge of their educations and to work on developing personal characteristics that will support their success.

Chapter 4 centers on the second step in self-advocacy: *assessing and reflecting on one's learner profile*. The five fields of information that make up the learner profile are explained:

- Cognitive functioning
- Learning strengths
- Interests
- Learning preferences
- Personality characteristics and traits

Student narratives and survey responses provide insights about the value of assessing and reflecting on each of these fields.

Chapter 5 gives details on the third step in self-advocacy: *investigating available options and opportunities and matching them to one's learner profile*. Examples are given in these categories of options most often sought by students:

- Finding more challenging work
- Exploring an interest
- Spending time with gifted peers
- Adjusting their environment to accommodate personal needs

The chapter distinguishes among students who are ready for change, students who are ready and willing, and students who are able to access needed options. Information is provided for each group that will help them choose, accept, or create opportunities that match their learner profiles. The addition of student survey responses underscores the value of educators talking with students about educational alternatives.

Chapter 6 outlines the fourth step in self-advocacy: *connecting with adult advocates who can help accomplish what needs to be done*. The three major responsibilities of these advocates are described:

◆ Communicating the concept of self-advocacy to others
◆ Supporting the practice of self-advocacy
◆ Initiating the individual student's attempts at self-advocacy

The chapter lists a wide range of resources that help each group of primary advocates—parents, educators, counselors, and gifted coordinators—understand and carry out their specific roles in building self-advocacy in students. Included is a chart indicating the possible roles and responsibilities of all stakeholders in the school district.

Chapter 7 provides concrete examples of individual students' plans for change and paths to graduation, demonstrating the value of careful and thoughtful planning. It includes questions that help students consider short- and long-term ramifications of their plans. It also describes the use of a simple Action Plan template.

Chapter 8 is a primer on teaching gifted students to self-advocate. While it lists several methods of direct instruction, the primary focus is the GT Carpe Diem Workshop model. The chapter includes workshop goals, activities, and timelines—all aligned to the NAGC PreK–Grade 12 Gifted Education Programming Standards. Post-workshop input from both students and advocates gives evidence of the model's success.

Chapter 9 concludes the book and reviews the entire self-advocacy process through a final look at Ryan's story.

Appendix A includes a list of useful resources to use with students and to find more information about gifted education and self-advocacy. Books, organizations, and websites are listed for gifted students and for their advocates. **Appendix B** provides the GT Carpe Diem Workshop materials and handouts, including the facilitator's guide and pre- and post-workshop surveys.

Lastly, the **digital content** accompanying this book includes:
◆ Customizable versions of all the reproducible forms
◆ The workshop facilitator's guide and workshop handouts
◆ A PDF presentation for use in the self-advocacy workshops

See page 194 for instructions on how to download these materials.

How to Use This Book

This book has the potential to be used in a variety of ways. First, it can be a resource for understanding the concept of self-advocacy and the information, insights, and tools that we need to share with gifted students for them to successfully self-advocate. If you are new to gifted education and have had few opportunities for professional development, it also may serve as an overview of crucial definitions, theories, characteristics, programming, and support for gifted students.

Experienced educators may find this book to be a good review of information as well as a guide to the next steps in partnering with your students. You may also find it useful in developing staff and parent sessions that prepare adults for their roles as advocates. As a gifted education coordinator, I frequently used books to create a series of monthly blog posts and newsletter articles to share with my staff and parents, each one a summary of a chapter so that by the end of the year we had "read" the book together.

Secondly, you might use this book to create learning experiences that guide students in developing the skill of self-advocacy. Whether you use the GT Carpe Diem Workshop format or design your own model, the key steps, processes, goals, and standards outlined in this book will help ensure that your direct instruction is systematic, continuous, and grounded in research and best practices.

Additionally, this guide can be used for book studies with gifted education staff or parent groups as they consider new ways to serve their students. Regional cooperative education services, especially those including rural schools, might read the book in a study group before conducting their own workshop to bring together students from various districts. **Download a free PLC/Book Study Guide at freespirit.com/PLC.**

Finally, educators and parents may find that one of the most productive uses of this book is to share it with an individual gifted learner. We sometimes underestimate the value of presenting a bright student with "adult" material. But gifted students who are ready for change need to be given clear information, insights, and tools.

My hope is that *The Power of Self-Advocacy for Gifted Learners* will allow us to put the power for change where it rightfully belongs: in the hands of the gifted individual.

I'd love to hear how this book has helped you in your work with gifted learners. If you have stories or questions for me, you can reach me through my publisher at help4kids@freespirit.com or visit my website at www.gtcarpediem.com.

Deb Douglas

1 CHANGE and CHANCE

Change happens. In fact, in the education system, change is the norm. In the time a gifted student journeys from kindergarten to graduation, almost everything changes. The national interest in addressing the needs of gifted students ebbs and flows. Sometimes there's federal funding for research and services, sometimes there isn't. Tracking, equity issues, achievement gaps, and international test scores all impact public perception and contribute to the fluctuating support. The field of gifted education itself shifts over time. Academic arguments persist regarding defining giftedness, talent development, labeling, identification, and best practices. And despite the turmoil, the truth is that the latest research may not impact students' daily lives for years, if at all.

Individual states' and provinces' support for gifted education also rises and falls with the economy, political interests, and assessment data. Often, laws and statutes

go unenforced and concerns such as programming and staffing are left up to individual districts. And those school districts also experience change. Administrators, with varying attitudes about gifted education, come and go. Classroom teachers, with varying preparation and experience in gifted education, come and go. Gifted coordinators and differentiated programming are seen as expendable when budgets are tight.

In short, the possibility of the education system meeting gifted students' unique needs is always in flux. Laws change, funding changes, staffing changes, and parent involvement changes. Educational trends come and go. Some trends are good for gifted kids. Some are not. Moreover, we now know students' abilities, strengths and weaknesses, interests, passions, and learning preferences can all change over time as well.

As advocates for gifted learners, it would be easy for educators and parents to be angry, stressed, anxious, confused, or just plain overwhelmed by all these changes. But rather than waste energy worrying or debating, it's crucial to keep our focus on the students themselves. One truth that doesn't change: In order to grow, each student needs an appropriately challenging education and effective social and emotional support. As John Fischer, former dean of Teachers College at Columbia University, stated: "The essence of our effort to see that every child has a chance must be to assure each an equal opportunity, not to become equal, but to become different—to realize whatever unique potential of body, mind, and spirit she or he possesses."[2]

No matter what the research says is best practice for gifted kids, in most public school districts in the United States and Canada, students are not put in gifted schools or even gifted classrooms or cluster groups. Most gifted students are in heterogeneous classrooms in which teachers may try to differentiate the curriculum and instruction semi-regularly. Many gifted students spend much of each day simply waiting. Waiting to be challenged, waiting to learn something new, waiting to interact with like minds. Many are plainly unaware that their route to graduation can and should be significantly different from that of their peers. Instead they slog on day after day, sometimes challenged and interested, but more frequently not.

While we hope for changes in the system, administration, teachers, budgets, laws, or initiatives that may eventually take place, *today* many gifted kids are starving for that "equal opportunity" to develop their unique potential. Instead of asking them to wait for the system to change, we must put the power of change-making into their hands. Yes, we sometimes forget that the students are primary players in the educational process. No one knows better than the students what is going on in their heads and hearts as they sit in class, walk the halls, complete assignments, and interact with their peers and teachers. As was the case with Ryan—from this book's introduction, who inspired my interest in self-advocacy—when given the information they need, students are best able to decide when, where, and how they want their education to be differentiated.

Our role must be to create and sustain a partnership with students. We must find ways to tell them, "There *is* something you can do right now to change tomorrow or next week or next month or next semester. You can self-advocate by speaking up for yourself, asking for what you need." Self-advocacy, as defined by the *Oxford Dictionary*, is simply "the action of representing oneself or one's views or interests." By sharing the four steps of self-advocacy detailed in this book, we can help gifted learners better navigate the education system and adapt it to meet their needs.

Gifted Profiles and the Education System

There is a myth that all gifted students are alike: they come from educated and supportive families, enjoy school, test well, earn good grades, and are admired by peers and teachers. The work of George Betts and Maureen Neihart, in *Profiles of the Gifted and Talented*, upends that misconception.[3] They describe six profiles of gifted learners, which I've summarized in the following sections and paired with real-life examples. Complete descriptions of all six profiles can be found in **Figure 1.1** on pages 9–12. *Note:* By using the monikers "Successful Learner," "At-Risk Learner," and others to refer to particular learners throughout the book, I don't intend to label students but rather to describe the different attributes and challenges they may possess at certain times during their school careers.

Type I: Successful Learners

Successful Learners have figured out how to adapt to the system. While Type I's are typically identified for gifted programs, frequently fit the stereotype described in the previous paragraph, and often have options at their disposal that allow them to grow, that doesn't mean they pursue those options. Sometimes they get bored, take the path of least resistance, or fail to develop their intellectual curiosity. Gifted students who earn good grades may seem successful, but may actually be underperforming. For instance, some students play the academic game, assuring they have just enough points for an A, but going no further. In the second semester of his senior year, Jason told me he was only taking PE, the last remaining half-credit he needed to graduate, because he'd already been accepted to his first-choice college and thought he deserved some "time off." For him, school was a chore, a means to an end. He hadn't yet recognized the intrinsic joy found in investigating new concepts, exploring a passion, or simply learning something challenging for fun.

Type II: Creative Learners

Creative Learners find the system overly rigid and haven't learned to use it to their advantage. Type IIs are often recognized for their nonconformity but not necessarily for attributes that would indicate a need for advanced programming. In fact, they are sometimes viewed as underperforming because their interests do not align with the school curriculum. Selena's passion for music led her to spend hours composing and playing drums with her garage band. But she refused to join the high school marching band ("Really, marching band? You've got to be kidding!"), even though district policy required it as a prerequisite to the advanced music courses in composition, theory, jazz, and independent study that would have engaged her.

Type III: Underground Learners

Underground Learners deny their abilities because their social milieu is at odds with the system. Type IIIs realize that friends, family, and/or their culture deem intellectual pursuits a lower priority. Nia's family expected her to fulfill traditional roles. Like other girls in her community, she spent after-school hours and weekends helping at home, babysitting for siblings, or hanging out with her girlfriends when she had time. She was expected to focus on her family's needs and prepare for marriage and motherhood. She brushed off recommendations to take honors courses, saying she just wasn't interested rather than admitting that her family and friends saw little need for her to pursue academic challenges. Students like Nia, who fail to accept challenges, may appear unmotivated or disinterested in academic pursuits.

Type IV: At-Risk Learners

At-Risk Learners find the system hostile and irrelevant. Type IVs are angry—with the adults around them and with themselves—because they have been in the education pipeline for years and their needs have not been met. They feel misunderstood and rejected and are often identified as underachieving rather than as gifted. Katie moved from district to district and school to school so often that no educator had a chance to know her well. School meant ubiquitous assessments to determine what she had been taught in the past and remediate what she'd missed through transferring. Even when her IQ was determined to be in the 99th percentile, acceleration and enrichment were never considered. With nothing more interesting on the horizon, she resorted to truancy and hanging out at the mall.

Type V: Twice/Multi-Exceptional (2E) Learners

2E Learners' time within the system is focused on their disabilities rather than strengths. Type Vs are frequently

overlooked when using traditional means of identifying gifts because their disabilities or learning differences overshadow their abilities. In other instances, their extraordinary aptitudes mask their struggles and their disabilities go undiagnosed because they appear "average." In second grade, Alex was diagnosed with dyslexia and ADHD, and he was already seeing a speech therapist twice a week at school. Although his teachers recognized his creativity, advanced vocabulary, and intellectual curiosity, the elementary enrichment program required high reading skills and time away from the regular classroom. Year after year there simply wasn't enough time in the day to address both Alex's special needs and his need for acceleration. Remediation took priority.

Type VI: Autonomous Learners

Autonomous Learners have figured out how to use the education system to create their unique educational paths. Type VIs do not work for the system, but instead make the system work for them (and sometimes in the process wind up changing the system itself!). Like many gifted students, school often seemed uninteresting and irrelevant to Tyler. But in middle school Spanish class, he discovered that he loved languages. No other languages were offered until high school so he found a free online Latin course and took it on his own. He also started a weekly lunch club where he and others could converse in Spanish. By demonstrating his commitment, he gained approval to begin French in eighth grade. He planned his four-year high school schedule to include as many elective language classes as possible. By the time he was accepted at a college with a renowned language program, he was fluent in Spanish, Latin, French, German, and Japanese.

Of course, students may fit into more than one of these profiles and can move between profiles over time as their lives and experiences change. Ultimately, I've found that the students most satisfied with school are those on the path to becoming Autonomous Learners. We can help all students move in that direction by teaching them to self-advocate.

continued ▲

FIGURE 1.1 Revised Profiles of the Gifted and Talented*

TYPE I: SUCCESSFUL LEARNERS

FEELINGS AND ATTITUDES	BEHAVIORS	NEEDS	METHODS USED FOR IDENTIFICATION	ADULT AND PEER PERCEPTIONS	HOME SUPPORT	SCHOOL SUPPORT
• Are complacent • Are dependent • Have good academic self-concept • Have fear of failure • Have extrinsic motivation • Are self-critical • Work for the grade • Are unsure about the future • Are eager for approval • Have an entity view of intelligence	• Achieve • Seek teacher approval • Avoid risks • Don't go beyond the syllabus • Accept and conform • Choose safe activities • Become consumers of knowledge	• To be challenged • To see deficiencies • To take risks • Assertiveness skills • Creativity development • Incremental view of intelligence • Self-knowledge • Independent learning skills	• Multiple criteria • Grades • Standardized test scores • Teacher nominations • Parent nominations • Peer nominations	• Are liked by teachers • Are admired by peers • Are generally liked and accepted by parents • Are overestimated in their abilities • Are believed to succeed on their own	• Parental space • Independence • Freedom to make choices • Risk-taking experiences • Permission to be distressed • Affirmation of their abilities to cope with challenges	• Subject and grade acceleration • More than AP, IB, and Honors courses • Time for personal curriculum • Activities that push them out of their comfort zone • Development of independent learning skills • In-depth studies • Mentorships • Cognitive coaching • Time with intellectual peers

Figure 1.1 (continued)

TYPE II: CREATIVE LEARNERS

FEELINGS AND ATTITUDES	BEHAVIORS	NEEDS	METHODS USED FOR IDENTIFICATION	ADULT AND PEER PERCEPTIONS	HOME SUPPORT	SCHOOL SUPPORT
• Are highly creative • Are bored and frustrated • Have fluctuating self-esteem • Are impatient and defensive • Have heightened sensitivity • Are uncertain about social roles • Are more psychologically vulnerable • Have strong motivation to follow inner convictions • Want to right wrongs • Have high energy	• Express impulses • Challenge teachers • Question rules and policies • Are honest and direct • Are emotionally liable • May have poor self-control • Have creative expression • Persevere in areas of interest (passions) • Stand up for convictions • May be in conflict with peers	• To connect with others • To learn tact, flexibility, self-awareness, and self-control • Support for creativity • Contractual systems • Less pressure to conform • Interpersonal skills to affirm others • Strategies to cope with potential psychological vulnerabilities	• Answer to: In what ways is this child creative? • Domain-specific, objective measures • Creative potential rather than achievement	• Are seldom liked by teachers • Are viewed as rebellious • Are engaged in power struggles • Are creative • Have discipline problems • Have others wanting them to change • Are not viewed as gifted • Are underestimated in their success • Have others wanting them to conform • Are viewed as entertaining by their peers	• Respect for their goals • Tolerance for higher levels of deviance • Freedom to pursue interests (passions) • Models of appropriate behavior • Family projects • Confidence in their abilities • Affirmation of their strengths • Recognition of their success • Recognition of their psychological vulnerability and intervention when necessary	• Tolerance • Rewards for new thinking • Placement with appropriate teachers • Direct and clear communication • Permission for feelings • Domain-specific training • Allowance for nonconformity • Mentorships • Direct instruction in interpersonal skills • Coaching for deliberate practice

TYPE III: UNDERGROUND LEARNERS

FEELINGS AND ATTITUDES	BEHAVIORS	NEEDS	METHODS USED FOR IDENTIFICATION	ADULT AND PEER PERCEPTIONS	HOME SUPPORT	SCHOOL SUPPORT
• Desire to belong socially • Feel unsure and pressured • Are conflicted, guilty, and insecure • Are unsure of their right to their emotions • Have diminished sense of self • Are ambivalent about achievement • Internalize and personalize societal ambiguities and conflicts • View some achievement behaviors as betrayal of social group	• Devalue, discount, and deny talent • Drop out of gifted and advanced classes • Reject challenges • Move from one peer group to the next • Are not connected to the teacher or the class • Are unsure of direction	• Freedom to make choices • Conflicts to be made explicit • To learn to code switch • Support for their abilities • Role models who cross cultures • Self-understanding and acceptance • An audience to listen to what they have to say (to be heard)	• Interviews • Parent nominations • Teacher nominations • Peer nominations (used with caution) • Demonstrated performance	• Are viewed as leaders or go unrecognized • Are viewed as average and successful • Are perceived to be compliant • Are viewed as quiet/shy • Are viewed as unwilling to take risks • Are viewed as resistant	• Normalization of their dissonance • College and career planning • Gifted role models • Models of lifelong learning • Freedom to make choices • No comparisons with siblings • Cultural brokering • Appreciation for multiculturalism and diversity	• Academic concepts framed as societal phenomena • Welcoming learning environments • Role models • Help for developing support groups • Open discussions about class, racism, sexism, etc. • Cultural brokering • Direct instruction of social skills • Teaching of the hidden curriculum • College planning • Discussion of the costs of success

continued ▲

Figure 1.1 (continued)

TYPE IV: AT-RISK LEARNERS

FEELINGS AND ATTITUDES	BEHAVIORS	NEEDS	METHODS USED FOR IDENTIFICATION	ADULT AND PEER PERCEPTIONS	HOME SUPPORT	SCHOOL SUPPORT
• Are resentful and angry • Are possibly depressed • Are reckless and manipulative • Have poor self-concept • Are defensive • Have unrealistic expectations • Feel unaccepted • Are resistant to authority • Are not motivated for teacher-driven rewards • May be antisocial	• Create crises and cause disruptions • Are thrill seeking • Have intermittent school attendance • Pursue outside interests • Have low academic achievement • May be self-isolating • Are often creative • Criticize themselves and others • Produce inconsistent work	• Safety and structure • Alternative learning environment • An individualized program • Confrontation and accountability • Professional counseling • Direction and short-term goals	• Individual IQ testing • Achievement subtests • Interviews • Auditions • Nonverbal measures of intelligence • Parent nominations • Teacher nominations	• May have adults angry with them • May have peers who are judgmental of them • Are viewed as troubled or irresponsible • Are viewed as rebellious • Have others who may be afraid of them • Have adults who feel powerless to help them	• Family counselling • Avoidance of power struggles • Involvement in extracurricular activities • Monitoring for dangerous behaviors • Open dialogue • Accountability • Minimal punishments • Confidence in their abilities to overcome obstacles • Preservation of relationships	• Expectations not to be lowered • Diagnostic testing • Nontraditional study skills • In-depth studies and mentorships • GED option • Academic coaching • Home visits • Promotion of resilience • Discussion of secondary options • Aggressive advocacy

TYPE V: TWICE/MULTI-EXCEPTIONAL LEARNERS (2E)

FEELINGS AND ATTITUDES	BEHAVIORS	NEEDS	METHODS USED FOR IDENTIFICATION	ADULT AND PEER PERCEPTIONS	HOME SUPPORT	SCHOOL SUPPORT
• Have learned helplessness • Have intense frustration and anger • Have possible mood disorders • Are prone to discouragement • Have poor academic self-support • Don't see themselves as successful • Don't know where they belong	• Make connections easily • Demonstrate inconsistent work • Seem average or below average • Are more like younger students in some aspects of social-emotional functioning • May be disruptive or off-task • Are good problem solvers • Have behavioral problems • Think conceptually • Enjoy novelty and complexity • Are disorganized • Are slow in information processing • May not be able to cope with gifted peer group	• Emphasis on strengths • Coping strategies • Monitoring for additional disorders, such as ADHD • To learn perseverance • To learn to self-advocate	• Measure of current classroom functioning • Achievement test scores • Curriculum-based assessment • Examination of performance over time • Evidence of declining performance paired with evidence of superior ability • Do not rely on IQ scatter analysis or test discrepancy analysis	• Are thought to require too many modifications because of disability • Are viewed as "weird" • Are underestimated for their potential • Are viewed as helpless • Are viewed as not belonging in a gifted program • Are perceived as needing a great deal of structure • Are seen only for their disabilities	• Focus on their strengths and accommodations for their disabilities • Development of their will to succeed • Recognition and affirmation of their gifted abilities • Challenges in their strength areas • Risk-taking opportunities • Assurance that college is a possibility • Family involvement • Nurturing of self-control • Information on how to set and reach realistic goals	• Challenges in their areas of strength • Acceleration in areas of strength • Accommodation for disabilities • Answers to: What will it take for this student to succeed here? • Teaching of self-regulation strategies • Time to be with gifted peers • Teaching of self-advocacy • Teaching of SMART goal setting

continued ▲

Figure 1.1 (continued)

TYPE VI: AUTONOMOUS LEARNERS

FEELINGS AND ATTITUDES	BEHAVIORS	NEEDS	METHODS USED FOR IDENTIFICATION	ADULT AND PEER PERCEPTIONS	HOME SUPPORT	SCHOOL SUPPORT
• Are self-confident • Are self-accepting • Hold incremental views of their abilities • Are optimistic • Are intrinsically motivated • Are ambitious and excited • May not view academics as one of their highest priorities • Are willing to fail and learn from it • Show tolerance and respect for others	• Have appropriate social skills • Work independently • Set SMART goals • Seek challenge • Are strongly self-directed • Follow strong areas of passion • Are good self-regulators • Stand up for convictions • Are resilient • Are producers of knowledge • Possess understanding and acceptance of themselves	• More support, not less • Advocacy for new directions and increasing independence • Feedback about strengths and possibilities • Facilitation of continuing growth • Support for risk-taking • Ongoing, facilitative relationships • To become more adept at managing themselves • A support team	• Demonstrated performance • Products • Nominations • Portfolios • Interviews • Standardized test scores • Awards	• Are admired and accepted • Are viewed as capable and responsible by parents • Are positive influences • Are successful in diverse environments • Are psychologically healthy • Have positive peer relationships	• Advocacy for students at school and in the community • Opportunities related to their passion areas • Permission to have friends of all ages • Absence of time and space restrictions for learning • A support team • Involvement in families' passions • Involvement in family decision-making • People to stay out of their way	• Development of long-term, integrated plan of study • Removal of time and space restrictions • Development of multiple, related, in-depth studies, including mentorships • Wide variety of accelerated options • Mentors and cultural brokers • Waiving of traditional school policies and regulations • Help to cope with psychological costs of success • People to stay out of their way

*Neihart, M., and Betts, G. (2011). *The Revised Profiles of the Gifted: A Research-Based Approach.* Keynote address; 19th Biennial World Conference of the World Council for Gifted and Talented Children, Prague, Czech Republic. Adapted and reprinted with permission.

Navigating the System

What information did each of these students need to help them better navigate the education system? How could their paths have been changed?

Jason (Type I: Successful Learner). Jason needed to reflect on his personal interests and passions. By "checking out" during the last semester of his senior year, he was foregoing one eighth of his high school experience, missing the chance to further investigate his interests and interact with knowledgeable teachers, career mentors, and intellectual peers. For him, high school courses and graduation requirements were just a checklist and he had ticked all the boxes. He hadn't stopped to consider what he was interested in pursuing beyond a diploma. What was he willing and eager to spend time on? What were his passions? What was intrinsically motivating to him? What enriching possibilities already existed in his school and the community? What exciting adventures could he create for himself?

Selena (Type II: Creative Learner). Selena needed to discover more about the system's rules, the marching band requirements, and the music department policy. For example, why was the policy in place? Could it be changed? If so, who could overrule it? How could Selena prove to the powers-that-be that she deserved a waiver?

Nia (Type III: Underground Learner). Nia needed to determine ways to bridge the gap between school and her cultural community. How could she have multiple peer groups? Who were the academic and intellectual role models within her community? How could she enlist these people to help her match her abilities to options her family would approve of?

Katie (Type IV: At-Risk Learner). Katie needed to connect with adult advocates. Who would take the time to hear her story and get to know her? Who had access to records from her past schools and could assure that they would transfer to the next school? Who could help her family discover ways to create consistency when changing schools? Is a residential school a possibility for Katie, so she could remain grounded at least part of the year if her family moves again?

Alex (Type V: 2E Learner). Alex also needed an advocate to help the school focus on his gifts, strengths, and abilities. How could he spend more time with gifted peers? How could the timing of various special services be coordinated? What alternative resources and programming options could provide him access to advanced skills and knowledge despite his reading difficulties?

Tyler (Type VI: Autonomous Learner). Tyler needed to take charge of his own education and he did. In fact, his path exemplifies autonomy and self-advocacy. He recognized his passion for language, understood his rights as a student, took responsibility for bringing about the change he wanted, worked with the adults who could support him, created a practical plan, and followed through with it.

It's important to note that Tyler wasn't always an Autonomous Learner, but provided with the information and support he needed as he worked through the process, he developed skills of self-advocacy and grew toward autonomy. Indeed, armed with basic self-advocacy skills, these students might have sought the help, solutions, resources, and support they needed to flourish.

Four Integral Assumptions About Gifted Students' Self-Advocacy

Regardless of their gifted profiles, gifted learners must begin the process of advocating for themselves, grounded in the following assumptions regarding their individuality, programming options, educational autonomy, and need for self-advocacy instruction.

1. Gifted students need to understand themselves as unique individuals.

Young people are empowered when we help them recognize what makes them different: their strengths and weaknesses, attitudes and interests, pleasures and passions. They may be aware they are different, but they often lack the self-reflection or even the vocabulary to describe the ways they feel different. In the first

edition of their book, *When Gifted Kids Don't Have All the Answers*, Jim Delisle and Judy Galbraith list the "Eight Great Gripes" expressed by students they surveyed.[4] What was number one? "No one explains what being gifted is all about—it's kept a big secret." That struck home for me because I knew that as a gifted coordinator I had not explained to my students exactly what it means (and does not mean) to be gifted. Yes, our district was systematic in identifying students for our gifted program and had communicated with parents what that programming would be and which assessments qualified their child for it. But in some ways, we had a *stealth* program, hoping that by not communicating too much or too loudly about what we were doing, no one would feel left out or raise charges of elitism or ask for something we couldn't provide. It now seems probable that our children and parents alike believed the common notion that *gifted* simply meant you were a good student and scored well on exams. That notion does a disservice to everyone. If, in an attempt to be egalitarian, we pretend that all children are alike, that all are gifted, or that all have the same abilities, then our children will think we're either lying or stupid. They are well aware of their differences.

Jean Sunde Peterson, counselor of gifted students and longtime coordinator of school counselor preparation at Purdue University, noted: "Gifted individuals are no different from anyone else in terms of needing to be heard and validated as a child, adolescent, adult, son, daughter, friend—certainly more than just an achiever, underachiever, delinquent, or star performer. They may even need to have their intelligence validated, because academic self-confidence in underachieving individuals, for instance, may have been eroded over time."[5] Understanding and accepting themselves as unique learners *outside* of the norm helps gifted students consider their educational desires *beyond* the norm.

> **Chapter 3: Rights and Responsibilities** provides specifics on what gifted students need to know about giftedness.

2. Gifted students need programming that is matched to their individual learner profiles and geared toward their academic, personal, social, and emotional readiness.

It's not unusual for the public to think of gifted education as giving more to those who already have a lot. But what would have been the future of Olympic medal–winner Michael Phelps if his practice had been confined to his parents' backyard pool? Or if a young Hilary Hahn were required to repeatedly rehearse "Twinkle, Twinkle Little Star" with the other budding musicians? As a high school English teacher, I discovered that too often the kids who had to work hardest each day in my classroom were those with below-grade-level skills. The gifted kids could whiz through the curriculum without breaking a sweat. That didn't seem fair. I wanted each of my students to work hard, learn something new every day, occasionally risk failing at something they found difficult, and then succeed when supported in their efforts. Gifted learners, like all other learners, can only grow when they are stretched. If they receive good grades with minimal effort, they can come to see themselves as impostors who are not as capable as other people believe them to be. Or they may become addicted to the success of high grades, rather than experiencing the joy of being successful at something they know to be difficult. Or, out of boredom, they may exhibit behavior challenges and therefore be less likely to be perceived as gifted. Without an appropriately challenging curriculum, gifted learners may not develop persistence, study skills, and self-efficacy. They may decide that school is simply something to be tolerated because meaningful learning takes place somewhere else, and sadly, they may lose interest in developing their abilities altogether.

Finding the right fit between student and programming is essential to gifted learners becoming autonomous. But the huge variation in their strengths, interests, learning preferences, and personal characteristics complicates the issue. In her seminal work, *Re-Forming Gifted Education: Matching the Program to the Child*, Karen Rogers explains the difficulty: "Educational planning for gifted youngsters . . . is somewhat like high-level negotiation in the business world. In simplest terms, it is matching the child's needs to the school's ability to meet those needs. But such planning is far from simple. And it requires advocacy, diplomacy, and persuasion . . . Such a plan is surely worth the effort."[6]

By matching gifted students' programming to their learner profiles and academic, personal, social, and emotional readiness, we ensure they have the intellectual challenge every student deserves.

> Ideas for matching the program to the student as well as examples of successful and unsuccessful attempts are included in **Chapter 5: Options and Opportunities**.

3. Gifted students need to grow toward autonomy and take charge of their own educations.

For gifted students to be challenged, they frequently must go beyond what is offered in the regular classroom. However, even if a wide array of high quality differentiated educational options is available, many gifted kids choose not to take advantage of those opportunities for a variety of reasons. Some fear they may not be successful at more difficult work and their grades may suffer. Others worry that doing something different from the rest of the class might increase the chances that they will be viewed as outsiders. Some are lazy, some unmotivated, and some complacent. It's also possible that the available options are no more rigorous or better at meeting their needs than the regular classroom work. Yet gifted learners remain unwitting captives of the status quo unless we help them take the lead in affecting change. As Rick Olenchak, head of the Department of Educational Studies at Purdue University, puts it: "Regardless of ability level, it seems that youth in our society rarely have the opportunity to take initiative, and their education largely encourages passive adaptation to external rules instead of extending opportunities for them to explore pathways toward personal fulfillment."[7]

While we might wish for all students of every ability level to become more autonomous, it's generally believed that intellectually gifted children are predisposed to it, especially those with a greater internal locus of control—the feeling that control of one's life rests in one's own hands. Yet while they may be intellectually ready, many gifted students do not have the information they need to be successful at crafting their own educational path. They need encouragement to drive their own education. When they become the driving force, they have much to gain. They grow to be more independent, responsible learners. They increase their knowledge base and decision-making skills. They develop more positive self-concepts and greater self-esteem. Over time, they move from consumers of knowledge to producers of knowledge.

4. Gifted students need specific, direct, and intentional instruction in self-advocacy.

I think it's fair to assume that educators and parents intend to provide young people with the information they need to be comfortable speaking up for themselves. But our attempts must be systematic, continuous, and specific for our message to come across as clear, consistent, and well-informed.

There are a variety of ways to teach the skills, concepts, and attitudes of self-advocacy—from extensive instructional models to simple ongoing conversations. The most comprehensive example of direct instruction in self-advocacy is found in *The Autonomous Learner Model* (ALM) developed by George Betts, who also identified the six gifted learner profiles with Maureen Neihart. The first of the ALM's five parts is Orientation, which encourages students to reflect on the concept of intelligence, the ways their school is helping them use their intelligence, and how they can work as partners in guiding their future. The Orientation phase includes understanding giftedness, talent, intelligence, and creativity;

group-building activities; personal development; and school opportunities and responsibilities.

Of course, not every school district is willing or able to adopt the Autonomous Learner Model. But the information acquisition, assessment, networking, and reflection can be achieved in other ways. For instance, it can be incorporated into a continuum of self-advocacy conversations—both individual and small group—that coordinators have with their students beginning in the early grades and continuing through high school. School counselors can include it in mentor/mentee programs, counseling sessions, or college and career planning. Classroom teachers could make it part of their differentiated curriculum. Parents, too, have an important role in this process, either by working in conjunction with the school or, if the district chooses not to encourage self-advocacy, by instructing their children at home on how to make the education system work for them. Key to the success of any method is that we are specific, direct, and intentional about the *who*, *why*, and *how* of self-advocacy.

Chapter 6: Advocates and Advisors details more of adults' responsibilities in teaching self-advocacy. **Chapter 8: Workshops and Ways Forward** includes several possible methods of delivering information about self-advocacy.

Talking About Giftedness

Over the last two decades, I've conducted countless GT Carpe Diem Workshops for gifted teens that mirror the Orientation component of the ALM, introducing teens to the possibilities of self-advocacy. Many of the examples and anecdotes and much of the data included in this book are taken from the surveys, activities, conversations, and student discussions that are part of the workshops. This is how the teens and preteens I surveyed in 2012–2016 responded:

FIGURE 1.2
Survey Responses: Talking About Giftedness

Number of Survey Respondents = 286

Has anyone talked with you about what it means to be gifted?

	Yes		No	
	#	%	#	%
	191	66.8	95	33.2

Have these people talked with you about giftedness?

	Yes		No	
	#	%	#	%
Parents	116	40.6	170	59.4
Teachers	105	36.7	181	63.3
Gifted Coordinators	89	31.1	197	68.9
School Counselors	26	9.1	260	90.9

It's surprising that almost a third of the students said no one had ever talked to them about giftedness, since all the students surveyed had been selected for the workshop on *gifted* self-advocacy by their parents or school personnel. Many said their first and only indication that they were considered gifted was receiving a letter informing them that they would be in a special group or class. Others were never told they were gifted or being singled out in any way and only realized inadvertently that they had been grouped according to their abilities.

Are these students' perceptions accurate? Do we talk with them about their exceptional abilities and high potential? If not, why not? There could be many reasons:

- We don't know what to say.
- We don't understand giftedness ourselves.
- We are grateful the occasion never presents itself (it's almost as hard as the "sex" talk!).
- We fear we might create elitists.
- We think that by being gifted, students already understand their giftedness.
- We feel we have too many students to speak with individually.
- We don't have a specific occasion to discuss the topic.
- We try to be egalitarian and imply that they are not different, such as "everyone is gifted."

The truth is, many young people know very little about the concept of giftedness. We must be specific and direct when talking with students about their giftedness. But what do we say? Since the educational community is at odds about defining giftedness and the terms we use to describe abilities (some even refuse to use the word *gifted*), students are best served if they are aware of the debate and allowed to reflect on a variety of definitions, descriptions, models, theories, and characteristics used for identification. When we talk to our kids about their exceptional abilities, we must make it a long, complete, ongoing conversation.

Some concepts to include in an initial conversation:
- Being gifted is not what you *do*, but who you *are*.
- There are many ways to be gifted and gifted people are not all alike.
- You have a combination of exceptional abilities; some may be intellectual, academic, creative, artistic, or leadership gifts. The mixture is different for every gifted person.
- Being gifted is not how well you do in school, what you become someday, or what you can contribute to society, but rather a unique set of characteristics you will have for your entire life.
- Because you're gifted you may experience life very intensely.
- You have definite strengths, but you also have underdeveloped areas that need some work.
- You are better *at* some things than others your age, but that doesn't mean you're better *than* they are.

- Being gifted is a good thing. It doesn't mean your life will always be easy, but it is part of what makes you uniquely valuable.

- Being gifted means you may often have different educational needs than some of your classmates. Every person needs to be challenged to grow and you can help your teachers and parents know when the challenge level feels right, when it's too tough, and when it's too easy.

> Much of the additional information that students and their advocates must have regarding giftedness is included in **Chapter 2: Basics and Beliefs** and **Chapter 3: Rights and Responsibilities.**

Increasing the Chances of Success

Chance plays a key role in determining whether a gifted learner will have the experiences that transform gifts into talents, as shown in **Figure 1.3**, a simplified version of Françoys Gagné's Differentiated Model of Giftedness and Talent. Notice that natural abilities (gifts) go through a developmental process to become competencies (talents). Many environmental and intrapersonal catalysts affect the process, but it is the shaded area labeled "chance" that undergirds (or overshadows) the process. When we assist kids in understanding themselves, expressing their needs, and accepting appropriate challenges, we act as catalysts that increase the chances that they will find fulfillment, joy, value, and success in using their talents.

For example, Ezra's life course was changed by chance. While his parents provided him with many enriching experiences, no one in the family was especially interested in music. When they moved to a new house with room to spare, they agreed to temporarily house a friend's grand piano. At first, it just sat closed in the middle of the living room. But nine-year-old Ezra's curiosity got the better of him and one day he opened the lid and tried a few notes. The attachment was immediate. Before long, he was spending hours on the piano bench, legs dangling, composing his own surprisingly complicated melodies. His parents supported his desire for formal instruction. By middle school he was competing in state music competitions; by high school he was winning them, along with a scholarship to the conservatory of music.

Emily, now a successful professional classical actress, wasn't interested in theater as a child. In middle school, she liked studying French but hated completing the repetitive workbook activities. Her teacher suggested she earn extra credit by participating in the French drama competition. And, *voilà*, a star was born. Without her teacher's fortuitous intervention, it's possible Emily would never have discovered her gift, her passion, or her professional calling.

Ezra and Emily were fortunate to have adults in their lives who supported their *aha!* moments. But what about all the children whose environmental and intrapersonal experiences *don't* include the catalysts described by Gagné? We can improve the odds that all children will grow their gifts into fully realized talents if we directly and intentionally instruct them in understanding their rights and responsibilities as gifted individuals. This includes assessing their personal learner profiles, investigating alternative experiences, and connecting them with the people who can bring about change in their lives.

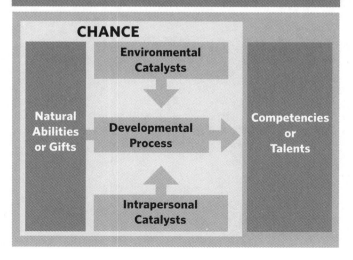

**FIGURE 1.3
Transforming Gifts into Talents**

Our goal in teaching self-advocacy is not necessarily to make every gifted learner successful in public school or even in life, but rather to give each learner the information he or she needs to make the wise decisions that contribute to a rich and fulfilling life.

Conclusion

No matter what changes to the education system may be promised, it's critical that gifted learners not wait for things to happen and instead make the changes that are best for them as the need arises. One of the first steps is to recognize themselves as gifted learners and determine which of the gifted profiles (or combination of profiles) best describes their current state. We better equip gifted learners to begin the journey of self-advocacy when we intentionally share what we know about them and lead them to understand their abilities and their struggles.

keyCONCEPTS IN CHAPTER 1

- ❖ Though changes in education are inevitable, the need for appropriately challenging educational experiences for gifted students is a constant.
- ❖ Gifted students vary greatly and need educational opportunities that match their unique needs.
- ❖ Gifted students can and should play a major role in designing their own paths to graduation and beyond.
- ❖ All students, no matter which profile or profiles describe them, can grow toward autonomy as they learn to self-advocate.
- ❖ We leave less to chance when we provide students with the information they need to understand themselves and make appropriate decisions.

2 BASICS and BELIEFS

My office phone rang in the middle of a busy Monday morning. "Hi, Mrs. Douglas. This is Peggy." Peggy had been a gifted student in my first self-advocacy workshop, but we hadn't talked since she transferred to a new school in Michigan and it took me a couple of seconds to place her voice. "I'm in the high school counselor's office," she continued. "I'm trying to arrange my senior year the way I want it to be but they think I'm just being stubborn. Would you please tell them about self-advocacy?"

Both we as advocates and the gifted students we're helping need to clearly understand what self-advocacy is, how it is accomplished, and how to talk to others about it. Undoubtedly all people would benefit from advocating for themselves, but for certain segments of our population, in certain situations, at certain times of their lives, there is greater urgency. In fact, the term most often refers to the practice of people with disabilities speaking for themselves and controlling their own affairs, rather than having others automatically assume responsibility for them. The self-advocacy movement is an effort to reduce the isolation of people with disabilities and give them the tools and experience to take greater control over their own lives, hence Loring Brinckerhoff's definition of self-advocacy quoted in this book's introduction and below. It seems logical then that every student with differing abilities, not just those with disabilities, should be empowered to speak up and act on his or her own best interests.

> "Self-advocacy is the process of recognizing and meeting the needs specific to one's learning ability without compromising the dignity of oneself or others."
> —*Loring Brinckerhoff, director of the Office of Disability Policy at Educational Testing Service*

Outliers: Why, How, and When to Self-Advocate

Within the education system, self-advocacy is especially necessary for an outlier, or anyone whose abilities fall outside the norm. The most common illustration of that norm is the bell curve, a concept historically used (sometimes for nefarious reasons) to describe varying intellectual ability. On most IQ tests, the average score is set at 100. With a normal distribution, 68 percent of scores fall between 85 and 115, and 95 percent fall between 70 and 130. Scores higher than 130 or lower than 70 are considered extreme outliers.

The normal distribution of any ability could likely be shown using a similar curve. For instance, ask 100 random people to race around a track. An average of 54 percent of the people would run somewhere in a pack in the middle, while 23 percent would run behind the pack and 23 percent would run ahead of the pack.

A few people, the outliers, will be either straggling far behind or else out-distancing everyone else. One person will end up last and one person will beat the other 99 runners to the finish line. Of course, the distribution would look different if we asked 100 Olympic athletes or even 100 high school cross-country stars to run the race as opposed to 100 random individuals who represent a cross section of the population (see **Figure 2.1**).

In much the same way, the academic abilities of children in our schools follow a similar distribution. In a group of random students at a grade level, 54 percent will have learning abilities clustered around grade level, while 23 percent will be struggling to keep up and 23 percent will be ahead of the pack, ready for more challenging work. The outliers are the students with exceptionally severe learning disabilities on one end and with exceptionally advanced learning abilities on the other.

FIGURE 2.1
Normal Distribution of Runners

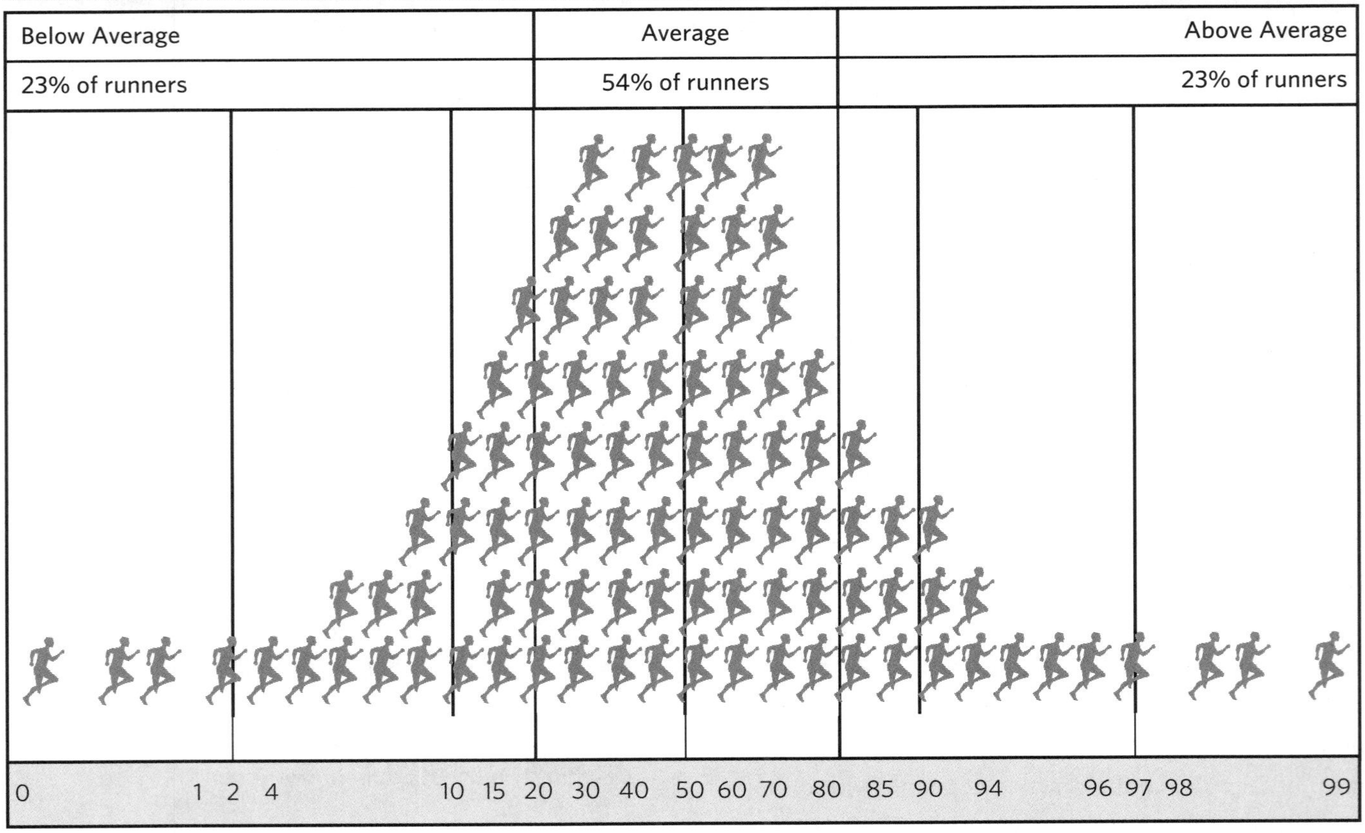

Below Average	Average	Above Average
23% of runners	54% of runners	23% of runners

0   1 2   4   10 15 20 30 40 50 60 70 80 85 90   94   96 97 98   99

Chapter 4: Profiles and Preferences includes a more detailed look at the specific characteristics of those intellectually and academically gifted outliers.

It's no secret that public education in our society is geared toward the norm by necessity. Most often in the regular heterogeneous classroom, the curriculum and instruction are directed at the largest group of students, the 54 percent in the middle. The further away the students are from the norm, the more they need differentiation of one kind or another. Those at the extreme ends need even greater accommodations.

While huge amounts of federal, state, and local funding are directed toward helping the least able and the underperforming, very little is directed toward students with the greatest abilities, who are just as far outside the norm and in just as great a need of appropriate challenges. In some ways, many of them are underperforming as well. They too must be empowered to self-advocate, to speak up for themselves, to make basic choices about their educations, and to be the experts in their own lives.

Self-advocacy is not just about students getting what they want; it is about students getting what they *need* to develop their potential. Our most able learners have to believe that they can change the things that aren't working for them and find a path through the educational system that provides them with academic challenges and effective social and emotional support. So while it's true that all people should be empowered to self-advocate, the greatest immediate need is for the outliers, those at both ends of the continuum.

In addition to learning *why* they should self-advocate, outliers need to learn *how* to self-advocate. While some gifted learners may be up-front about stating their needs, their egotism can keep them from being tactful or subtle. Meanwhile, others may suffer from self-esteem issues and their requests may be overly subtle or vague. Consider again Brinckerhoff's definition: "the process of recognizing and meeting the needs specific to

one's learning ability *without compromising the dignity of oneself or others.*" Since self-advocacy is all about relationships (students, parents, teachers, administrators, counselors, mentors, school board members, legislators, and so on), maintaining dignity is extremely important. Whose dignity might be compromised in the process of self-advocacy? Who might feel insulted or disrespected? During GT Carpe Diem Workshop discussions, students were quick to respond to these questions (see Chapter 8 for details). Their answers named a variety of stakeholders in the system. This young woman's story sums it up well:

> "My dignity was compromised when my algebra teacher said there wasn't anything he could do to pick up the pace and that I shouldn't be asking for special treatment. And I think the teacher felt insulted, like I was questioning what he was doing and his teaching wasn't good enough. Some of the other kids in my class probably felt worse about their own math skills when I said it was too easy and they thought it was too hard. My parents were embarrassed when my teacher emailed to tell them I was being disrespectful. When I asked to be switched to a different teacher, the principal thought I was criticizing his staff and I got a lecture on what a good school district we have and how their job was to serve all students. So everyone's dignity was compromised and I never got anything changed." —*Maria, age 14*

So much depends on how students ask for change and how the adults who have the power to make that change perceive their request.

There is more about diplomatic communication of wants and needs and the roles and responsibilities of supportive parents and educators in **Chapter 6: Advocates and Advisors**.

Some teachers and parents have wondered what the best age is for children to begin self-advocating. Since gifted children are as different from each other as they are similar, and because a common characteristic is asynchronous development, the age for self-advocacy varies greatly. A gifted child in fourth grade may have the argumentative skills of a lawyer, be able to solve complex mathematical equations, or compose sonatas, but still have the emotional sensitivity, vulnerability, and temperamental moments of a six-year-old. Still, encouraging gifted children's self-advocacy can begin in some form when they are very young and just entering formal education, and it should continue throughout their school years. Self-advocacy is an ongoing process that, once learned, students will use consciously or subconsciously whenever they need it throughout their lives.

From early on, children can and need to understand their giftedness, their right to ask for what they need, and their responsibility to develop attributes of good character. It is equally important for them to feel comfortable venting their frustrations with the education system and seeking ways to rectify the situation. Developing the skills of negotiation and clear verbal communication in young children will help increase their comfort with and success in self-advocating.

For many gifted students, the critical time to take charge of their own educations is when they are in grades five through twelve, especially as they transition into middle and high school. During these years, the typical adolescent urge for less dependence on parents makes it particularly important to begin advocating for themselves. Frequently, it is also at these ages that gifted students discover they have exhausted the advanced learning opportunities in their elementary or middle school and are ready to make the transition into the next level earlier than their classmates. Even students entering their senior year may need or want changes to their curriculum that better prepare them for their post-graduation lives.

Benefits of Self-Advocacy for Gifted Students

One of the characteristics distinguishing students with special learning needs who are successful from those who are not is the ability to advocate for themselves.

When self-advocating, students are choosing their own paths, weighing the alternatives, and making choices. Having those choices is a primary motivational tool that encourages learning.[8] Gifted students who self-advocate are more likely to find and select suitable academic and personal choices. Using one's own voice has other invaluable benefits as well.

Benefit 1. More Appropriate Academic Challenges

For gifted students to be appropriately challenged in school, the level of that challenge must be just slightly greater than their ability. Students rightly rebel against *more* of the same low-level work but sometimes shy away from tasks that don't come easily.

The Theory of Flow

If we share with students the theory of flow, developed by Mihaly Csikszentmihalyi, that states an appropriate challenge leads to total involvement and joy in learning, they are more apt to accept and even seek out those demanding experiences that require real effort. According to this theory, six factors are present in a flow experience:[9]

1. Intense and focused concentration on the present moment
2. Merging of action and awareness
3. Loss of reflective self-consciousness
4. Sense of personal control over the activity
5. Distortion of temporal experience
6. Awareness of the activity as intrinsically rewarding

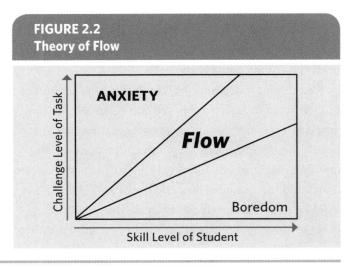

FIGURE 2.2
Theory of Flow

In short, flow happens when a challenge we're facing is in sync with our skill level. For example, an appropriate effort for an inexperienced skier might be slowly traversing a bunny hill, seeking a slow, safe, and steady descent. If she were somehow transported to the top of an Olympic ski jump, she might freeze there—literally and figuratively—never attempting the feat at all. An Olympic skier, on the other hand, would be bored to tears on the bunny hill but would find flow in the challenge of a perfectly executed jump down a 90-meter slope.

Most often the gifted teens in my workshops report that they experience flow when playing video games in which the difficulty increases with each step of their success. That's not surprising since software developers build flow into their games. While we can't and probably shouldn't turn every learning experience into a video game, it is possible to provide gifted students with choices that allow them to experience flow more regularly.

> Many of these alternatives are discussed in
> **Chapter 5: Options and Opportunities**.

Students who have been introduced to the theory of flow also understand that a more appropriate challenge doesn't necessarily mean *more* work, but rather more interesting, intrinsically rewarding work. Whether one is gaming, skiing, or solving quadratic equations, three conditions have to be met to achieve a flow state:[10]

1. A clear set of goals and sense of progress.
2. Clear and immediate feedback that helps a person work through changing demands.
3. A balance between a person's *perceived* challenges of the task and their own *perceived* skills (i.e., a confidence in one's ability to complete the task successfully).

If you've ever worked out on a treadmill, you know there are preset modes but you also can customize the program or create a new one to fit your personal needs. You can set your own pace, adjust the incline, and run or walk or jog for as long as you like. The goal and progress are clearly displayed. You can even monitor your pulse and adjust your workout as needed. You can choose to be super challenged . . . or not. We exercise best and we learn best when we're in control of our options and are neither bored by lack of effort nor frustrated by being pushed too far, too fast. Gifted students who have figured out their own learner needs can adjust the pace and depth and breadth of their instruction accordingly, allowing them to make progress in their intellectual fitness workout.

> "My science teacher thought that working with a group of other smart kids would make the project more intriguing. It was fun, but I already knew a lot of what we were doing and ended up just helping the other kids understand concepts. For the next unit my teacher let me choose from a list of online college-level anatomy projects. Going my own pace let me dive in more deeply when I wanted and move more quickly when I needed. I know I must have spent hours and hours and hours on the assignments, but I don't really know. The three weeks just flew by!"
> —*Shahree, age 15*

Benefit 2. Increased Motivation

Gifted students may be motivated by extrinsic rewards (those originating outside the individual, such as grades, test scores, praise, and other honors). Or they may be motivated by experiences they find intrinsically rewarding, engaging, challenging, fun, and interesting (motivation that arises from within the individual). To some extent, it depends upon how much choice students have and how well we guide them in making suitable choices. Successful Learners lean toward extrinsic motivation while Autonomous Learners more often derive intrinsic motivation from the pleasure they get from working on and/or completing a task that they have chosen themselves.

> Assessing sources and levels of motivation is discussed in **Chapter 4: Profiles and Preferences**.

According to the work of Del Siegle and Betsy McCoach, students who have chosen their educational experiences through self-advocacy find value in their school experiences, believe they have the skills to be successful, and trust their environment and expect they can succeed in it. They also develop greater self-regulation, have more realistic expectations, and continue to apply appropriate strategies for success. Success leads to greater motivation that leads to more success.[11]

> "We were studying Japan in social studies class and everybody got assigned a topic for their research project. Mine was traditional Japanese musical instruments. I thought that was pretty cool because I'm really into music, but all I had to do was Google it and it was all there. Easy A . . . but boring! So instead I asked my teacher if I could compose a piece of music that incorporated both Western and Japanese tonal systems. He didn't know what I was talking about, but said 'sure.' I can't believe how complex it all was and how much I loved digging into it and then demonstrating it to the rest of the class!"
> —Luke, age 14

Benefit 3. Greater Independence and Self-Direction

In a typical classroom, students pursue what they are told to study and move along in that study according to a prescribed schedule. In this way, the education system hopes to build similar skills and impart the required knowledge to all students. While this process often achieves that end, there is a danger that students will only learn to do what they are told to do and not learn to love the act of learning itself. When learners are given greater independence and become partners in directing their own curriculum, the benefits are great. They pursue subjects and experiences that they find interesting, discover their passions, and develop into lifelong learners.

Students who choose and successfully complete more demanding challenges through self-advocacy increase their independence and self-direction, two of the critical personal characteristics required for success in many programming options recommended for gifted learners. Self-directed learners take the initiative in selecting, managing, and assessing their own learning experiences rather than relying on a parent or teacher to oversee each step. Some children seem to be born with these skills, but others need to be guided there.

> "The best semester I ever had was in ninth-grade honors English. All the teacher gave us was a rubric and the language arts standards we needed to achieve. Then we had to set up our own plan to meet them and be very specific about what we would research, read, and write. My research question was 'What is the historical and cultural significance of the Foo Fighters?'—my favorite band. You know what? Even though that semester ended and I got an A, this project is ongoing. You'd be surprised how much of language arts skills and life in general can be related to the Foo Fighters! And by the way, I *exceeded the state standards*."
> —Jessie, age 17

Benefit 4. Improved Academic Performance

For gifted students who are underachievers, self-advocacy may be the key to becoming achievers. However, some may be reluctant to take the risk of asking for something different when they know they have not met teacher and/or parent expectations in the past. They need encouragement and support in finding and choosing the best options and places where they will find the flow that leads to success. Teachers frequently complain that underachieving students simply won't do their work. I've seen many instances, however, in which gifted learners won't do the class assignments but will spend hours working on their own self-selected "nonschool" projects. In seventh grade, for instance, Leah was in danger of failing all her classes. The A's on all her exams couldn't balance out the F's on all her incomplete homework. "I just didn't have time for all that pointless work," she told me. "I was too busy at night watching Kahn Academy economics videos." Together we began to look for ways she could find engagement and flow in her required classes.

Even students who appear to be academically successful based on good grades may be under-achieving if the tasks they're doing require little or no effort. They may not develop study skills, work ethic, or persistence if they stop producing when they hit the artificial ceiling of an A grade. They may become satisfied with inferior work and devalue the high quality they are capable of doing. But their true academic capabilities will be revealed when they are encouraged to take risks and ask for more appropriate educational choices.

> "I always got everything right on my math homework, but the teacher started out each day going through every one of our 20 or 30 homework problems. By the time we got through three or four of them I knew I had it figured out. I guess I got kind of restless and screwed around a lot. I started getting kicked out of class. I quit doing the pointless homework and got an F in a class where I already knew everything! Then my counselor set up a computerized math program for me where I could go at my own speed and by the end of the year I was getting A's and had finished two full years of math." —*Chet, age 13*

Benefit 5. Greater Equanimity, Less Frustration

In *The Survival Guide for Gifted Kids: For Ages 10 & Under,* Judy Galbraith reports that gifted students' "Eight Great Gripes" have morphed a bit since they first began surveying over thirty years ago. Some have changed, but many frustrations remain:[12]

1. We miss out on activities other kids get to do while we're in our gifted class.
2. We have to do extra work in school.
3. Other kids ask us for too much help.
4. The stuff we do in school is too easy and it's boring.
5. When we finish our schoolwork early, we often aren't allowed to work ahead.
6. Our friends and classmates don't always understand us, and they don't see all of our different sides.
7. Parents, teachers, and even our friends expect too much of us. We're supposed to get A's and do our best all the time.
8. Tests, tests, and more tests!

In my own recent surveys of over 300 gifted teens who attended GT Carpe Diem Workshops, similar feelings toward school came through loud and clear:

- Classes simply move too slowly. It's hard to act like I'm paying attention in class.
- Teachers think you automatically get stuff if you're gifted, but sometimes you do need help and it's hard to ask for it.
- Sometimes you are afraid to do extra work that you enjoy because people think you are crazy.
- People depend on me to do all the work in groups.
- I hate it when I get one bad grade on a test and other people make fun of me.
- My parents don't praise me if I get good grades or do well but they make a big deal if my grades start to slip a little bit, for example, 100% goes down to 95%.

It's apparent these students' concerns are universal and timeless. It's normal for gifted kids to feel frustrated sometimes. But how do we help? First, we can acknowledge that their gripes are legitimate. Too often they hear the equivalent of, "Quit complaining. Just think of those kids who struggle to learn." It's important for gifted learners to be able to express those frustrations to people who understand and can help them resolve their grievances. Secondly, we can assure them that there are other options, more choices. Students who feel hopeful are happier and less stressed.

> "I couldn't wait to get to middle school where I thought my English teacher would be a specialist who loved literary analysis as much as me. But on the first day of class she announced apples would be the integrated theme for the next six weeks. Apples! I guess I was naively hoping for a chance to discuss Shakespeare and Jane Austen and Sylvia Plath. I sat in silence as the rest of the class eagerly brainstormed all the possible ways that apples could be related to language arts. I talked to the teacher after class and over the next several days we developed a plan. We went to the department head with my writing portfolio and the work I had done in a summer enrichment program at Northwestern University. He agreed that I could enroll in ninth-grade English. It still wasn't all I'd hoped, but the acceleration allowed me to enjoy all the high school English electives offered over the next several years." —Mariah, age 12

Benefits to Others When Gifted Students Self-Advocate

Self-advocacy is not just a personal struggle for individual gifted kids. I've observed time and time again how one student's success in self-advocating can bring huge benefits to others. So, who benefits and how?

Other Gifted Students

What begins as a successful experience for one learner may allow other students to follow the same path. In the last quarter of seventh grade, science whiz Bart asked if he could skip the next year of science and take a high school course, integrated physical science (IPS), instead. He proposed taking the eighth-grade text home over the summer, answering all the chapter questions, and passing the final exam before the next school year began. The science teachers agreed to the plan but were

pretty sure it wouldn't work. What kid would spend his summer independently working his way through a whole year of science curriculum? Well, Bart would, and did, passing the exam with flying colors. What's more, the option Bart created expanded to others since he had demonstrated to teachers that some students are ready for a faster pace and greater depth. It wasn't long before the science department compacted two years of middle school general science into one year for identified advanced learners. Eventually, accelerated students were given the choice of IPS and/or biology, with both high school courses taught in the middle school.

Other Students with Varying Abilities

The accommodations stemming from the successful self-advocacy of a gifted student may also lead to differentiation for all students. When her family and consumer science teacher announced a dough art project, gifted artist Bev got permission to ramp it up, creating highly original and complex designs. Other students took notice and requested their own variations on the tasks. With their input, the teacher created a fully differentiated unit with options to match student abilities across the spectrum, from more effective scaffolding for struggling students to open-ended alternatives for self-directed learners.

Parents

Parents want their children to stretch their minds, enjoy learning, and feel safe in the school environment. But since parents aren't beside their kids every step of the way, it's difficult to know if and when that is happening. Student self-advocacy can help reassure parents that their children will get what they need when they need it. Several years ago, when our district decided to earnestly focus on classroom differentiation and self-advocacy, we eliminated the weekly gifted pullout program in the elementary schools. Zena, mother of three gifted children, was dismayed. "That one hour a week is the only time my kids really enjoy school," she said (a sad but frequent experience for many gifted children). A tireless advocate, she had met with their regular classroom teachers, year after year trying to ensure their needs were understood and addressed, sometimes effecting change, but more often running into resistance from staff who had no training in addressing the needs of gifted youth. But once Zena's kids were empowered with the skills of self-advocacy and could create their own paths through the system, each day became an interesting challenge for them. Together with their teachers, they discovered independent study, curriculum compacting, interest explorations, online classes, mentorships, and contests and competitions, each one matched to their individual learner profiles. They also learned to acknowledge and work on areas where they struggled. Zena could relax and enjoy supporting each child's unique path.

Teachers

Teachers want their students to succeed. Less is left to chance in the traditional classroom when students feel empowered to talk with teachers about their needs. Micah, a high school world literature teacher, was unsure which of his students were "getting it" and which were left behind in daily discussions. His students rarely asked for different work, so he was always on the lookout for the silent signs that one of his gifted learners might need more depth or greater pace: the jiggling foot, glazed-over eyes, pencil tapping, window-staring. His task was made easier when he posted Galbraith and Delisle's "Ten Tips for Talking to Teachers" on his bulletin board (see page 173).

The very next day Amber, Marta, and Josh approached him with a request to form an independent advanced study group. Meanwhile, two struggling students asked him for additional resources that would help them more easily approach a complex text. For many years teachers have been encouraged to differentiate curriculum and instruction to address the wide range of abilities in their heterogeneous classrooms. This daunting task is made much easier when students self-advocate. When they experience the delight and satisfaction in meaningful work, all students can become partners in designing and implementing their own accommodations.

Gifted Education Coordinators

Self-advocacy gives coordinators another tool for their toolbox, allowing them to develop partnerships with their students. Coordinators' responsibilities often include scheduling programs, compiling identification data, conducting professional development for staff, updating records, and evaluating programming—duties that allow few opportunities for direct contact with students. When self-advocacy becomes the focus of gifted programming, coordinators become active advocates, working together with their students. After attending the workshop on self-advocacy with her students, gifted coordinator Janell reflected on their experience together: "This day provided a first step for many of my students—they began a conversation with me that they hadn't felt comfortable initiating and are now speaking up for themselves and ensuring their voices are heard!" Her colleague Laura wrote, "[This was] an informative and exciting day for students and teachers alike! Our discussions gave me great ideas about how to grow my role in working with students, and my students felt empowered and inspired by the self-discovery process." Both coordinators began to conduct similar yearly workshops within their districts, helping them get to know all their students and their students' needs more fully.

Counselors

With their huge workload and responsibility for hundreds of students, school counselors don't have to go looking for problems; problems are usually lining up at their doors. Often the needs of seemingly successful students get lost in the shuffle. But when gifted learners better understand their own academic, social, and emotional concerns, they can more clearly and effectively present those issues to their counselors and work together on a solution before a crisis arises. For instance, in assessing her learner profile, gifted student Jenna realized her perfectionistic tendencies were leading to a lot of stress. She knew a few friends who seemed to be struggling with the same issue. So together they asked a counselor to set up a weekly lunch group to read and discuss Thomas Greenspon's book, *What* to Do When Good Enough Isn't Good Enough. When word got out about the group, a couple staff members who were dealing with their own perfectionism joined the students. It became not just an intervention support group, but also a way to network with like minds.

School Districts

Most public school districts have mission statements that include phrases like, "to provide each student with an equal opportunity to succeed." Districts are more apt to accomplish that mission when students become partners in their educations and have input into their own routes to success. While many states have unfunded or unmonitored mandates for gifted education, districts that encourage self-advocacy have greater assurance of fulfilling the spirit as well as the letter of the law. Ultimately there are fewer student gripes and less pressure from parents who can see firsthand that their children's needs are being addressed.

So Why Don't Students Ask for Change?

Do gifted students self-advocate? If not, why not? Judging from the GT Carpe Diem Workshop survey responses, we have to assume that most students are not in the habit of asking for what they want and need. A whopping 92 percent of students in fifth through twelfth grade report that they have never/almost never/ occasionally talked with a teacher about differentiating work for them, even though 81 percent said they were very comfortable or at least okay asking a teacher for something different. Sadly, a great majority (86 percent) said they occasionally/frequently/always wished a teacher would modify their work. Also, it's telling that while over half of the respondents frequently/always *wish* for modifications, only 8 percent frequently/ always *ask*.

FIGURE 2.3
Survey Responses: Asking for Change

How often have you asked a teacher to modify something for you?

Number of survey respondents = 323	# of students	% of students	
Never/Almost never	201	62.3	92
Occasionally	96	29.7	
Frequently/Always	26	8.0	

How comfortable are you asking a teacher to modify something for you to make your work more challenging or more interesting?

Number of survey respondents = 323	# of students	% of students	
Very Uncomfortable	59	18.3	
Okay	165	51.0	81.7
Very Comfortable	99	30.7	

How often have you wished a teacher would modify something for you?

Number of survey respondents = 323	# of students	% of students	
Never/Almost never	43	13.3	
Occasionally	110	34.0	86.6
Frequently/Always	170	52.6	

So, if gifted students are uniquely capable of self-advocacy, why don't they do it? Do they need permission to ask for what they need? Do they not know how? Are they uncomfortable with the etiquette of speaking with authority figures? Are they afraid of being ridiculed? The answer is: All the above. Too often students feel that education is something that is done *to* them, not *with* them. It simply doesn't occur to them that things could be different if they asked. When some try to self-advocate without having self-advocacy skills or training, their unskilled attempts may get them into trouble. Many a well-meaning-but-harried teacher has reacted negatively to the claim, "This is boring!" and piled on *more* rather than *different* work. Success in self-advocacy requires developing a specific vocabulary, learning effective ways of communicating, and engaging in lots of practice.

> "If many gifted youth are not inclined to ask for help, perhaps it is because they are concerned with protecting an image of excellence, do not want to disappoint those who are highly invested in them, or simply believe that they should be able to 'figure it out'—even when experiencing depression."
> —*Jean Sunde Peterson, "The Burdens of Capability"*

It also could be that, like many adults, gifted kids have been conditioned to believe that only struggling students have special academic needs. These students buy into the myth that because they are bright they should be able to get by without special programming, or they believe the falsehood that gifted education programs are elitist. In reality, programs that provide appropriate challenges for advanced learners are no more elitist than those that address the needs of struggling learners or talented athletes.

Some gifted learners fail to ask for what they need because they erroneously believe these and other widespread myths, such as those listed by Sandra Berger in *College Planning for Gifted Students*:[13]

- Gifted students have (or should have) fewer problems than others because their intelligence and abilities somehow exempt them from the hassles of daily life.
- Gifted students are (or should be) self-directed; they know where they are heading.
- Gifted students need to serve as examples to others and they should always assume extra responsibility.
- Gifted students can accomplish anything they put their minds to. All they have to do is apply themselves.

Many traits associated with high intellectual ability may also play a role. Introversion, perfectionism, and overexcitabilities may directly affect one's desire and ability to self-advocate. Assertiveness is not an innate talent. In fact, introversion is a common characteristic within the gifted population. It's especially difficult for quiet gifted students to speak up for themselves when they often have been admonished to be courteous, respectful, humble, and "not act like you're better than anyone else." However, that doesn't keep them from wishing things could be different.

> Introversion, perfectionism, and overexcitabilities are all discussed in greater detail in **Chapter 4: Profiles and Preferences**.

George Betts and Maureen Neihart's *Profiles of the Gifted* discussed in Chapter 1 provides further clues about different types of gifted students' reluctance to self-advocate.

Successful Learners are more apt to be extrinsically motivated, complacent, and dependent. They may fear failure, work for the grade, and be more eager for approval than challenge.

Creative Learners may be bored and frustrated but uncertain about social roles and more psychologically vulnerable. Poor self-control may lead to outbursts rather than effective self-advocacy.

Underground Learners may feel unsure and pressured and have a diminished sense of self. Ambivalence about achievement and viewing some achievement behaviors as betraying their social group may undermine their desire for change.

At-Risk Learners may have a tendency toward depression, recklessness, manipulation, and defensiveness. Unrealistic expectations, resistance to authority, and aversion to teacher-driven rewards further erode any desire to work for change.

2E Learners may experience learned helplessness and depend on others to advocate for them. If they feel intense frustration and anger, they are prone to discouragement and a poor academic self-image. They may not believe they deserve services that address their gifts and talents.

Autonomous Learners may be intrinsically motivated and strongly self-directed in their own pursuits and may not feel that changing traditional academics is a high priority.

"Adults can be tempted to think that children and teens who are exceptionally bright and academically successful will have all the confidence and intelligence they need to figure out the rest of life. The fact is, learning to live well in this world—to be happy, to have strong personal relationships, to know oneself, and to belong to small and large communities—requires skills, practice, missteps from which we learn, and time."

—Lisa Rivero, *A Parent's Guide to Gifted Teens*

Student Comfort with Parent Advocacy

Many gifted learners do not self-advocate because they are accustomed to their parents advocating for them. They have never had to speak up for themselves or practice tactful approaches that will bring about change. However, students often shun this parental involvement just when they need it most as they move into the greater independence of secondary school.

When asked about their comfort level in having a parent talk with their teacher, students in my GT Carpe Diem Workshop were fairly evenly divided with almost a third indicating they wouldn't want their parents talking to their teachers.

FIGURE 2.4
Survey Responses: Comfort with Parental Advocacy

How comfortable are you having a parent ask your teacher to modify something for you to make your work more challenging or more interesting?		
Number of respondents = 323	# of students	% of students
Very Uncomfortable	93	29
Okay	118	36
Very Comfortable	112	35

While parent advocacy continues to be important throughout the school years, gifted learners benefit more from learning how to self-advocate rather than relying on parent advocacy. How can we increase students' comfort with advocating for themselves? The simple answer is that we must talk with them. Often, educators are the gatekeepers of the information students need to feel confident about speaking up for themselves. Most learners will have access to appropriately challenging educational experiences only if we give them the knowledge and know-how they need to advocate for themselves, explain their rights and responsibilities, help them recognize their own learner needs, and point them to the opportunities that match those needs.

We have an increased responsibility to encourage gifted students from underserved groups who may not have parents able to advocate for them and may be uncomfortable self-advocating because of the various barriers they face. The National Association for Gifted Children uses the term "special populations" in reference to gifted children whose circumstances may interfere with their academic achievement and social and emotional growth. These groups include children from cultural, linguistic, or ethnically diverse backgrounds; those who are gay, lesbian, bisexual, transgendered, or questioning; twice-exceptional gifted children; highly and profoundly gifted children; children from low socioeconomic status backgrounds; and those impacted by geographic issues, such as urban and rural settings. We must insure that all gifted learners have access to the specific information and tools they need to self-advocate.

Talking to Students About Self-Advocacy

Do we talk to students about self-advocacy? If not, why not? Students' responses in the GT Carpe Diem Workshop survey clearly show adults' lack of communication on this subject with well over half of the respondents saying no one has ever encouraged them to ask for what they need.

FIGURE 2.5
Survey Responses: Encouraged to Ask for Change

Number of respondents = 323				
Has anyone encouraged you to talk with your school about better meeting your needs?				
	Yes		**No**	
	#	**%**	**#**	**%**
	142	44.0	181	56.0
Have these people encouraged you to talk with your school about your needs?				
	Yes		**No**	
	#	**%**	**#**	**%**
Parents	101	31.3	222	68.7
Teachers	59	18.3	264	81.7
Gifted Coordinators	51	15.8	272	84.2
School Counselors	12	3.7	311	96.3

Parents seem to speak with children most often, but less than a third of the students reported having been encouraged at home. Adults in the schools are even less apt to promote self-advocacy. This is not just the students' perspective. Many teachers, counselors, and parents I've surveyed admit they seldom discuss self-advocacy with children. Parents claim they just don't know what to say, don't know how things could be different, don't understand their children's rights, and don't know enough about the education system. It is the duty

of educators to ensure that parents have the information they need to share with their children. But many educators fail to fulfill this duty and also remain silent on the topic. The adults who accompany students to GT Carpe Diem Workshops often discuss their reasons for not encouraging students' self-advocacy. Their concerns fall into several generalized responses:

◆ *"It would be elitist."* The common definition of elitism is "the belief that certain persons deserve favored treatment by virtue of their superiority." Having access to an appropriately challenging education, whether one is advanced or struggling, is not favored treatment. It is equity. Gifted learners need to self-advocate not because they are superior, but because their needs are outside the norm.

◆ *"If we tell them they're smart, they'll just get big heads."* Gifted learners already know they're smart and are usually not arrogant about it. Our goal should be to help them understand their exceptional abilities and the related responsibilities they have to themselves and to others.

◆ *"They'll ask for something we can't offer them."* Addressing students' needs is often about compromise. Our discussions should focus on what they need and what alternatives we can realistically provide.

◆ *"We don't have time."* It's true that educators will need to reallocate time to get self-advocacy started and to support student initiative, but in the long run, it is far more efficient and effective when students learn to take the lead.

◆ *"School counselors already do it for all kids."* Most school counselors would like to give gifted kids' concerns an equal share of their time, but they are responsible for helping hundreds of students. Dealing with absenteeism, substance abuse, bullying, career counseling, college admissions, scheduling, and a host of other issues often takes precedence.

◆ *"If we do something different when one kid asks, we'll have to do it for everybody."* Not if we match the program to the student, using the data (numerical and anecdotal) to understand the need. On the other hand, it is not unusual to find that what begins as a solution

for one student paves the way for other students with similar needs.

◆ **"We've never done it before."** aka **"We don't do that in our district."** This implies that students/education/life/communities don't change and that whatever worked (or sometimes hasn't worked) in the past is good enough. Yet change is inevitable and just as we expect students to grow and adapt, schools must be willing to do the same.

There may be other factors, as well, specifically affecting teachers' and coordinators' ability to communicate with students regarding self-advocacy. For instance, it's not uncommon for gifted education positions to have a high rate of turnover, and in many states, no special certification or course work is required. That means those who work with gifted students may have little expertise or training in gifted education, may lack in-depth knowledge of gifted issues, and may have little time to study the research on any topic, let alone self-advocacy. In fact, while there is a wealth of research on identification, curriculum and instruction, underrepresented groups, underachievement, and assessment, research on gifted student empowerment is far less common. Additionally, coordinators' jobs generally require that most of their time be spent on identifying, providing curriculum, instructing, and managing programming. Plus, "hot" issues can arise daily and

putting out those fires takes priority. Understanding and addressing individual gifted students' social and emotional needs often take a back seat.

Gifted Students and Decision-Making

Effective self-advocacy is reliant on effective decision-making, and research indicates that gifted students should be especially good at making decisions. According to a study by Christopher Ball and colleagues, intellectually gifted high school students, relative to non-gifted students, had superior metacognition, were faster in making decisions, made greater use of efficient search strategies, were better at "tuning" information about probabilities, and reported a more competent decision style. Yet despite all that potential, it's not unusual for smart people to make poor decisions.[14]

The following common constraints affect everyone's ability to make decisions and may preclude gifted students from choosing what is ultimately best for them.

◆ **We often have less-than-perfect information.** Gifted students may have insufficient information about resources, processes, or priorities that would help them find clear solutions to the issues that are negatively affecting their education. The information they do have may be incomplete, overwhelming, too late in coming, or simply wrong.

◆ **Our perceptual processes can lead to distortions.** For example, we tend to warp incoming information to make it consistent with our preconceptions. All of us, including gifted students, are subject to biases, stereotyping, and selective attention to cues. Impatience with a lack of clear-cut answers, options, or decisions could drive the gifted student to seek answers where none readily exist.

◆ **We have limited cognitive ability.** To varying degrees, we all have restricted short-term memory and computational ability, and we process information slowly. Since gifted students tend to perceive more environmental cues and can often see both sides to an argument, they may feel overwhelmed by vast amounts of information.

◆ **We often face time and cost constraints.** We feel pressure to be decisive and to act rather than to analyze. Frequently facing the high expectations of others, gifted students may rush to make decisions to demonstrate quick problem-solving ability. This predisposition for impulsive decision-making can also make them intolerant of ambiguous, unresolved situations.

◆ **Unlike computers, we care about the outcomes of our decisions.** This can lead to distortions. For example, to enhance our confidence, we tend to perceive what we expect to perceive and we seek information confirming our position while avoiding contrary information. This is a critical issue for gifted students who have come to believe they must always be right.

◆ **We often make decisions under great psychological stress.** Such stress can lead to anger or depression. Gifted students also may be extremely sensitive to the judgments of others (both real and perceived), adding more stress to an already difficult process. It can be challenging to recover from the disappointment and shame when resolutions fail, especially when others gloat about those failures.

In order for wise decisions to be made, every person invested in the self-advocacy process needs to know what giftedness is, what rights and responsibilities students have, which characteristics constitute their learner profiles, which educational options and opportunities match a specific profile, and how to communicate effectively with others who are supporting students' attempts at changing their world. However, we adults sometimes do a less-than-stellar job of sharing this information with children, as evidenced by students' responses to the following questions on the GT Carpe Diem Workshop survey.

FIGURE 2.6
Survey Responses: Communicating About Options

Number of respondents = 286				
Has anyone talked with you about programming for gifted students in your district?				
	Yes		No	
	#	%	#	%
	166	58.0	120	42.0
Have these people talked with you about programming for gifted students in your district?				
	Yes		No	
	#	%	#	%
Parents	61	21.3	225	78.7
Teachers	84	29.4	202	70.6
Gifted Coordinators	91	31.8	195	68.2
School Counselors	22	7.7	264	92.3

Close to half of the students say they have never had a conversation with an adult about what options for gifted children are available at their school. Coordinators and classroom teachers seem to do it most often, but less than one third of the students have learned about options from them. Parents may be less able to convey the information in part because the school hasn't shared programming details with them. School counselors are least likely to have talked with the students, perhaps because they haven't been trained to address the specific needs of gifted children. Without this knowledge and other information crucial to self-advocacy, students may feel there are no alternatives to what they are currently experiencing.

How a Lack of Information Affects Gifted Learners

Consider how the lack of information affected the decision-making of the following six students, described by their gifted profiles (see Chapter 1 for more details on the profiles of gifted learners).

Jaime, who exhibited attributes of a **Successful Learner**, decided not to take honors, AP, or IB classes, because he believed they were more difficult and earning less than an A would wreck his GPA, lower his class rank, and minimize his chances of getting into the university of his choice. He didn't know about the national survey of important factors in college admission. As shown in **Figure 2.7**, only 14 percent of admission counselors rated class rank as having "considerable importance" in the selection process, compared to 60.2 percent who rated strength of curriculum. Grades in college prep courses (79.2 percent) received the highest ranking, while grades in all courses was much less important (60.3 percent).[15] If he had known this, Jaime could have increased his chances of college acceptance by taking the more difficult courses.

FIGURE 2.7
College Acceptance Factors

Factor	Considerable Importance
Grades in college prep courses	79.2%
Grades in all courses	60.3%
Strength of curriculum	60.2%
Class rank	14.0%

Bui, a **Creative Learner** and brilliant musician, assumed that "gifted" only applied to kids who were smart in math. She was unaware that the law in her state required school districts to provide appropriate programming for students with high potential in five areas: intellectual ability, academic subjects, creativity, the arts, and leadership. Bored and frustrated, she dropped out of her middle school orchestra not knowing that she had the right to several alternatives, including practicing and performing with her ability peers at the high school level.

Crystal, an **Underground Learner**, hung out with kids from her neighborhood who didn't see the importance of a traditional school experience and were content with meeting minimal graduation requirements. Like most of their older siblings, Crystal and her friends opted for the afternoon-only alternative school program that allowed them to sleep in or watch television all morning. She hadn't heard of the other more enticing educational options available to gifted kids throughout the city and therefore missed the individualized programming that was right for her. Her desire to belong outweighed her desire (and need) to be academically challenged.

Finn, an **At-Risk Learner**, had great intellectual and academic ability but faced almost insurmountable problems at home: addictive behaviors, incarcerations, absentee parents, and poverty. Though his teachers were encouraging, it didn't compensate for his life outside of school. Disciplinary issues and poor attendance led to his low achievement. He was caught up in his present struggle and didn't have the information that could enable him to see a different future. Unaware of alternatives that could have changed his course, such as residential schools with merit- and need-based scholarships, he took the path of least resistance and eventually dropped out of school.

Kenneth, a **2E Learner** with dysgraphia (a deficiency in writing and transcription ability), went unidentified for most of his elementary years because he scored in the midrange on achievement tests. But when his fourth-grade teacher recognized his intellectual strengths, the school psychologist correctly described him as twice-exceptional. Fearful of the special education label, he and his parents refused any interventions, not realizing that classroom and testing accommodations could have opened the door to many interesting, engaging, and challenging opportunities.

Alyssa, an **Autonomous Learner**, was determined to craft her own route through school, but she too lacked one piece of important information—an effective and respectful way of communicating with the advocates who could support her plans. Self-directed and independent, she came up with highly creative ideas, but her teachers, counselor, and principal had some reservations. When they asked for more specifics and questioned parts of the plan, her assertiveness turned to aggression and her requests for change were denied.

Information is the key to solve many of the problems gifted learners face.

Gifted Learners and the Problem-Solving Process

Along with their advocates, gifted students must gather and discuss the required information to make wise, rational, logical decisions at each stage of the problem-solving process (see **Figure 2.8**, and the following descriptions of the five stages).

Stage 1: Define the Problem.

At the initial stage, students gather information to answer these questions: What would you like to change? What about your education frustrates, bothers, or worries you? Is it a school issue? Home issue? Peer issue? Personal issue? Is this a typical concern for gifted students? What is your specific goal?

Stage 2: Identify Alternative Solutions.

During this stage students collect data that corresponds to these queries: What options are available? What opportunities could you create? What rights do you have? What are related district policies? Are there state laws or regulations that apply? What alternatives are recommended specifically for gifted students?

Stage 3: Evaluate and Choose an Alternative.

Next, students determine answers to the following questions: How well will the alternative match your learning styles and preferences? Will you find it interesting? Will it challenge you appropriately or will it be too difficult or too easy? What resources or physical space is needed? Will you have the time for it? Will this affect graduation or college? Do you have the skills you need to be successful?

Stage 4: Implement the Decision.

Students now gather information to respond to these inquiries: What is the best plan for implementation? Where do you begin? Who needs to give approval? Who else could or should be involved? Who will support your efforts? What is the best timeline?

Stage 5: Monitor and Control Decision Outcomes.

Finally, students compile answers to these questions: Who can help you monitor objectively? What will happen if you change your mind, don't follow through, or don't succeed? Who can you turn to for help? What will be your next step, your next goal?

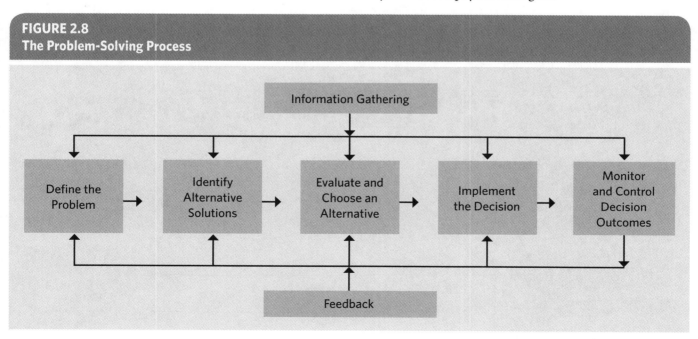

FIGURE 2.8
The Problem-Solving Process

Throughout this process, discussions with parents, peers, teachers, counselors, and gifted coordinators provide essential feedback. Students gain from others' perspectives when drafting and refining their plans, monitoring their progress, and evaluating their outcomes. A caring, knowledgeable support team adds to the success of any project.

Four Simple Steps to Self-Advocacy

In order for gifted learners to engage in effective decision-making and problem solving, they must feel comfortable advocating for themselves. They achieve this comfort by following the four simple steps of self-advocacy, each of which will be discussed more completely in the chapters to come.

1. Students understand their rights and responsibilities as gifted individuals.
2. Students develop their learner profiles by assessing their abilities and interests, strengths and weaknesses, learning styles, and personal characteristics.
3. Students investigate available options and opportunities and match them to their learner profiles.
4. Students connect with advocates who can help them accomplish what needs to be done.

Figure 2.9 shows that following these steps will lead students to a newfound comfort level and knowledge that will enhance their decision-making and, in turn, enable self-advocacy. As we've discussed, effective self-advocacy can lead to increased motivation, greater independence and self-direction, improved academic performance, more appropriate academic challenges, greater equanimity, and less frustration.

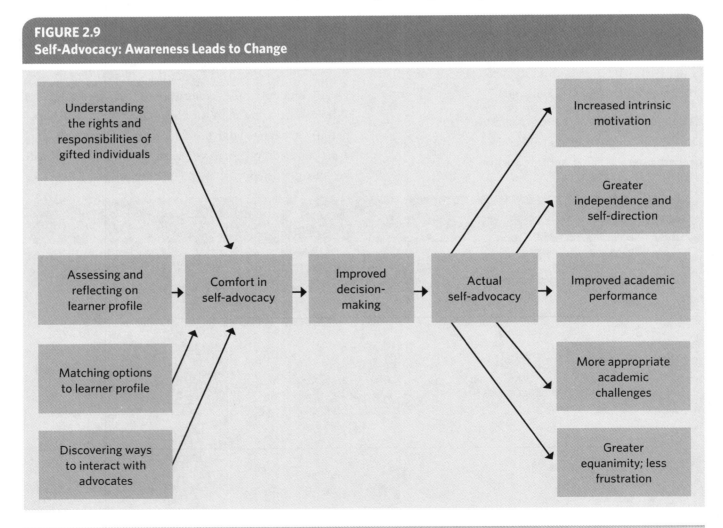

FIGURE 2.9
Self-Advocacy: Awareness Leads to Change

Conclusion

Empowering our gifted students to self-advocate is not some new educational initiative. It is about ensuring that all children know how to make the education system work for them, no matter which initiative is currently trending. Speaking up for themselves is how empowered learners throughout history have attained the education they deserve. However, most gifted children will not work through these steps on their own. Parents can help, but educators are the first line of defense for students in schools, making sure that each has continuous and systematic support. Direct teaching of self-advocacy ensures that everyone has access to all that they need to succeed.

key CONCEPTS IN CHAPTER 2

❖ Self-advocacy is the process of recognizing and meeting the needs specific to one's ability without compromising the dignity of oneself or others.

❖ As outliers, gifted children must be empowered to self-advocate for options that address their academic, social, and emotional needs.

❖ Without encouragement, gifted children are unlikely to ask for what they need.

❖ The four simple steps to self-advocacy include knowing one's rights and responsibilities, developing one's learner profile, investigating available options that match one's profile, and connecting with advocates to help achieve one's goals.

❖ The benefits of self-advocacy include more appropriate academic challenges, increased motivation, greater independence and self-direction, improved academic performance, greater equanimity, and less frustration.

❖ Adults can increase students' self-advocacy by helping students discover the information they need at each step of the decision-making process.

3 RIGHTS and RESPONSIBILITIES

I've been known to make brilliant adults cry. For instance, a few months ago I was telling my child-hood friend Jean about my work on this book and why I was so impassioned about helping gifted people self-advocate. "Of course," I said, "you know exactly what I'm talking about." She looked at me astonished, tears welling up in her eyes. "Do you think I might have been gifted?" she asked quite sincerely. I didn't know where to begin responding. *Might have been* gifted? This from a woman who grew up in a small rural community and spent her life questing for knowl-edge, with advanced degrees in music, physics, finance, and psychiatry; a woman who had studied Buddhism, volunteered with Mother Teresa, and learned Native American healing practices in New Mexico; a woman who wrote sonnets, concertos, and medieval murder mysteries. One might think she knew she was gifted, but in truth, she understood very little about the concept.

We had no gifted education per se in the little town where Jean and I were raised. No one was identified, no one was in a special program, no one was encouraged to reflect on how they might be different. Rather, the edu-cation system encouraged conformity. And so, through-out her school years—in fact, throughout her life—Jean had seen herself as a lonely, weird outsider.

Having spent my professional career working with people just like Jean, I was eager to help her discover the universal community of gifted individuals where she would see herself as an insider. That's one key reason why it is so crucial for gifted children to have information about giftedness early on. Not only do they gain self-knowledge, they also find a place where they belong. This information introduces them to a world where they feel known, understood, and accepted. It allows them to begin to focus on their rights as a unique subset of learners as well as on their responsibilities to themselves, to others, and to the world around them. In the frame of the problem-solving process discussed in Chapter 2, understanding giftedness provides students with "Define the Problem" information.

Self-Advocacy Step 1: Students Understand Their Rights and Responsibilities

As gifted individuals, students have the right to:

◆ understand giftedness and how it relates to their unique selves

◆ an appropriately challenging education

As gifted individuals, students are responsible for:

◆ taking charge of their own educations

◆ developing personal characteristics that support their success

Right #1: To Understand Giftedness and How It Relates to Their Unique Selves

If we are to empower students' self-advocacy, we must go beyond labeling to help them understand the specifics of their giftedness and the ways they differ from and are like other students. By law, we couldn't put a student with learning disabilities into a special program without detailing their needs in an Individualized Educational Plan (IEP), an explanation of their abilities and the accommodations prescribed to address those needs. We understand that dyslexia is not the same as dysgraphia; an emotional disturbance (ED) is not the same as a behavioral disorder (BD); and autism is not the same as ADHD. In the same way, intellectual talent is not the same as creative talent or leadership ability. A gifted mathematician may not be gifted with words. A gifted writer may not be fascinated by astrophysics. A gifted musician has different talents than a gifted visual artist. The interventions that help a Successful Learner navigate the education system vary from those for Creative, Underground, At-Risk, 2E, and Autonomous learners. To ask for what they need, students must understand themselves as gifted individuals. Most, however, do not, and, sadly, this is not a new concern. The results of research conducted almost twenty-five years ago

are surprisingly similar to what I've learned from the students I recently surveyed. Neither they nor their advocates clearly understand the concept of giftedness or how it applies to them and their educations.

In a 1992 study, researchers Mark Kunkel, Beatrice Chapa, Greg Patterson, and Derald Walling questioned middle school students at a summer program for the gifted. More than half of the children expressed confusion when they were asked, "What is it like to be gifted?"

Comments included:

◆ I have never been told I am gifted . . . people just call me smart.

◆ I've always been told I was hardworking. If I am gifted, it doesn't feel any different than being non-gifted.

◆ I cannot judge being "gifted" for I am confused on the matter myself.

◆ I don't think "gifted" is the right word—how about just easy learner?

◆ I'll admit that I have a few qualities and talents that others don't have, but does that make me gifted? If yes, then everybody is gifted.

Kunkel and his colleagues found that students' confusion about giftedness was an abiding and overriding theme.[16] For some, denial of giftedness seemed to serve as an important way to conform to their age peers. Others were eager to diminish their own uniqueness to promote equality. While this may seem admirable, it doesn't indicate a true understanding of giftedness nor does it help the students find the equity in education that is necessary for them to grow.

My friend Jean's comment, "Do you think I might have been gifted?" reflects the same confusion of the students in the 1992 study, as well as the confusion many people today have about the meaning of giftedness. After reflecting on her own gifts, one workshop student recently told me, "You know, my mom said she was gifted when she was young, too," as if giftedness is just a "school" thing that ends at graduation. It is not merely a label stamped on the foreheads of children who are identified for enrichment or acceleration in

education (at public expense and under public supervision and direction) for elementary and secondary students. In Canada, Special Education Policy 1.3 identifies giftedness as one of the exceptionalities that may require program planning and services, but it lets each province write its own definition.

Giftedness, however, is more than just "high achievement capability" in school. While there is no one easy way of defining giftedness, helping students reflect on several wide-ranging descriptions (some competing with and some corroborating each other) may give students a sense of its complexity and lead them away from the good grades, high-achieving, exam-acing stereotype.

National Association for Gifted Children (NAGC) Definition of Giftedness

Gifted individuals are those who demonstrate outstanding levels of aptitude (defined as an exceptional ability to reason and learn) or competence (documented performance or achievement in top 10% or rarer) in one or more domains. Domains include any structured area of activity with its own symbol system (e.g., mathematics, music, language) and/or set of sensorimotor skills (e.g., painting, dance, sports)."[18]

NAGC also maintains a list of state definitions of giftedness on their website (nagc.org), which are mostly variations of the U.S. federal definition. While state, provincial, federal, and organizational definitions may aid in systematizing formal identification procedures, they do little to help us understand the more personal—intellectual, social, and emotional—characteristics of each gifted individual. The following descriptions help us place our focus on the whole person.

school. Giftedness is a set of characteristics that they carry with them throughout their lives. Perhaps much of this confusion comes from the most common definition of giftedness, provided by the U.S. government as part of the former No Child Left Behind Act (NCLB) and the current Every Student Succeeds Act (ESSA), a reauthorization and revision of the earlier Elementary and Secondary Education Act (ESEA).

United States Federal Definition of Giftedness

The term "gifted and talented," when used with respect to students, children, or youth, means [those] who give evidence of high achievement capability in areas such as intellectual, creative, artistic, or leadership capacity, or in specific academic fields, and who need services or activities not ordinarily provided by the school in order to fully develop those capabilities.[17]

This federal definition necessarily focuses on schools and academics because the government is charged with assuring that each state provides a free

The Columbus Group's Definition of Giftedness

Giftedness is asynchronous development in which advanced cognitive abilities and heightened intensity combine to create inner experiences and awareness that are qualitatively different from the norm. This asynchrony increases with higher intellectual capacity. The uniqueness of the gifted renders them particularly vulnerable and requires modifications in parenting, teaching, and counseling in order for them to develop optimally.[19]

Annemarie Roeper's Definition of Giftedness

Giftedness is a greater awareness, a greater sensitivity, and a greater ability to understand and transform perceptions into intellectual and emotional experiences.[20]

Michael Piechowski's Definition of Giftedness

One of the basic characteristics of the gifted is their intensity and an expanded field of their subjective experience. The intensity, in particular, must be understood as a qualitatively distinct characteristic. It is not a matter of degree but of a different quality of experiencing: vivid, absorbing, penetrating, encompassing, complex, commanding—a way of being quiveringly alive.[21]

On a lighter note, many gifted individuals I've met can relate to this more visual definition:

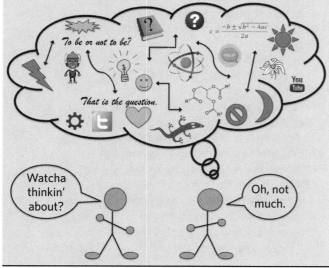

**FIGURE 3.1
A Visual Definition of Giftedness**

© Deb Douglas, gtcarpediem.com

What is inherent, but not necessarily explicit, in every definition is that no two individuals are gifted in the same way due to varying areas of giftedness, degrees of abilities, combinations of gifts and talents, experiences, interests, strengths, motivations, and other personal characteristics. It is an amalgamation of all those pieces that makes every person one-of-a-kind and contributes to an individual's unique learner profile. No wonder attempting to define *giftedness* is so messy, so elusive, and so fascinating.

Chapter 4: Profiles and Preferences more specifically addresses the five areas of information that comprise a learner profile.

The G Word

No attempt to understand the concept of giftedness would be complete without discussing the semantics of the word *gifted*. While official definitions use it without apology, it's a loaded term for many—hinting at injustice, elitism, and entitlement.

Several years ago, a colleague and I were attending the Illinois Association for Gifted Children (IAGC) conference in Chicago. We headed back to our hotel room after a very full day and stepped into the elevator with three middle-aged men in business suits. After glancing at our nametags, one asked what IAGC stood for. No sooner was the word *gifted* out of my mouth than he began a tirade on the gifted kids in his grade school "who had thought they were so smart with their special program." His face turned red, his lips quivered, and his hands shook with anger. He continued his rant, following us off the elevator and down the hallway, complaining that nobody ever did anything for kids like him in the middle. "I'm just glad my son isn't gifted," he said. "He would have turned into a jerk just like the kids I knew." We slipped into our room as quickly as possible, amazed at the power of one small word to release so much repressed emotion.

In retrospect, I understand that lack of information—about giftedness and the education system in general—is to blame for much of that man's anger and much of the misunderstanding and resentment surrounding the term *gifted*. To get around it, educators often revert to using euphemisms for gifted, like *able, capable, proficient, talented, high potential, bright,* or *advanced.* I use *gifted* in my work because I know that the students I serve are more than just advanced/able learners or high functioning or highly capable. They all have an array of other outlier qualities in addition to their high intellectual ability that affects their lives at home and school, at work and play. In GT

Carpe Diem Workshops, I simply announce that I'm going to use the term *gifted* and that the students, by being invited to the event, should know they are gifted, even if no one has ever told them so.

Several years ago, I discovered Jim Delisle's poem "Don't Mention the 'G' Word (Shhh!)" (see **Figure 3.2**). The poem helped me decide to embrace the word, using it in context and, when necessary, helping others understand its complexity. Plus, it's easier than trying to think up alternatives!

FIGURE 3.2
Don't Mention the "G" Word (Shhh!) by James R. Delisle

This poem is dedicated to Dr. Seuss.

It used to be, when folks were bold
And words weren't minced, and truth was told,
That people spoke a common tongue
They used a term we all once heard,
Simply put, the big "g" word.

But now... shhh!... you can't say "gifted,"
For if you do, you will have drifted
To a place of ill repute
Where malcontented folks refute
There's such a thing as a higher state
Of mind, of heart, of depth or rate
Of thinking, feeling, knowing, being,
Sensing, asking, crying, seeing.
These "g" word critics have lost their balance.
They think that "gifted" equates with "talents."
And the "g" word (shhh!) is just taboo.

Away! Away! They say to gifts

Thinking this denial lifts
All children to a common place
Where people do not have to face
The truth, that some have deeper thoughts
Than others, not by plans or plots,
To use their wits and thus, have gained
A higher ground of greater knowing,
A deeper depth, a profound showing
Of empathy, knowledge, wisdom, wit
That "g" word (shhh!), it still doth fit
These children, who've become a part
Of a world that's known right from the start
That some are gifted, in both mind and heart.

Sadly, though, too few take heed,
They spout "All children can succeed!"
"... Yes, that is true!" in haste I add
But when did it become so bad
To use the "g" word to define

Those able few whose intact minds
Race forward, faster, ever strong,
'Tis not a question of right or wrong,
Or better than, or me 'gainst you.
"But I know that the gifted, too,
Have special needs" we must now say
For if we don't, they'll go away
To a place where "gifted" equates with "bad."
It's way too wrong, and downright sad.
For when all are treated just the same
In this "multiple talents" or "inclusion" game
Then no one need be tagged or labeled,
That "g" word (shhh!), it can be tabled,
Pushed far into the deep, dark past,
That "g" word (shhh!) might breathe its last.
(Some may be happy, I'm aghast!)

For the gifted (shhh!) have always been
They always shall, for it's no sin
To be smarter than some, more able than most.
My dream? To someday serve as host
Of a feast where famous athletes talk
Of that new sensation, the "knowledge jock,"
And swim for miles in big, deep pools
Of learning, hoping that others see
That knowledge rocks. Yes, they deserve to be
Applauded and cheered, as their minds are set free.

And if it should happen that this day should come,
I'll lead a parade with a big, bold bass drum
With a rat-a-tat loudness that gives out a cheer
That the gifted are with us, they've always been here.

They won't go away, never will, never can,
So let us just hope that each woman and man
Will embrace the idea "It's OK to be smart."
And my idea of a good place to start?
Let's deliver the "g" word from persona non grata
And make it a good term, for it truly does matter
That the "Shhhing" ends soon, so our children can know
That it's OK to be gifted; it's OK to grow.

This poem originally appeared in *Understanding Our Gifted*, 13, 3 (2001): 8. Reprinted with permission.

Not only are we afraid to use the G word to describe individuals, but school districts often disguise their gifted programming with what they consider more acceptable acronyms. Not so long ago, GATE (Gifted and Talented Education) and TAG (Talented and Gifted) were most commonly used, but here are several I've run across recently:

- ACE (Accelerated Curriculum and Enrichment)
- ALPHA (Advanced Learning Programs for High Achievers)
- FOCUS (Facilitation of Options Centering Upon Scholarly Students)
- IDEA (Interesting Dimensions that Extend Abilities) or (Interdisciplinary Enrichment and Academics)
- LEAP (Learning Enrichment Activities Program)
- PACE (Program for Academic Challenge in Education)
- PEP (Personal Enrichment Program)
- PROBE (Pupils Reaching Out for Broader Education)
- RISE (Recognizing Individual Student Excellence)
- SEMI (Schoolwide Enrichment Model Initiative)

Much of our conflict with the word *gifted* may come from a belief in the equality of all people. We don't want gifted education to seem exclusive or elitist. I confess I've succumbed to the same verbal gymnastics. On my first day as district gifted education coordinator, I received a call from an irate parent. "I hope you're going to change the name of your GATE program," she said. "It just proves you're trying to slam that gate and keep some kids out." As a parent and teacher, I'd never viewed it that way, but if a name was going to stand in the way of progress and understanding, that was an easy fix. So we changed it to EXCEL, and described it as "programming to identify and develop student talent." At the time, I didn't feel it was a sell-out since the name also signaled a new direction in what we were doing—using more varied methods of identification, expanding beyond intellectual and academic gifts, and targeting underrepresented groups. It's also true that, fueled by society's misconceptions, gifted students are sometimes more willing to participate in enriching or accelerated alternatives if something other than *gifted* is used in the title or description.

Why do so many of us feel the need to beat around the bush when it may be futile? In her blog post "What's in a Name?" Stephanie Tolan, author and expert on exceptionally gifted children, concludes, "We could certainly change the word we use, but we can't change the underlying stories and beliefs of a whole culture or alleviate the strains and pains of human experience."[22]

Views of Giftedness Through Time

Students are further empowered with "Define the Problem" information when they can place their giftedness into historical context. It isn't just about them feeling different or a score they received on an ability test or an activity their school has put together. There is a breadth and depth to the concept of giftedness that has long been recognized. Gifted individuals fit into a timeless mosaic of "otherness."

> "Across centuries and cultures, exceptional performances and performers have intrigued scholars, practitioners, and the general public. Whatever the domain, high-level achievements interest people, sometimes as a model to emulate, sometimes as an area of inquiry, sometimes as a curiosity."
> —*Ann Robinson and Pamela Clinkenbeard, "History of Giftedness: Perspectives from the Past Presage Modern Scholarship"*

A brief history of the education of gifted students in the United States can be found at the NAGC website. Some students may be fascinated, others disinterested. But even a brief introduction to a historical perspective will allow young people to see themselves as part of a larger picture and help them understand the various hills and valleys (such as the uses and misuses of IQ testing) and perceived pros and cons that have led to our nation's love-hate relationship with giftedness. In their essay, "History of Giftedness," Ann Robinson and Pamela Clinkenbeard describe three general epochs of interest in giftedness that affect our thinking:[23]

◆ **Giftedness and divinity.** According to the early Greeks and Romans, to excel at something was to be divinely inspired in the tradition of the muses.

◆ **Giftedness and neuroses.** During the Renaissance, practitioners of medicine discovered a linkage between great intellectual ability and nervous instability.

◆ **Giftedness and the rise of mental tests.** In the 19th and 20th centuries, growth of compulsory education in the United States and Britain and recruitment for World War I ushered in the use of intelligence testing as well as the study of giftedness.

Each of these periods has impacted the perception of giftedness by individuals, schools, and society today.

So how important is it for children to learn about themselves through the lens of giftedness? Students in my self-advocacy workshops felt it was fundamental to understanding themselves. When asked to name the most important thing they had learned during the day-long event, over one third of the students indicated it was an increased understanding of giftedness. The following insights from students who self-identified as one of the six gifted learner profiles (See Chapter 1) typify the views shared by many workshop participants.

Successful Learners
"I need to step outside my comfort zone more often." —*Cierra, grade 9*

"I do not need to go with the flow of everyone else; I can make my own decisions." —*Sid, grade 8*

"It might be harder if I'm challenged, but that doesn't mean I'm not smart." —*Joy, grade 8*

Creative Learners
"Gifted people are really different from each other." —*Olivia, grade 6*

"You don't have to be mathematically or stereotypically smart to be gifted." —*Parker, grade 8*

"I'm not weird or different in a bad way, but different in a unique way." —*Lindley, grade 8*

Underground Learners
"I have a gift and I should use those benefits in the best way possible and be who I am and not feel I need to change myself to be more like everyone else." —*Jonathan, grade 6*

"I have a right to be challenged and my opinion does matter." —*James, grade 7*

"I need to believe in myself and make a goal to be successful." —*Kaia, grade 6*

At-Risk Learners
"I'm not alone in this world. I have a lot of people around me that can help." —*Josh, grade 6*

"I am the key to my education and I can stand up for myself." —*Teagan, grade 7*

"There are so many other kids out there who feel exactly the same about some situations as I do." —*Jackie, grade 8*

2E Learners
"I am, in fact, gifted, and that is okay." —*Mia, grade 6*

"No one in this room is exactly the same although each of us is gifted." —*Garret, grade 11*

"Because I am different than others, I require different things." —*Kiersten, grade 7*

Autonomous Learners
"I don't have to be gifted in everything." —*Nayely, grade 7*

"Although I'm not alone, I am the only one who really knows what I need." —*Stephan, grade 9*

"I have the power to change the future. My goals are within reach." —*Hans, grade 9*

As we help students define and own their giftedness, it's essential for us to remind them that being gifted might give them some advantages, but it doesn't guarantee top grades, academic achievement, acceptance at a prestigious university, or access to a meaningful career. It's important for them to remember that all people, including those who are gifted, need to work hard to get whatever it is they want in life—be it happiness, relationships, respect, success, or celebrity.

Right #2: An Appropriately Challenging Education

What information do gifted learners need to believe that they too have the right to an education that is meaningful, engaging, and challenging? Over thirty years ago, author Judy Galbraith spelled out the right of our brightest learners: "You have the right to a rigorous education, which stretches your skills and thinking every day."

Gifted students have a right:[24]

◆ to be in classes that are challenging and interesting
◆ to know about giftedness and why they're in or should be in an enriched or accelerated class
◆ to make mistakes and "not do their best" if they feel like it
◆ to be with other kids who really understand them
◆ to be treated with respect by friends, teachers, and parents
◆ to be different

Where does this right originate? No federal mandate exists for gifted education in either the United States or Canada. While the governments may define gifted students and their special education needs, it is left up to each state and province to provide for those needs and it is not unusual for states and provinces to defer to individual school districts.

State Laws Regarding Gifted Programming

When considering, evaluating, and choosing alternative solutions, students need the crucial information regarding their own state or province definitions, policies, mandates, and funding regarding gifted education. In the United States, NAGC collects this data regularly and posts it on their website. The recent biennial report,

2014–2015 State of the States in Gifted Education, found that while most states do have policies or laws requiring districts to identify or serve their high-ability students, most of the policies are partially or totally unfunded. State oversight of local district activities is also uneven, with only about half of the states monitoring or auditing the local gifted programs.[25]

District Mission Statements on Gifted Education

With so much ambiguity in the states' commitment to gifted education, the most direct way for gifted students to access their rights is through their local school district. Even though programming varies tremendously (or doesn't exist at all), often it is the stated intent of the district to assure that gifted learners' needs are addressed. Almost every district across the nation has a mission or vision statement that, if read carefully, includes the rights of gifted students. Here are a few exemplars I've collected recently. The emphasis in each is my own.

◆ **Chicago Public Schools:** At Chicago Public Schools, our mission is to provide a **high-quality** public education for **every** child in every neighborhood, that prepares them for success in college, career, and community.[26]

◆ **Cleveland Metropolitan School District:** (We) envision 21st Century Schools of Choice where students will be **challenged** with a **rigorous** curriculum that considers the **individual learning styles, program preferences and academic capabilities of each student,** while utilizing the highest quality professional educators, administrators and support staff available.[27]

◆ **Minneapolis Public Schools:** We exist to ensure that **all** students learn. We support their growth into knowledgeable, skilled, and confident citizens capable of succeeding in their work, personal, and family lives into the 21st century. (We) promise an **inspirational education experience** in a safe, welcoming environment **for all diverse learners** to acquire the tools and skills necessary to confidently engage in the global community.[28]

◆ **San Francisco Unified School District:** Our mission is to provide **each** student with an equal opportunity to succeed by promoting **intellectual growth**, creativity, self-discipline, cultural and linguistic sensitivity, democratic responsibility, economic competence, and physical and mental health so that **each student can achieve his or her maximum potential.**[29]

Many gifted learners don't understand that their school's vision for *all* students applies to them. But it is important that each district makes an effort to assure gifted students that they have as much right as others to have their needs met.

On a less optimistic note, it's possible that old biases and misunderstandings of giftedness provide an unintended subtext in some mission statements:

◆ "Providing high quality education for all" may imply "except for the brightest kids who have already hit the ceiling."

◆ "Encouraging everyone to be his or her personal best" could be finished with "because the underground/at-risk/creative/2E kids probably won't be successful in the traditional 'valedictorian' way."

◆ "Access to a high-quality education" may not include the encouragement and support that culturally, linguistically, ethnically, or socioeconomically diverse gifted students need to succeed.

It's easier for students to respond to biases like these when they have the information that helps them understand giftedness in general and how it relates to their needs.

The Power of Student Voices in Schools

It is relatively rare for school districts to give a lot of weight to student input when making curriculum and instruction decisions. That may be changing. An issue of *Education Week* highlighted an exemplary program that uses student voices to help fulfill a district's mission statement. Vickie Reed, superintendent of the high-poverty Murray County schools in Georgia, created a program that supports self-advocacy. In part, her school improvement plan relies on input from student-perception surveys that ask, "Do your teachers know you? Do they care about you? Do they challenge you?" There is also a district-wide council of students from every grade and every school, charged with listening to their classmates and making suggestions for change. Reed has found that when students feel their voices are being heard and are making a difference, they are more confident to take ownership of their educations. Since Reed became superintendent more than a decade ago, student achievement in the district has risen across the board and the graduation rate has increased over 30 percent.[30]

All students must claim their right to an education that is engaging and challenging and differentiated for their needs. They must believe that when other issues or concerns appear to take precedence in their schools, they have a right to speak up for themselves with assistance from adults and peers who support them.

Gifted Student Advocacy Organizations

Many state, provincial, national, and international organizations have been advocating for the rights of gifted children for a very long time, albeit with varying levels of success. Awareness of this larger group can make a gifted student's desire for change feel less like a personal struggle and more like a universal cause. Hoagies' Gifted Education Page, the "all things gifted" website at hoagiesgifted.org, lists well over 100 groups that support gifted individuals, including the most prominent ones:

◆ **National Association for Gifted Children (NAGC)** is an organization of parents, teachers, educators, other professionals, and community leaders in the United States who unite to address the unique needs of children and teens with demonstrated gifts and talents, as well as those children who may be able to develop their talent potential with appropriate educational experiences.

> *Past NAGC president, Del Siegle, has written a Gifted Children's Bill of Rights that can be downloaded from the NAGC website:*[31]
>
> You have a right
> ❖ to know about your giftedness
> ❖ to learn something new every day
> ❖ to be passionate about your talent area without apologies
> ❖ to have an identity beyond your talent area
> ❖ to feel good about your accomplishments
> ❖ to make mistakes
> ❖ to seek guidance in the development of your talent
> ❖ to have multiple peer groups and a variety of friends
> ❖ to choose which of your talent areas you wish to pursue
> ❖ not to be gifted at everything

◆ **Supporting the Emotional Needs of the Gifted (SENG)** has a mission to empower families and communities to guide gifted and talented individuals to reach their intellectual, physical, emotional, social, and spiritual goals.

◆ **The World Council for Gifted and Talented Children (WCGTC)** is a worldwide nonprofit organization that provides advocacy and support for gifted children. The WCGTC is a diverse networking organization with an active international membership of educators, scholars, researchers, parents, and others interested in the development and education of gifted and talented children of all ages.

◆ **State and Provincial Organizations** and NAGC affiliates also support the needs of gifted students and advocate for their rights at the state and national level. Since the U.S. and Canadian federal governments have left it up to the states and provinces to determine gifted programming, identification, and funding in public schools, educators and parents in almost every state and province have joined together to form a united voice. Both Hoagies' and NAGC websites have links to each.

As we teach our students to self-advocate, we must convince them that asking for an appropriately challenging curriculum is not asking for more than they deserve; rather it is a right defended by their advocates around the world. After a day focused on understanding their right to self-advocate, my workshop participants did indeed seem to get it. Common responses to the prompt, "The most important thing learned about myself today" reveal their insights:

> "I have a right to be challenged."
> —Devin, grade 8
>
> "I have the right to pursue an individualized education." —Kiana, grade 10
>
> "I have the right to ask for harder work from my teachers." —Alec, grade 7
>
> "It's okay to ask for more because it's required by law." —Joy, grade 8
>
> And my favorite comment . . . "I'm legally supposed to be getting more stuff."
> —Nate, grade 8

Responsibility #1: Take Charge of Your Own Education

In addition to their rights, gifted individuals must recognize their responsibilities if they want to self-advocate effectively. While each person may want (and has the right) to be the expert on themselves and their own educational needs, it takes more than desire. A gifted learner seeking to self-advocate has a responsibility to:

1. Acquire the information that contributes to each step of the problem-solving process.
2. Create a workable plan.
3. Follow through on the plan.
4. Seek help when needed.
5. Assess and reflect on the experience.

Two basic types of knowledge are needed to do this:

- **Self-knowledge.** Who are you and what do you need?
- **System-knowledge.** How does (and doesn't) the education system work?

Students gain these insights as they take charge and tackle one concern after another using the problem-solving process (see page 35 for a graphic).

Each of these concerns is discussed in greater detail in **Chapter 4: Profiles and Preferences, Chapter 5: Options and Opportunities, Chapter 6: Advocates and Advisors**, and **Chapter 7: Paths and Plans**.

Responsibility #2: Develop Personal Characteristics that Support Your Success

Gifted students need to develop positive character attributes and thoughtful risk-taking habits to advocate for themselves effectively.

Acquire Attributes of Good Character

Like all students, gifted learners are expected by educators to demonstrate what are considered "good student" attributes, the traits that lead to school success. It's common, however, for parents, students, and educators to confuse those qualities with a different set of attributes typically present in gifted individuals. On page 53, a brief quiz illustrates this point, followed by answers.

The misconceptions and confusion regarding these two sets of traits repeatedly shows up in my work with gifted learners. Mrs. Miller, a third-grade teacher, told me her student Perry wouldn't be ready for our enrichment program until he improved his handwriting. Francine's mother bemoaned her daughter, "If she's so smart, why is her room always such a mess?" Ashley's school counselor told her she wouldn't be so bored in school if she joined a sports team and made more friends her age. Michael told me that he was sure he wasn't gifted because he hated homework and almost always got Cs. All the attributes referred to here relate to good character, not necessarily to giftedness.

While it's true our children must work on the attributes of good character, that should be *while* they are being appropriately challenged, not *before*. Being a "good student" is not a prerequisite to getting the education one needs. On the other hand, gifted students must remember that being bored is not an excuse for turning in unimpressive homework or surreptitiously playing a video game instead of participating in class. Likewise, frustration with the inequities of group work is not a reason to deride other students, criticize the teacher, or abandon the assignment. A gifted person who also has good character finds a way to change an unsatisfying situation.

Make and Take Positive Risks

Self-advocacy requires risk-taking, an essential part of the journey toward autonomy. We learn from risks that take us outside our comfort zone, open up a world of possibilities, and lead us in important new directions. Gifted students are responsible for *taking* educational risks that are offered and *making* risks that correspond to their personal wants and needs.

Author Jim Delisle described the distinction between the two:[32]

◆ *Risk-taking* emanates from an outside source—a parent, teacher, or coach, for example—who asks a child to try something new or to take a current activity and "ramp it up" to a higher level. When the risk is offered, the child has the option of taking it or not.

◆ *Risk-making* arises from the child feeling compelled to initiate a new activity or expand an existing one. The child takes the proverbial bull by the horns and elects to enter the activity due to his or her own interest in doing so.

However, even if a wide array of high quality educational options is available, some learners choose not to take risks. Many under-challenged gifted students mistakenly believe that all schoolwork is or should be easy and that any task that requires more than a minimum amount of effort is too difficult. This belief may lead to a student's failure to develop study and problem-solving skills and an unwillingness to put forth the effort to develop those skills. It can also lead to what has been dubbed "the impostor syndrome," which occurs when true effort and perseverance is needed to successfully complete a task or understand a concept. Running into this intellectual wall may cause gifted students to doubt their abilities. What used to seem effortless has become difficult and they begin to doubt their native ability, leading some to wonder, "Am I as smart as I thought I was? What will people think if I fail or if they find out I'm not really gifted?"

Sometimes the best first step for gifted students—especially for those who fit the profiles of Successful, Underground, At-Risk, and 2E learners—is to accept the risk-*taking* suggested by others. Meanwhile, Autonomous and Creative learners may be ready for more independent risk-*making*. All students, however, need to approach risks with thought and preparation and should understand the importance of implementation and follow-through.

Mindset Theory

On a related note, gifted students also have the responsibility to pursue these risk-taking/making opportunities with a "growth mindset." Popularized by Stanford professor Carol Dweck, the theory of mindset proposes two different perceptions of learning: fixed mindset and growth mindset. With a *fixed mindset*, a person believes his basic qualities, like intelligence or talent, are fixed traits and that talent alone creates success, without apparent effort. With a *growth mindset*, a person believes her most basic qualities can be developed through dedication and hard work. This belief is supported by much of the recent research in brain development, which has found that important parts of intelligence can be developed over time and that the brain has huge potential for growth and change throughout one's life. Gifted students with a fixed mindset may feel that having to work hard indicates they aren't gifted, as described in the preceding paragraphs. They are fearful of making mistakes and often try to hide failure rather than facing and overcoming it. Students with a growth mindset are more apt to take and make risks, seek challenges, work hard, recognize their deficiencies, and work to correct or overcome them.

While risks are sometimes regarded as dangerous, wisely taking/making positive risks can be an opportunity to succeed rather than a path to failure. Of course, even experiencing failure can be positive since risk-taking/making leads to resilience. Successful risk-taking/making allows us to overcome fear of failure and provides an opportunity for internal growth. Current educational initiatives emphasize the need for resilience, sometimes referred to as "grit." According to Dweck and her colleague David Yeager, "Resilience—or whether students respond positively to challenges—is crucial for success in school and life."[33] As gifted students self-advocate for greater challenges and new experiences, it's imperative that they understand their own mindset and work on developing a risk-taking/risk-making mentality. They need to believe in their capacity to succeed at work they find difficult or challenging.

A word of caution: Lest we take the concept of valuing grit too far, recent articles with titles like "Grit and Perseverance Mean More Than Talent and High Aptitude" do more harm than good. It's not one or the other. But for gifted students to develop grit, we must ensure they are provided with educational options that allow them to persevere and eventually succeed at tasks they know to be difficult.

The Question of Gifted Students' Social Responsibility

Some people have posited that gifted individuals not only have a responsibility to themselves, but also to society. If we, as a society, provide them with the educational opportunities they need, then they owe us something. James Borland at Teachers College, Columbia University, calls this the "national-resource approach," in which gifted students are considered a commodity that needs to be identified and developed for the common good, with a focus on their future contributions to society. The alternative, Borland says, is the "special-education approach," where the emphasis is on the present and gifted children are seen as exceptional learners requiring special-educational opportunities simply in order to receive the education they, like all children, deserve.[34]

Jane Piirto, director of talent development education at Ashland University in Ohio, has long held a perspective that falls in the special-education camp: "Gifted children have no greater obligation than any

other children to be future leaders or world-class geniuses. They should just be given a chance to be themselves, children who might like to classify their collections of baseball cards by the middle initials of the players, or who might like to spend endless afternoon hours in dreamy reading of novels, and to have an education that appreciates and serves these behaviors."[35]

On the other hand, Norman Augustine, retired CEO of Lockheed Martin, appears to support the national-resource viewpoint: "Our K–12 education system has not yet determined how best to nurture extraordinary individuals so that they can become extraordinary contributors to society—and feel rewarded in doing so."[36]

The debate concerning the practical purpose of gifted programming goes on.

- ◆ Should our emphasis be on igniting each bright mind for its own sake or on preparing students to contribute meaningfully to society?
- ◆ Are gifted individuals a natural resource whose intellect we leverage to benefit other students and eventually the global community?
- ◆ Is developing each student's abilities important in and of itself, worthy of our time and effort, or is school largely preparation for college acceptance and future careers?
- ◆ Should students be encouraged to follow their passions regardless of the societal importance?

These are questions we could ask about any student, but they gain a special importance regarding gifted individuals who may do "just fine" (relatively) in school without tailored programming, but who never realize their true potential or find and follow their true passion.

Many of my first lessons about teaching gifted kids came through my work with Lucy, a brilliant young woman with amazing talents in many areas, but she had a true passion for math. For instance, as a sixth grader in the Talent Search program she answered all the ACT geometry questions correctly because, as she said, "It just makes sense." We worked hard together over her public school years to make sure she had appropriate challenges, enrichment, and social and emotional support. Subject-accelerated many times, she took courses at the local college while still in high school and finished her degree at a prestigious university in record time. But instead of accepting a fellowship or one of several job offers, she married her college sweetheart and chose to be a stay-at-home mom. A colleague of mine said she found that disappointing. I find it refreshing. Lucy followed her heart, not others' expectations. Who knows what the future holds for her, but for now she continues her quest for knowledge, grappling with profound issues while changing diapers, serving others, making the world a better place, and sharing her brilliance in many ways—both large and small—with those around her.

Chris Hedges wrote in *Empire of Illusion: The End of Literacy and the Triumph of Spectacle*: "We've bought into the idea that education is about training and 'success,' defined monetarily, rather than learning to think critically and to challenge. We should not forget that the true purpose of education is to make minds, not careers."[37]

The Perils of Choosing Not to Self-Advocate

When I first espoused self-advocacy in my district several years ago, one parent questioned, "But why does my daughter have to ask for what she needs?" My response? "Because she can." She has the right to ask for what she wants and the obligation to let her educators and parents know when things aren't going well. She has the requisite intellectual ability and can acquire the skills and diplomacy needed to be successful. She will be developing an important capacity she will use for the rest of her life. Plus, no one knows what a gifted child needs better than the child herself, especially if we help her acquire the information she needs to make wise decisions.

Parents sometimes forget that even the most attentive teachers may not recognize our students' needs all day, every day. While elementary teachers may have a

class of twenty to thirty students that they get to know quite well over the course of a year, secondary school teachers may see a student fewer than five hours a week during one semester in a classroom full of thirty to forty learners. That makes it even more imperative that students speak up for themselves. If they hadn't investigated their rights and fulfilled their responsibilities, none of the following gifted individuals would have reaped the benefits of self-advocacy:

- Matteo wouldn't have found out that his state law allowed dual enrollment, enabling him to earn credit toward graduation while still in middle school.
- Carrie wouldn't have realized that intellectual and academic enrichment should be written into her IEP along with the interventions for her high-functioning autism.
- Jeremy, wanting to fill his senior year with science and math electives, wouldn't have discovered a precedent in his school district that permitted him to squeeze in the required P.E. credit as an out-of-school independent study, an accommodation originally created for pregnant teens.
- Dayana, a talented seventh-grade cellist, wouldn't have known that her district's gifted programming included the arts and that she could be provided with music lessons during the school day and be accelerated into the high school orchestra.

The truth is, all of us who advocate for gifted students have the right and the responsibility to adapt the education system to better address their wants and needs. But, as Carol Ann Tomlinson wrote, "In instances when a child's suggestions fall on unwilling ears, I would want the child to understand the limitless possibilities that exist in his or her own mind to craft opportunities that are better than the ones that currently exist."[38]

When my self-advocacy workshop students were asked to name the most important thing they had learned about themselves during our day together, many spoke of an increased understanding of their responsibilities.

"I need to create my own path through the system." —*Samantha, grade 6*

"I want to make goals for myself."
—*Kurt, grade 8*

"I should speak up, not sit back and wait, and be courageous." —*Rebekah, grade 6*

"I won't be afraid to tell a teacher how I am feeling but I'll do it nicely." —*Maia, grade 6*

"If there are areas too easy for me I have to ask for new assignments and there are people I can talk with to help me improve my learning environment." —*Izzy, grade 6*

"I can make every day of my life better according to my learner profile by working things out with counselors. —*Jenna, grade 8*

Conclusion

Students have the right and the duty to ask for what they need. It's not too much of a stretch to say that gifted individuals have a fundamental right to self-advocate. The United States *Declaration of Independence* affirms every person's unalienable right to the pursuit of happiness and the right to pursue any legal activity as long as it does not infringe on the rights of others nor compromise "the dignity of oneself or others." In *Happiness by Design*, Paul Dolan proposed that happiness is "experiences of pleasure and purpose over time."[39] It follows that when gifted learners are allowed to take charge of their educations, they are able to pursue the *pleasure* of challenges that match their ability and find *purpose* in doing work that interests them, stretches their minds, and leads to greater challenges. We need to ensure they understand that right and their responsibility to claim it. There are no guarantees, of course, but individuals' informed pursuit of their goals yields a greater chance of leading them to happiness.

key CONCEPTS
IN CHAPTER 3

❖ The first step in self-advocacy is understanding one's rights and responsibilities.
❖ Gifted students have the right to know what giftedness is and how the term applies to them.
❖ Gifted students have the right to an appropriately challenging education.
❖ Gifted students also have the responsibility to take charge of their own educations and to develop the attributes of good character.
❖ Self-advocacy requires risk-taking that leads to risk-making; both are essential on the journey toward autonomy.
❖ While it's important for adult advocates to be familiar with the rights and responsibilities of gifted students, it is even more important that the students themselves are well informed.

Attributes Quiz

Which of the characteristics listed below are generally true of people of good character but not necessarily true of all gifted individuals? Which are generally true of gifted individuals but not necessarily true of all people?

Attribute	Good Character	Giftedness
1. Works hard		
2. Learns rapidly		
3. Turns in work on time		
4. Is considerate of others		
5. Prefers older companions/adults		
6. Is a keen observer		
7. Is attentive		
8. Is highly alert		
9. Listens with interest		
10. Has a vivid imagination		
11. Is intense		
12. Craves learning		
13. Is an early or avid reader		
14. Is organized		
15. Has an excellent memory		
16. Is perfectionistic		
17. Copies neatly and accurately		
18. Completes assignments		
19. Displays deep curiosity		
20. Is fascinated by puzzles		
21. Enjoys peers		
22. Works well in a group		

ANSWERS TO THE ATTRIBUTES QUIZ

❖ A person exhibits signs of *good character* when he or she 1) works hard, 3) turns in work on time, 4) is considerate of others, 7) is attentive, 9) listens with interest, 14) is organized, 17) copies neatly and accurately, 18) completes assignments, 21) enjoys peers, and 22) works well in a group.

❖ A person exhibits signs of *giftedness* when he or she 2) learns rapidly, 5) prefers older companions/adults, 6) is a keen observer, 8) is highly alert, 10) has a vivid imagination, 11) is intense, 12) craves learning, 13) is an early or avid reader, 15) has an excellent memory, 16) is perfectionistic, 19) displays deep curiosity, and 20) is fascinated by puzzles.

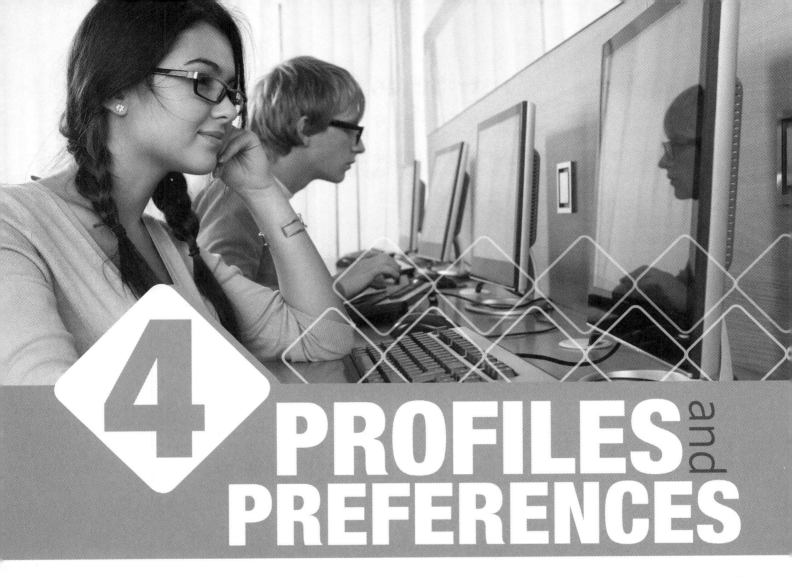

4 PROFILES and PREFERENCES

In my first year as a gifted education coordinator, a third-grade teacher approached me. "Will you talk to one of my students?" she asked. "Josh is the brightest boy I've taught in a long time, but something's wrong. When I nominated him for the gifted program, he didn't score well enough to get in."

I assured her I'd look into it but jumped to the conclusion that Josh was probably a very nice kid, a teacher pleaser, and a good student whose needs easily could be met in the regular classroom. When I met him, my error was immediately apparent. Beyond a doubt he was a gifted outlier: funny, articulate, curious, creative, and brilliant. Josh told me, "I'm really good at school stuff and coming up with new ideas, but the problem with tests is that I get so nervous I feel sick and can't pay attention." Then this eight-year-old continued to describe his learner profile to me, detailing his strengths (math, reading, and chess) and weaknesses (handwriting), his learning preferences (reading alone in a quiet room), interests (fractals and mythological beasts), and personality traits (optimistic, motivated, and introverted). His personal awareness amazed me. He knew his learning needs far better than any standardized test could reveal.

And so Josh was placed in the program without the test data. I know it might not always be easy or even possible to ignore policy, to look beyond test scores and simply admit a student into a gifted program. But identifying giftedness is so much more than parsing numerical data. I trusted Josh's teacher who truly understood his abilities, and I trusted Josh who knew himself better than many adults I know. Funny thing, six months after he was identified, Josh agreed to take the achievement and ability tests again "just for fun." This time, the pressure was off. His IQ? 152. Achievement scores in reading and math? Both in the 99th percentile.

Some people like Josh are naturally reflective, but many are not. As advocates for gifted students, it's our duty to help them recognize the specific aspects of their learner profiles, insights that will enable them to self-advocate more effectively.

BEWARE THE RIGID ID PROCESS!

For giving Josh a "free pass," I took some heat from the people who created the "sift down" method of identification that had kept him out of gifted programming. In that system, students needed to perform at or above the 95th percentile on the Iowa Test of Basic Skills to proceed with the identification process. Those who didn't were never considered. The eligible kids were then given the Otis-Lennon group IQ test, on which they also needed to achieve a certain score. Those who didn't were rejected. Finally, the remaining few students had to achieve a specific minimum score or better on the Scales for Rating the Behavioral Characteristics of Superior Students (SRBCSS), completed by a teacher. In essence, we were looking for the fewest possible students and only those who were good at taking tests and, often, at pleasing teachers. I'm happy to say that it wasn't too long before we changed this process to a talent pool model, where even one indicator of giftedness was enough to start an assessment of what a student needed to be appropriately challenged.

Self-Advocacy Step 2: Students Develop Their Learner Profiles

In order to self-advocate, gifted students must understand themselves as learners and reflect on their learner profiles. A learner profile is simply a collection of information about the ways in which a student learns (not to be confused with the six profiles of gifted learners identified by Neihart and Betts; see Chapter 1). The profile enables students to understand and celebrate their similarities and differences while uncovering areas in need of change. Within the problem-solving process (see the graphic on page 35), a learner profile contains

"Define the Problem" information. It describes how well an individual student's needs match the expectations of the education system.

We can't assume that all students automatically know themselves as learners and independently reflect on their personal characteristics. In fact, I've found that most gifted students I have worked with, especially those Successful Learners (see the six profiles of gifted learners in Chapter 1), have not been encouraged to assess their learner profiles. Creative, Underground, At-Risk, and 2E learners may have been led to examine some of the traits that are negatively affecting their academic achievement. Autonomous Learners, on the other hand, are likely to be self-reflective and to use what they understand about themselves to get what they want and need.

Even gifted educators—whose jobs are to define, assess, and identify gifts and talents—confess they seldom collect information beyond test data and teacher/parent checklists, tools that primarily assess only two parts of a learner profile: cognitive functioning and learning strengths. Typically, it's only when a problem arises that we begin to dig deeper. Yet it's impossible to match students to appropriate programming options *without* using their learner profiles. And even when no formalized gifted program is in place, leading students to better understand their profiles will encourage them to seek whatever opportunities are the best fit. This reflective process also helps students understand the ways in which their learner profiles affect their personal lives at home and school.

"If gifted children understand the reasons their minds react in different ways than how their friends may be reacting, or the traits they have that make them more intensely interested in some things than in others, they are more likely to speak up and request support for their needs than if they feel like they are just 'odd' and try to fit in or dwell on the things as if they are negative traits."

—*Kathleen Casper, "The Ultimate Plan to Help Gifted Education"*

Five Areas of the Learner Profile

It's not complicated. Gifted students just need to be encouraged to spend time thinking about themselves as learners and provided with the activities and assessments that help them focus their investigation. As eighth-grader Connor wrote in his evaluation of the workshop he attended, "When I first heard about this it seemed like it would be kind of weird, but it turned out to be really, really fun. What could be more interesting to me than me? ☺"

Karen Rogers identifies five distinct categories that should be considered when creating a learner profile:[40]

1. **Cognitive Functioning:** rate, ease, and depth of one's learning

2. **Learning Strengths:** specific areas of high performance

3. **Interests:** hobbies and favorite activities that indicate advanced development

4. **Learning Preferences:** preferred learning formats and ways to acquire information

5. **Personality Characteristics and Traits:** behaviors and attitudes that enhance or limit school success

Each of these categories is discussed in the following sections with suggestions for gathering more information and assessing traits. I have included a self-assessment for each area as an example of how an individual student might reflect on his or her profile characteristics outside of a facilitated self-advocacy workshop. Keep in mind that use of assessment tools is not intended to identify whether a student is gifted, but rather to determine specific strengths and to help students understand their own facets of giftedness that may require changes to their educational program. It's helpful for learners to evaluate each category and to document or journal their discoveries and personal impressions. They could respond to questions like these:

◆ What are your perceptions of your ability?

◆ What evidence do you have?

◆ How do the assessment results compare with what you know to be true about yourself?

◆ In what ways might your learner profile affect your school or home life on a regular/daily basis?

And remember to tell students:

◆ It's okay not to be gifted at everything.

◆ It's okay not to be interested in everything.

◆ It's okay not to be like other gifted people you know.

CAVEATS TO LEARNER PROFILE ASSESSMENTS

❖ Adult advocates should complete assessments themselves before recommending them to students.

❖ Assessments are not absolute. They're intended to get students thinking about various aspects of their learner profiles.

❖ It might be helpful for students to think of assessments as a social media quiz, such as, "Which Star Wars character are you?"

❖ There is no black or white, right or wrong, perfect or imperfect.

❖ Some parts of students' learner profiles will change over time as they grow and have new experiences.

❖ On completing an assessment, students should always ask themselves, "Is this really true about me?"

Learner Profile Category 1: Cognitive Functioning Assessments

Students can glean information about their cognitive functioning from several possible places.

Cumulative School Record

The most readily available yet least utilized resource is the cumulative record maintained by school districts throughout the student's years of attendance. Generally, the cumulative record contains ability and achievement test scores, report cards, grades, teacher comments, disciplinary actions, and communications with parents or guardians. Today, it is likely to exist as electronic files. Test results may be available in one software program, while report cards, attendance, and parent/teacher communications are in others. Reviewing their cumulative school record with a parent, counselor, or gifted education coordinator can give students important insights into their formally assessed cognitive functioning as well as their teachers' perceptions. While it may be a cumbersome process and some schools initially may be reluctant to share this information, parents and students do have a legal right to view it. Depending on the individual student, it might be wise for the parent and educator to preview the record and choose the data that's most pertinent to share with the child.

Differentiated Educational Plan (DEP)

Some school districts create DEPs for gifted students who need accommodations beyond the regular classroom. These plans take into consideration the student's intellectual abilities, current level of knowledge mastered, social and emotional concerns, and special interests and skills. They lay out appropriate academic differentiation, in-school accommodations, routes for nurturing social and emotional development, and enrichment and/or acceleration opportunities. Usually a DEP is developed at the time of initial identification and is reviewed annually. Students who are fortunate enough to have a DEP they can peruse will discover details that help them understand their cognitive functioning.

Individualized Educational Plan (IEP)

Students who are twice- or multi-exceptional should have an IEP that gives further indications of cognitive functioning. An inclusive, well-written IEP contains plans for addressing a student's gifts as part of his or her differing abilities.

IQ Scores and Online IQ Tests

For over 100 years, cognitive ability has been measured by IQ tests. Though some school districts continue to use IQ scores for identification, others do not. Yet many gifted learners are curious about IQ and since online tests are easily accessible (and vary greatly in quality), it's helpful to put the numbers in perspective. Students should know that IQ is actually an "intelligence quotient," derived through an equation: mental age divided by chronological age multiplied by 100. For example:

$$\frac{16 \text{ (mental age)}}{13 \text{ (chronological age)}} \times 100 = 123 \text{ IQ}$$

The average IQ score is 100. Just over two thirds of the population score between 85 and 115, and about 2.1 percent of the population scores above 130. The distribution of IQ scores forms a bell curve (see **Figure 4.1**).

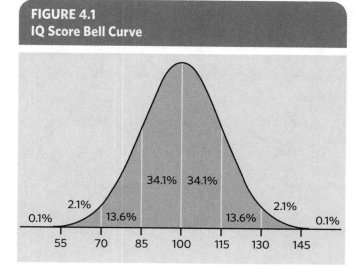

FIGURE 4.1
IQ Score Bell Curve

A Word of Caution About IQ Scores

It's important to remember that giftedness is not just an IQ score and an IQ score may not be all it's cracked up to be. Early on, part of my job as a gifted education resource teacher was to administer group IQ tests to second graders who had scored exceptionally well on the state achievement test. My doubts about the reliability of this method of determining intelligence were confirmed one day at Stangel Elementary School. My group of ten second graders and I were packed into a small conference room adjacent to the noisy office. It was stuffy and the lights buzzed. One nervous kid repeatedly kicked the leg of his chair. Another tapped her pencil on the desktop. A third hummed quietly to herself. The testing period was seventy-five minutes—a long time for ten little kids to sit still, listen, follow along in their test booklets, ignore each others' wiggling and jiggling and sniffling and sighing, and think deep thoughts.

Thirty minutes into the session the fire alarm sounded so we all traipsed outside and stood on the playground with 300 other animated students and staff until the "all clear" was sounded. I called my supervisor who said, "Oh, just pick up where you left off. It won't make much of a difference." But I knew it would. Gifted kids are not test-taking robots. They are intense human beings who, especially at that age, are distracted by the possibility of disaster, energized by the change of location and presence of hundreds of other excited kids, worried about doing well, and anxious to please the adults around them. How important is a tested IQ? It's something, but it's definitely not everything and depending on the testing experience, it's not always reliable or valid.

ONLINE IQ TESTS

To check their inherent value, I personally took six online IQ tests one evening and compared the results to my ages-old eighth-grade Otis-Lennon score. Two of the tests returned scores roughly equal to that. One was slightly higher. One was slightly lower. But one put me thirty points lower and the lowest put me just above average. During that particular test I remember thinking, "This is all numerical. Where are the analogies, the verbal questions, the 'which-of-these-things-is-not-like-the-others' that I know I'm good at?" I admit I was getting tired toward the end and giving up rather than thinking long and hard about the questions. And obviously, that can affect students' scores as well. We need to ensure that students who try online IQ tests are aware of their fallibility. The most valid and reliable IQ tests are those individually administered by trained professionals. Group tests, more frequently used by schools, may not be as dependable and provide less information for a learner profile.

Student Self-Assessment of Cognitive Functioning

Considering the attributes of high cognitive functioning allows students to think about their own abilities anecdotally rather than numerically. They can reflect on the extent to which each of the qualities in the self-assessment on page 73 is true about them in relation to others.

Following the learner profile assessments in my workshops, students summarize what they've discovered about themselves and then the group discusses the ramifications of these assets on their daily lives at home and in school.

Students' Insights on Cognitive Functioning

Following is one student's reflection on her cognitive ability, as well as various comments from my GT Carpe Diem Workshop discussions.

"My school district doesn't do IQ tests but I was really curious so I tried one online during our lunch break today. I scored 148, which it said is in the 99th percentile, so I guess that's pretty good. I know I could read before I started preschool because I remember reading books to the other kids. My parents, teachers, and friends have always told me I'm smart and I almost always top out on standardized tests. I really like learning new stuff but I don't always like school. Sometimes it's just plain boring, especially when we go over and over something that I understood the first time around. I'm kind of embarrassed to say that I can get interested in almost anything. I'm not real focused I guess, just curious about a whole lot of things. There's just not enough time to dig into everything. I read a lot of science books and science fiction and I'm writing a novel about a girl who's kind of like me and comes back from the future to show people how to cure cancer. All in all, I'd say I have fairly strong cognitive functioning."
—Liana, grade 10

"A lot of the time I don't have to study much because things come quickly and easily."
—Andrew, grade 6

"In order to learn something, I have to go beyond what the rest of the class is doing."
—Madelyn, grade 7

"People don't always understand what I'm saying unless I simplify it." —Shonda, grade 9

> "Some kids think I'm showing off when I'm really just excited about the topic and already know a lot about it." —*Nathan, grade 6*
>
> "It's easy for me to do well in school but not always so easy to be excited about it." —*Rachael, grade 7*

Ultimately, for students to use the education system to get what they need, it may be less important for them to know how gifted they are than to understand in what ways they are gifted and where their learning strengths lie.

Learner Profile Category 2: Learning Strength Assessments

Information on learning strengths can be found in several ways, including the following.

Out-of-Level Assessments

It's not unusual for gifted students to reach the ceiling of grade-level exams, scoring as high as the 99th percentile. Top scores may seem like success, but are useless in matching the learner to appropriate programming. The results do not reveal the full extent of students' abilities in specific areas, nor do they give us a valid measure of their academic growth. A more reliable way to assess learning strengths is an out-of-level test that removes the ceiling. Some districts may administer an achievement test battery (like the Iowa Tests of Basic Skills or the Woodcock-Johnson Tests of Achievement) that is scored two or more grade levels above the student's current grade level. In essence, their results would be compared to those of students two to three years older. The Woodcock-Johnson provides achievement information in reading, oral language, mathematics, written language, and academic knowledge. The Iowa Tests offer a look at how students are progressing in key academic areas and provide diagnostic data that can be used to make decisions on differentiation for a variety of academic strengths.

If a district has done this type of assessment, the results would be in the student's cumulative file. If it has not been done, many classroom teachers, school counselors and psychologists, as well as other licensed educators, are qualified to oversee the testing.

Talent Searches

Talent searches for academically gifted students in third through ninth grades conducted by colleges and universities also use out-of-level testing to help determine specific learning strengths and appropriate accelerated programming. For example, as part of Northwestern University's Midwest Academic Talent Search, the EXPLORE test, designed for students in eighth grade, is administered to gifted children in third through sixth grade. Students in sixth through ninth grade take the ACT and/or SAT, college entrance exams intended for high school juniors and seniors. The ACT and EXPLORE tests can identify learning strengths in English, reading, math, and science. The SAT includes reading, writing, and math assessments, and individual subject tests (SAT II) are also available. While it's good to remember that talent search test scores are only one piece of the puzzle, they are an important piece backed up by years of research. Awareness of what test scores indicate about students' abilities is vital for gifted students as they develop their learner profiles.

Student Self-Assessment of Learning Strengths

The following resources can help students identify their learning strengths.

Scales for Rating the Behavioral Characteristics of Superior Students (SRBCSS)

These scales were designed as a tool for identifying gifted and talented learners, allowing teachers and/or parents to evaluate a student's characteristics. While some districts use the scales as part of their identification process, students can also use them to discover specific learning strengths. Most helpful are the scales for art, music, drama, communication, mathematics, reading, technology, and science. Students can see their strengths broken down into identifiable characteristics and weigh the scales' results with their own self-knowledge. For instance, rather than simply thinking "I like music," students can rate themselves on seven traits on the Musical Characteristics scale, including these:

◆ shows a sustained interest in music; seeks out opportunities to hear and create music.

◆ perceives fine differences in musical tone (pitch, loudness, timbre, duration).

◆ is sensitive to the rhythm of music; responds to changes in the tempo of music through body movements.

Five of the SRBCSS scales—creativity, leadership, learning, motivation, and planning—may more accurately detect other aspects of a learner profile, such as cognitive ability or personality traits. Samples of all fourteen scales can be found at: prufrock.com/assets/clientpages/pdfs/Renzulli_Scales_Sample_Copyright_Prufrock_Press_2013.pdf.

Purdue Academic Rating Scales (PARS) and Purdue Vocational Talent Scales (PVTS)

These assessments were designed by John Feldhusen and associates to allow teachers to evaluate secondary school students' performances in specific subject areas: science, social studies, English, mathematics, foreign languages, agriculture, business, home economics, and trade and industrial arts. Though created in the 1990s, these scales are still valuable today in helping students analyze their learning strengths. For example, a student who believes science to be a learning strength could rate herself on the PARS Science Scale containing traits such as:

◆ sees relationship of science to real world.

◆ is interested in science books and TV programs; enjoys science fiction.

◆ has science hobbies, is a collector, likes gadgets.

◆ comes up with good questions or ideas for experiments.

◆ is interested in numerical analysis, is good at measurement and data analysis.

◆ understands scientific method, is able to formulate hypotheses and conduct experiments carefully.

Both the PARS and the PVTS are available online at: iu19giftednetwork.wikispaces.com/file/view/Purdue_scales.doc.

Students' Insights on Learning Strengths

Following is one student's reflection on his learning strengths, as well as various comments from my GT Carpe Diem Workshop discussions.

"I always score high on all parts of our state tests—reading, writing, math, science, and social studies—but I know I'm better at some things than others. Like, I'm great in science and math (I should be since my dad teaches both), but, in all humility, I think I have a real gift for languages and the social sciences and the arts. Anything that is directly related to people and the way they live and have lived. In 7th grade I took the SAT as part of the NUMATS and my reading score was higher than my math score so I guess that confirms it!"
—*Tyler, grade 9*

"Sometimes a learning strength is not really something you're most passionate about."
—*Abby, grade 9*

"In high school it's hard to work out a course schedule that lets me take all the really challenging classes." —*Jackson, grade 10*

"I want to have as many science classes as I can, which means I won't have time for music or art." —*Lynn, grade 9*

"My strength is in social studies, but our middle school only has accelerated math and language arts." —*Billy, grade 7*

"A kid whose strength is in the arts may seem very different from a kid whose strength is math and science, but both can be gifted."
—*Luther, grade 5*

A deeper understanding of one's learning strengths leads quite naturally to an examination of one's interests and passions.

Learner Profile Category 3: Interest/Passion Assessments

It's common for gifted kids to be interested in a wide range of things. But frequently when asked about their interests, they speak in general terms, such as math, writing, sports, or video games. It's important when assessing their learning profiles that they look more deeply at what they are passionate about and how those passions can be part of their educational plan. "Visual Preferences" is one of my GT Carpe Diem Workshop activities. Students line up across the room forming a continuum that shows their interest in a particular subject. When the workshop leader calls out "math," those who absolutely love math move to one end of the room, those who dislike it move to the other, and those students who have less adamant feelings fill in the rest of the continuum. The lineup changes, however, when the leader says "geometry," and it morphs again when interest in "algebra" is measured. The same thing happens when topics range from "writing" to "writing poetry" to "writing short stories" to "writing essays." When sports is the subject, the continuum changes in relation to playing sports versus watching sports, and also regarding involvement in specific sports activities. The value of this exercise is twofold: it reinforces that gifted kids differ in their interests and abilities, and it also helps students weigh their priorities. Several more formal tools have been developed to help gifted students assess their interests and passions. Two of the most popular are listed here.

Rogers's Interest Inventory

This tool helps gifted students reflect on the kinds of programs and enrichment activities they might be interested in pursuing. It is most appropriate for upper elementary and middle grades. It presents several scenarios for students to react to based on their interests. For instance, in one situation the student has been hired by a magazine to oversee a monthly special feature and must rank her top three choices from a list of twenty-two possibilities. Other inventory items ask more direct questions, such as: "What are some things you would do if you had more time and money?" As

students contemplate their responses, they may begin to see patterns that will help them choose or design their educational options.

This inventory is published in Karen Rogers's book, *Re-Forming Gifted Education* and is also included in Rogers's *The Gifted Education Planner*.

Renzulli's Interest-A-Lyzers

The Interest-A-Lyzer, designed by Joseph Renzulli, is for use with gifted students ages six to twelve to identify their interests in fine and performing arts, literature, science, mathematics, history, business and management, and athletics. Thomas Hébert, Michele Sorensen, and Renzulli later created the Secondary Interest-A-Lyzer for students in middle school and high school. The stated purpose of the questionnaires is to help students become more familiar with their interests and potential interests, helping them more quickly and easily choose topics to pursue during individual or small-group projects. Similar to Rogers's inventory, the Interest-A-Lyzer asks students to imagine themselves in certain situations and to choose between various options.

Different versions of the Interest-A-Lyzer can be found online:

- Interest-A-Lyzer (search researchgate.net)
- Secondary Interest-A-Lyzer (search prufrock.com)
- Reading Interest-A-Lyzer (search nrcgt.uconn.edu)

Student Self-Assessment of Interests and Passions

As is often the case, having a one-on-one conversation with gifted students is the best method to help them zero in on their passions and to both narrow and broaden their list of interests. Possible questions you might ask include:

- What do you spend a lot of time doing?
- What do you wish you could spend more time on?
- What are you currently spending time on that isn't interesting to you?
- Which of your involvements are family interests? Which are peer group interests? Which are your own personal interests?
- What new areas would you like to explore?

Students' Insights on Interests and Passions

Following is one student's reflection on his interests and passions, as well as various comments from my GT Carpe Diem Workshop discussions.

"I think I need to categorize my interests into three groups: family interests, friend interests, and my personal interests. There's some stuff I know I love because of my family, like running and orchestra, two things I got from my mom and dad. And my friends and I are really into computer programming, old-school hip-hop, and college football. But here, in no particular order, are the things that I'm currently passionate about: astrophysics, time travel, science fiction, Miles Davis, Ta-Nehisi Coates, and voter rights. Do you think they'll cover any of this in 8th grade next year?"
—*Levar, grade 7*

"A lot of what I'm interested in doesn't come up in class during the school year."
—*Mario, grade 6*

"I spend a ton of time outside of school reading and investigating the things I'm really passionate about." —*Clare, grade 9*

"Sometimes I wish science class would go slower and we'd spend more time going deeper into something that really interests me, but then I find out no one else really cares about it." —*Anthony, grade 11*

"Sometimes I'm happy to just be the same as every other kid my age who likes sports, music, and girls." —*Johann, grade 8*

As with all of us, gifted students' interests change over time, sometimes becoming very linear, sometimes growing very deep, and sometimes fanning out across several disciplines. Some interests are short-lived, some last for a lifetime.

Learner Profile Category 4: Learning Preference Assessments

The best way for students to gather information on learning preferences is to reflect on what works and doesn't work in the classroom and when studying at home. Areas to think about include the instructional practices they have experienced in the classroom, their personal learning modes, the environment that allows them to focus on the task at hand, and the ways in which they are most successful at demonstrating what they have learned. Following are five categories of learning preferences: classroom, grouping, learning mode, learning environment, and learning assessment.

Classroom Learning Preferences

The most common classroom instructional techniques include:

◆ Lecture and discussion
◆ Research and inquiry
◆ Experiments and simulations
◆ Games and competitions
◆ Projects and independent study

Students can self-assess their classroom learning preferences by asking themselves, "What was the best learning activity I've ever experienced and what made it so great?" They should also consider the worst learning activities they've experienced and what made them so bad. Which strategies inspire them to persevere? Which do they find frustrating? An honest introspection is important here. For some students, a change in instructional strategy may provide a better challenge. For others, however, a change in the student's attitude and self-discipline might be required.

For example, three students once told me that they hated lab work in science classes, but each had a different reason. Kennedy said he didn't like all the setup and cleanup work. Quinn said she thought it took too much time to write up the lab reports. But Bree's reason for hating labs was that she was already adept at setting them up and in most cases they seemed like a waste of time because she could easily predict the results. Gifted kids need to determine if their reason for disliking a learning strategy is because it is too *much* work or too *little* work.

Chapter 5: Options and Opportunities provides suggestions for working with teachers to adjust instructional techniques to match student preferences.

Grouping and Learning Preferences

Grouping also plays an important role in gifted students' classroom learning preferences. For a wide variety of reasons, some students always choose to work alone; some love peer learning, especially if their partners have similar academic or intellectual abilities or interests; and some prefer group learning, but generally in a small group of like-ability peers. Whole-class learning can also be exciting for gifted students if the teacher is skilled in differentiation and tiered questioning.

In every GT Carpe Diem Workshop, participants are surveyed regarding their group experiences. The following set of responses is particularly telling.

FIGURE 4.2 Survey Responses: Group Experiences				
Number of respondents = 288				
During the last year, how often have you been grouped to work with other students of your ability level?				
Never	Seldom	Occasionally	Often	Always
9%	18%	31%	36%	7%

Over half of the students never, seldom, or only occasionally get to work with like-ability peers. Those who said they often or always work with like-ability peers indicated they are in gifted schools or homogeneous classrooms.

The topic of group work often generates energetic discussion among workshop participants. A typical conversation goes something like this:

Anna: "I hate group projects. Everyone always expects me to do all the work. Slackers really drag me down."

Carlos: "Yes, but sometimes other kids need help and can't do it as well as I can so if I'm not the leader we'll get a lousy grade."

Anna: "But are the other kids learning anything if you do all the work?"

Carlos: "Well, sometimes they understand better when I explain something than when the teacher does."

Anna: "Maybe the question should be: Are *you* learning anything if you're teaching other kids?"

Carlos: "I guess if I were working alone I could get the assignment done in half the time."

Anna: "So you're not learning much and you're wasting a lot of time."

Carlos: "But I like helping other people and I don't want it to look like I think I'm better than anyone else."

Anna: "Me either, but I just wish I could work with someone who's smarter than I am once in a while, someone who would push me to ask harder questions and dig deeper."

Carlos: "I know. My ideas really start to fly when I'm working with other smart people. But is that fair?"

Anna: "Fair to whom? To others or to me?"

Carlos: "Well, if all the smartest kids work together they'll do a lot better than the other groups and get the best grades. But if we're in mixed groups we wind up doing most of the work, but don't really get inspired or learn much."

Anna: "So our job is to slow down, average out the grades, and try to keep the other kids from hating us?"

Carlos: "Not really, but that's what always seems to happen."

Anna: "And that's why I hate group projects!"

Learning Mode Preferences

Although there are a variety of learning style theories and descriptions, the simplest assessment is determining if one favors visual, auditory, or kinesthetic learning (VAK, as it is sometimes called).

- ◆ **Visual Preference.** Learning by seeing. Do you study best by reading notes or headlines in a book and studying diagrams or illustrations? Do you see the information in your "mind's eye"?

- ◆ **Auditory Preference.** Learning by hearing. Do you study best by having someone ask you questions and saying facts silently to yourself? Do you actually hear the information repeated in your mind?

- ◆ **Kinesthetic Preference.** Learning by doing. Do you study best by acting out things or building models or creating diagrams?

Most learners use all three modes to receive and process new information and experiences, but one or two of these is typically dominant. The dominant mode or modes, however, may not always be the same for every task; a person may prefer one or more modes of learning for one task, and a different mode or modes for another task.

It's important for adult advocates to remember that the students we help may have different learning mode preferences than ours. I tried in vain to help my son memorize vocabulary words for his German class. But as he patiently reminded me, the visual mnemonics I suggested were of little help to a young person who favors auditory learning.

During GT Carpe Diem Workshops, I help students focus on their learning mode preferences by asking them to remember a random ten-digit phone number. I repeat it twice and then am silent. After fifteen seconds I call "stop" and ask them to share what they're doing to memorize the number, which preferred method is their "go-to." Their responses relate closely to Howard Gardner's theory of multiple intelligences. Some are writing the number on paper or repeating it over and over in their heads (verbal-linguistic); some are rhythmically chanting it (musical); some are relating it to the phone number of someone else they know and call frequently (interpersonal); some are finding numerical patterns (logical-mathematical); some are indicating the numbers on their outstretched fingers (bodily-kinesthetic); and some are visualizing the numbers like movie credits scrolling across their minds (visual-spatial). Most are using a combination of styles. In the days of touch-tone phone dialing, one musically gifted young man memorized the phone number by singing the corresponding tones to himself. Whichever learning mode or modes students prefer, it's helpful for them to be aware of their strengths and to be able to call them into play, especially when tasks become more difficult.

Learning Environment Preferences

Students also should reflect on when and where they study most effectively. Some may fare best in the school environment while others prefer working at home. The best place for a person to study is often determined by a combination of conditions, including noise level, lighting, time of day, presence of other people, and furniture arrangement. Self-directed students may be surprisingly successful studying in environments that we adults might question. Instead of absolute quiet, they might prefer background noise, such as music, television, or conversation. Sprawling on a bed or in a comfy chair may be the best place to read or review. And since many gifted individuals are night owls, their brains might be most alert later in the evening, while others may prefer rising early and studying in the predawn hours. Conversely, an under-motivated gifted student may prefer to begin homework at midnight, stretched out on a bed with rap music blaring, but that may not be the most conducive to academic achievement. An honest reflection of their learning environment preferences enables students to plan for success.

Learning Assessment Preferences

While tests remain the most common way of assessing learning, a variety of other ways allows students to demonstrate their understanding:

◆ Essays, term papers, written compositions
◆ Performance tasks: exhibitions, presentations, and demonstrations
◆ Projects
◆ Portfolios and journals
◆ Rubrics
◆ Interviews with teacher
◆ Peer-evaluation
◆ Self-evaluation

In many instances, the form of assessment is dictated by the school or teacher. However, when given a choice, gifted students should have an idea of which form is their preference. Jake was struggling with a paper he had chosen to write for history class. Since I knew him to be highly creative, verbally articulate, and a keen actor and comedian, I asked why he'd chosen a written form of assessment. Our conversation went something like this:

Me: "Do you like writing? Are you good at it?"
Jake: "No, I hate it. It just seemed like the easiest option."
Me: "And is it easy?"
Jake: "No, it's really hard."
Me: "Then why don't you ask your teacher if you can change to an oral presentation? Use your strengths and abilities to show what you know in the best way you can."

That's not to say that Jake didn't need to work on improving his writing skills if he expected to succeed in high school and college. But until he was more proficient at it, he had a better chance of demonstrating his understanding using an assessment that he truly preferred.

Student Self-Assessment of Learning Preferences

As stated earlier, the most direct way for students to assess their learning preferences is to recall an educational experience that was truly satisfying. What conditions contributed to its success? Where, when, and how did students do most of the work? What happened during class time? What materials did students use and what method did they choose to demonstrate what they learned? Since it's critical for us to gain insight from both our successes and failures, students also could recall a project they considered a disappointment and respond to the same questions.

As another part of the "Visual Preferences" activity during GT Carpe Diem Workshops, students specify their learning preferences by moving around the room in response to questions from the facilitator. For instance, students indicate their preference for classroom activities by walking to one of the four corners designated as: 1) lecture, 2) demonstration, 3) group project, and 4) independent study. This simple activity serves two purposes: students reflect on the ways they prefer to learn and they observe the variety of preferences that exist within a group of gifted individuals. They are often surprised that what works best for them is less than optimal for others.

Students' Insights on Learning Preferences

Following is one student's reflection on her learning preferences, as well as various comments from my GT Carpe Diem Workshop discussions.

> "The most important thing I realized is that I'm a night owl (or as I like to say, a nightingale), and while the majority of people don't understand that, it's not wrong. Around midnight, my most creative ideas begin to flow. That makes it hard to be alert at 7:45 a.m., when first hour begins, so I've got to find some imaginative ways to resolve that. I like to study alone at the desk in my bedroom with quiet music playing in the background. No lyrics! I know I'm a visual learner rather than auditory. For example, in French class I have trouble following along with the conversation, but reading and writing are easy for me. And I hate group work, especially when I'm expected to do it all. Given an assessment choice, I would always write, maybe an essay or poem or short story." —*Cassy, grade 10*

"Neither home nor school is a good place for me to study, so I get most of my work done at the public library." —*Vang, grade 8*

"I love lectures when the speaker really knows the subject well and is excited about it. But I fall asleep when people just drone on and on." —*Helen, grade 10*

"It took some convincing but my parents now let me have the TV on while I study. I don't really watch it, but somehow it helps me focus." —*Ramon, grade 8*

"We have study hall but I never get anything done because it's so noisy. Maybe I should see if I can go someplace else." —*Song, grade 7*

A clear understanding of their learning preferences helps gifted learners create the environment in which they can be most successful.

Learner Profile Category 5: Personality Characteristic and Trait Assessments

Gifted students are often fascinated with psychology and especially enjoy personality assessments that let them explore who they are and what makes them tick. It's a great opportunity for students to become acquainted with the "Big Five" framework of personality traits, the most widely used and extensively researched model in the field of psychology. The Big Five were described in the 1970s by two independent research teams: Paul Costa and Robert McCrae at the National Institutes of Health, and Warren Norman at the University of Michigan with Lewis Goldberg at the University of Oregon. As the name implies, the framework has five big dimensions, often referred to using the acronym OCEAN:

- **Openness to experience** can be viewed as inventive/curious versus consistent/cautious. It includes an appreciation for art, adventure, unusual ideas, curiosity, and a variety of experiences.
- **Conscientiousness** refers to the tendency to be organized, dependable, self-disciplined, dutiful, and achievement-oriented, and to prefer planned activities to spontaneous ones. The dichotomy could be described as efficient/organized versus easygoing/careless.
- **Extroversion** is defined as energy, talkativeness, positive emotions, assertiveness, sociability, and the desire to seek stimulation in the company of others. It is often seen as outgoing/energetic versus solitary/reserved.
- **Agreeableness** is friendly/compassionate versus analytical/detached. It is exemplified by compassion and cooperation rather than suspicion and antagonism toward others.
- **Neuroticism** is reflected in the tendency to experience unpleasant emotions easily, such as depression, anxiety, anger, and vulnerability. It is described as sensitive/nervous versus secure/confident and is sometimes referred to by its inverse, emotional stability.

Inventories based on the Big Five traits can be accessed online; some are quick and easy, some more extensive. Here are links to the most reliable instruments available at the time of publication:

Ten Item Personality Measure (TIPI):
gosling.psy.utexas.edu/scales-weve-developed/ten-item-personality-measure-tipi

The Big Five Project: outofservice.com/bigfive

50-Item Set of IPIP Big-Five Factor Markers:
personality-testing.info/tests/BIG5.php

Truity Personality Tests:
truity.com/test/big-five-personality-test

Short Form for the IPIP-NEO:
personal.psu.edu/~j5j/IPIP/ipipneo120.htm

The Six Most Relevant Personality Characteristics of Gifted Learners

Over time, my GT Carpe Diem Workshop students have indicated that within the Big Five dimensions are six specific characteristics they feel are especially relevant in helping them understand their own giftedness.

Characteristic #1: Analytical Mind/Creative Mind (related to the Big Five's "Openness to Experience")

People often prefer one type of thinking to the other. For example, one person might display a more analytical mind (logical and objective) while another person has a more creative mind (intuitive, thoughtful, and subjective). People with strong analytical minds are often described as left-brained, and people with strong creative minds as right-brained. However, the validity of this right brain/left brain dichotomy has been debated over and over again and most scientists agree that it is merely a myth. For instance, abilities in subjects such as math are actually strongest when both halves of the brain work together. While we might have a natural tendency toward one way of thinking, the various parts of our brain work together in very complex ways. Because analytical thinking is akin to the stereotypical vision of giftedness, it's important for students all along the analytical-creative spectrum to also see themselves as gifted learners.

Characteristic #2: Motivation, Self-Direction, Independence (related to the Big Five's "Conscientiousness")

Motivation includes deciding which goal to pursue, beginning to work on that goal, and being persistent in working toward that goal. The characteristics evaluated in the "Motivation" section of the Scales for Rating the Behavioral Characteristics of Superior Students (SRBCSS) help students assess their attributes of motivation, self-direction, and independence:[41]

- persistence when pursuing goals
- little direction required from teachers
- little need for external motivation to follow through
- intense concentration on a topic for an extended period
- sustained interest in certain topics or problems
- tenacity and persistence even when setbacks occur
- commitment to long-term projects

When it comes to school and academic work, gifted students' motivation varies greatly. Successful Learners (see the profiles of gifted learners in Chapter 1) often are extrinsically motivated—studying because they want to get good grades and please their parents, participating in a sport to win awards, or entering a competition to get a scholarship. Autonomous Learners tend to be more intrinsically motivated—researching a topic because it's interesting to them, participating in a sport because they find it enjoyable, competing because the challenge is exciting. What we do know is that motivated students find value in their school experience, believe they have the skills to be successful, and trust their environment and expect they can succeed in it.[42]

Characteristic #3: Optimism/Pessimism (related to the Big Five's "Neuroticism and Agreeableness")

The most common metaphor for this characteristic is the half-full versus half-empty glass. Those who are optimistic generally foresee the best possible outcome to a situation, while pessimists anticipate undesirable outcomes. For gifted students to realize their potential, they need to adopt an optimistic outlook. In Chapter 7 of *Peak Performance for Smart Kids*, Maureen Neihart details helpful ways for advocates to talk with learners about this trait. She suggests we begin by measuring our own optimism using a tool such as the Optimism Test created by Martin Seligman (available at: www .authentichappiness.sas.upenn.edu/home). When we recognize what we are modeling, we also become more conscious of our students' optimism and pessimism when they talk about their own successes and disappointments. Teaching them to consider more than one explanation for what happened engenders a more optimistic viewpoint that can have lifelong positive effects.[43] As they work through the self-advocacy process, optimistic gifted students believe that change is possible and the outcome they seek is attainable.

Characteristic #4: Perfectionism
(related to the Big Five's "Conscientiousness")

Gifted people tend to exhibit perfectionism at higher levels than the general population. When used adaptively, as a striving for excellence, perfectionism can motivate students to reach their goals. But unhealthy, maladaptive perfectionism could drive them to attempt an unattainable ideal. The research of Thomas Buescher and Sharon Higham asked gifted children about perfectionism: "By their own admission, talented adolescents often feel like perfectionists. They have learned to set their standards high, to expect to do more and be more than their abilities might allow. Childhood desires to do demanding tasks *perfectly* become compounded during adolescence. It is not uncommon for talented adolescents to experience real dissonance between what is actually done and how well they expected it to be accomplished. Often the dissonance perceived by young people is far greater than most parents or teachers realize."[44]

The father of a seventh grader once called me late in the evening of the first day of the school year. "Would you please talk to Jenna?" he pleaded. "She's been working on her English paper for hours and says it still isn't good enough. We can't get her to go to bed." He put Jenna on the phone and I asked her to describe the assignment. "Well," she said, "our teacher told us to write a five-paragraph essay on something fun we did during the summer. She said to do our best job because she was going to use the essay to set our individual writing workshop goals for the whole semester. I'm just trying to show her what my best writing is like." To her credit, Jenna was striving for excellence, but her perfectionism was keeping her from setting realistic limits on the amount of work required for that particular assignment. No doubt the teacher had instructed the class to "do your best work" as an encouragement for undermotivated students. Jenna, however, took the words to heart and felt the assignment was not complete until it was her *very best* work, a task that proved endless because she couldn't tell when "good enough" was good enough.

Author Thomas Greenspon has spent much of his professional life researching, counseling, and writing about perfectionism. In his book, *What to Do When Good Enough Isn't Good Enough*, he helps students like Jenna recognize the difference between striving for excellence and succumbing to paralyzing perfectionism (see **Figure 4.3** on page 69 for an excerpt). Since perfectionism can sometimes run in families, another of Greenspon's books, *Moving Past Perfect: How Perfectionism May Be Holding Back Your Kids (and You!) and What You Can Do About It*, helps parents and children work together to free themselves from perfectionism.

Characteristic #5: Overexcitabilities/Intensities
(related to the Big Five's "Neuroticism")

Kazimierz Dabrowski, a Polish psychiatrist and psychologist, first identified overexcitability (OE) as the inborn intensities that indicate a heightened response to stimuli. He described five specific areas of OE: psychomotor, intellectual, emotional, sensual, and imaginational. While not all gifted individuals have overexcitabilities in each area, research and observation have both shown that these increased sensitivities are indeed primary characteristics of gifted people.

In his book *"Mellow Out," They Say. If I Only Could*, Michael Piechowski writes, "It is unfortunate that the stronger these excitabilities are, the less peers and teachers welcome them. Children exhibiting strong excitabilities are often made to feel embarrassed and guilty for being 'different.' Criticized and teased for what they cannot help, they begin to believe there is something wrong with them."[45]

FIGURE 4.3
Trying to Do Well vs. Perfectionism

Trying to Do Well	Perfectionism
Doing the research you have to do for a project, working hard on it, turning it in on time, and feeling good about what you learned.	Writing your report over three times, staying up two nights in a row, and handing it in late because you had to get it right (and still feeling bad about your report).
Studying for a test, taking it with confidence, and feeling good about your score of 9 out of 10, or getting a B+ instead of an A.	Cramming at the last minute, taking the test with sweaty palms, and feeling bad about your B+ because a friend got an A.
Choosing to work on group projects because you enjoy learning from different people's experiences and ways of doing things.	Always working alone because no one can do as good a job as you—and you're not about to let anyone else slide by on *your* A.
Accepting an award with pride, even though your name is misspelled on it. (You know it can be fixed later.)	Being grumpy about the award because the officials didn't get your name right.
Getting together with people who are interesting, likable, and fun to be with.	Refusing to be with people who aren't star athletes, smart, and popular.
Being willing to try new things, even when they're a little scary, and learning from your experiences and mistakes.	Avoiding experiences because you are terrified of making mistakes—especially in public.
Keeping your room cleaner and neater, making your bed more often, and putting your clothes away.	Not being able to leave the room until the bed and room are just so.
Joining a soccer team and playing two or three times a week to have fun and compete with other teams.	Taking lessons as often as you can, practicing every day, and not feeling satisfied until you can beat every other team in your league.

From *What to Do When Good Enough Isn't Good Enough* by Thomas S. Greenspon, Ph.D. (Free Spirit Publishing, 2007): 36–37. Reprinted with permission from the publisher.

This belief is borne out in my self-advocacy workshops. Initially, most students aren't familiar with the concept but quickly identify themselves as experiencing OE in one or more areas. They discover that what they once felt might be abnormal is actually very normal. They also begin to recognize the ways in which OE might affect their time in school. The following student quotes illustrate each area of overexcitability.

Sensual OE: "It's hard to concentrate in class with the buzzing fluorescent light above me, my desk rocking on the uneven floor, and the smells coming up from the cafeteria."
—*Brynn, grade 6*

Intellectual OE: "Sometimes I get really excited about a subject and have a million questions I want to ask, but I just keep them to myself because I don't want the other kids to think I'm an overachiever."
—*Miles, grade 5*

Emotional OE: "I was really, really disappointed when the teacher handed back a test that I'd screwed up. I could hardly read his comments because I was fighting back the tears so no one else would know."
—*Javier, grade 10*

Psychomotor OE: "Other kids call me hyper because when I'm excited about something I always talk fast and wave my hands around and it's hard for me to sit still."
—*Mika, grade 8*

Imaginational OE: "When class gets boring I tune out and disappear into my own world. I got in trouble for sketching out the map for the fantasy game I'm creating instead of finishing my math homework."

—JP, grade 7

Characteristic #6: Introversion/Extroversion
(related to the Big Five's "Extroversion")

An important difference between introverts and extroverts is the source of their energy: extroverts get energy from people and objects outside themselves, whereas introverts gain energy from within themselves. Once again, most people fall somewhere on the continuum, but gifted individuals are often outliers. Linda Silverman of the Gifted Development Center reports, "About 60 percent of gifted children are introverted compared with 30 percent of the general population. Approximately 75 percent of highly gifted children are introverted." However, introversion "is very likely to be misunderstood and 'corrected' in children by well-meaning adults."[46]

Following a recent workshop, one introverted student emailed me: "Thanks for helping me realize that I don't need fixing," he wrote. He included the link to a website and suggested that all introverts pass it on to their families and friends. As an introvert myself, I'm happy to oblige: "10 Myths About Introverts": carlkingdom.com/10-myths-about-introverts.

Student Self-Assessment of Personality Characteristics and Traits

Following are ideas for self-assessment related to each of the six characteristics just discussed.

Analytical Mind/Creative Mind: Although most assessments still use the right brain/left brain terminology, they actually are identifying where one lies on the continuum between analytical and creative thinking. A version of a simple assessment, the Open Hemispheric Brain Dominance Scale, can be found at: personality-testing.info/tests/OHBDS.

Motivation, Self-Direction, Independence: An internet search will reveal several reliable motivation scales. My past workshop students have favored this one at See My

Personality: www.seemypersonality.com/personality.asp?p=Motivation-Test.

Optimism/Pessimism: The Authentic Happiness website, developed by the University of Pennsylvania's Positive Psychology Center, directed by Dr. Martin Seligman, offers an Optimism Test. As referenced earlier in this chapter, the test is available here: www.authentichappiness.sas.upenn.edu/home.

Perfectionism: There are many online perfectionism quizzes, but you'll find a useful checklist, "Perfectionism at a Glance," from Thomas Greenspon's book, *Moving Past Perfect*. It helps family members weigh the level of their own perfectionism. Download the checklist at: freespirit.com/counseling-and-social-emotional-learning/moving-past-perfect-thomas-greenspon.

Overexcitabilities/Intensities: The most authoritative assessment, the Overexcitability Questionnaire-II developed by the Institute for the Study of Advanced Development (ISAD), is primarily used for academic research and not readily available for student self-assessment. However, several informal rating scales can be found online, such as this one at PowerWood: powerwood.org.uk/overexcitability-test.

Introversion/Extroversion: Daniel Pink, popular author and speaker on the topics of business, work, and behavior, has a simple introvert/extrovert/ambivert quiz at his website: danpink.com/assessment.

Students' Insights on Personality Characteristics and Traits

Following is one student's reflection on her personality characteristics and traits, as well as various comments from my GT Carpe Diem Workshop discussions.

"So this is really crazy, but I feel like I've uncovered the real me. I'm not just shy, I'm introverted. And that's why I don't like to raise my hand or speak up in class. I like group work with other motivated kids, but it exhausts me. I can't wait to get home and curl up with a good book in my own room. I guess I'm also a bit of a perfectionist. I remember in third grade my parents set a limit on how many times I could erase my homework answers because I was wearing through the paper. It just seems like I could rewrite and rewrite and it could always be improved. I'm more Successful than Autonomous and I sometimes go Underground. I don't want to make it sound like everything I learned about myself is negative. I'm a really optimistic person. I'm open to new experiences and creative. My art and music are enhanced by my sensual, emotional, and imaginational overexcitabilities. My inner life is vivid and intense, even though it doesn't always show on the outside." —*Olivia, grade 10*

"I always felt that other people didn't understand me and now I know I didn't totally understand myself either!" —*Darryl, grade 10*

"The reason why I'm always so happy is that I am not a perfectionist and I am an optimist." —*Sasha, grade 6*

"I tend to have extrinsic motivation because I take on challenges just to get a specific result instead of actually appreciating the challenge. This is something I want to work on." —*Casey, grade 9*

"Teachers and parents should know that gifted kids come in all personality 'shapes and sizes.' We need to help them understand us better, even if that's hard because we're introverts." —*Dalia, grade 7*

Links to a wide variety of resources and more details on ways that each of the common personality traits directly relates to gifted individuals can be found on Hoagies' Gifted Education Page:

◆ Characteristics of the Gifted Child: hoagiesgifted.org/characteristics.htm
◆ Personality Type: hoagiesgifted.org/personality_type.htm
◆ Overexcitabilities: hoagiesgifted.org/dabrowski.htm
◆ The Social/Emotional Aspects of Giftedness: hoagiesgifted.org/social_emotional.htm
◆ Gifted Underachievement: hoagiesgifted.org/underachievement.htm

THE MOST COMPLETE RESOURCES FOR LEARNER PROFILE ASSESSMENTS

Here are the two best tools for assessing gifted students' learner profiles.

Rogers's Gifted Education Planner (GEP)

The planner is available on its own and also included in Karen Rogers's book, *Re-Forming Gifted Education,* Appendix A: Supplementary Materials.[47] Used in conjunction with the recommendations in the book, the GEP allows students (and their advocates) to gather the information they need to better understand themselves as learners and plan accordingly.

The GEP includes these inventories and data collection forms:

❖ Parent Inventory for Finding Potential (PIP)
❖ Teacher Inventory of Learning Strengths (TILS)
❖ Attitudes About School and Learning (for students)
❖ Reading/Language Interest and Attitudes (for students)
❖ Mathematics Interest and Attitudes (for students)
❖ Science Interest and Attitudes (for students)
❖ Social Studies Interest and Attitudes (for students)
❖ Interest and Attitudes About Arts Learning (for students)
❖ How Do You Like to Learn? (for students)
❖ Rogers's Interest Inventory
❖ The Data Collector
❖ Yearly Educational Planner

Renzulli's Total Talent Portfolio (TTP)

The TTP is a component of the Schoolwide Enrichment Model (SEM) developed by Joseph Renzulli. It includes assessments of abilities, interests, and learning style preferences (instruction, environment, thinking, and expression), and enables the student to work together with the teacher to decide which acceleration and/or enrichment options to use. The TTP also provides valuable information for educational, personal, and career counseling. A link to all the SEM resources and forms created by Joseph Renzulli and Sally Reis can be found at: gifted.uconn.edu/schoolwide-enrichment-model/sem3rd.

Conclusion

All five dimensions of the learner profile—cognitive functioning, learning strengths, interests and passions, learning preferences, and personality characteristics and traits—provide crucial information about a gifted learner's problem-solving process. Gifted students who have a realistic picture of their unique learner profiles are better prepared to self-advocate, to adapt the education system to meet their needs, and to make strides toward becoming Autonomous Learners.

key CONCEPTS
IN CHAPTER 4

❖ The second step in self-advocacy is assessing and reflecting on one's learner profile.

❖ Five fields of information make up the learner profile: 1) cognitive functioning, 2) learning strengths, 3) interests/passions, 4) learning preferences, and 5) personality characteristics/traits.

❖ Learner profiles are fluid and change over time.

❖ Students who are aware of their learner profiles better understand their need for educational alternatives at home and in school.

Cognitive Functioning Self-Assessment

	Disagree strongly	Disagree a little	Neither agree nor disagree	Agree a little	Agree strongly
I reason well.					
I learn rapidly.					
I have an extensive vocabulary.					
I have an excellent memory.					
I have a long attention span.					
I am highly curious.					
I have a wide range of interests.					
I was an early reader and/or I am an avid reader.					
I am a keen observer.					
I have a vivid imagination.					
I am highly creative.					

5 OPTIONS and OPPORTUNITIES

Sometimes I mess up. And I readily admit to messing up in my early attempts to help seventh grader Ari, one of my gifted At-Risk students. Though bright, curious, and articulate, he might have been deemed just "another one of the kids in *that* family," since his older siblings were frequently in trouble, truant, defiant, and leaders of the wrong kind. But teachers recognized that Ari was different—quiet, attentive, and intense. Classroom differentiation seemed to provide appropriate challenges during his elementary years. By middle school, however, Ari began emulating his siblings: frequent tardiness, unfinished homework, a negative attitude toward authority, and rapidly declining grades, despite achievement test scores at the 99th percentile.

In my naïveté, I honestly believed there was an easy answer for Ari. We tried compacting, alternative assignments, online programming, and independent study.

But nothing held his attention for long. Nothing was supported at home. Nothing changed. When I heard of a residential school across the state, I took him to visit. His enthusiasm grew as the tour progressed and, to my surprise, the headmaster offered Ari a full scholarship for the next year if he could maintain at least a C average for the rest of the year in his current school. In the car on the way home, he eagerly began filling out the application. But even that future possibility was not enough motivation. As the first semester flowed into the second, it became obvious that Ari's grades, attitude, attention, and willingness to work with me on a solution were in continual decline. I felt that both of us had failed.

Yes, sometimes I mess up, but I've messed up less often since I discovered the importance of matching the program to the child and learned to recognize the varying needs of gifted kids, including the At-Risk ones. With this wisdom, both Ari and I eventually understood his specific learner needs and, together, we matched them to programming that allowed him to succeed. Stay tuned for more of Ari's story later in the chapter.

Self-Advocacy Step 3: Students Investigate Available Options and Opportunities

This step is broken down into two parts:

1. investigating options
2. matching those options to the individual

Both parts are essential. For a student to customize her own education, she needs problem-solving information about the education system and the learning opportunities that may be available. She then needs to know the personal characteristics she'll need to succeed in those opportunities, evaluate the options in regards to her learner profile, and, finally, choose an alternative that is right for her.

Investigating Options for Enrichment and Acceleration

With no national mandate for gifted education in the United States or Canada, and inconsistent (or non-existent) state and provincial funding, program offerings vary greatly across North America. Some of the students I work with come from rural districts so small that all students at a grade level are in one heterogeneous English, science, math, or history class. At the other end of the spectrum, some students in affluent suburban schools have seemingly endless opportunities for enrichment and acceleration. What is optimum? An extensive list of secondary school options can be found in *Programs and Services for Gifted Secondary Students: A Guide to Recommended Practices,* edited by Felicia A. Dixon. Dixon and her colleagues suggest that even the most basic program for gifted students should include the following:

◆ AP and/or IB options
◆ independent study
◆ access to distance education
◆ opportunity to place out of courses based on rigorous independent/summer study

◆ required advanced study in a second language
◆ differentiation in the regular classroom
◆ flexible access based on ability scores and/or demonstrated achievement
◆ opportunities for students capable of moving faster/ higher than average

In addition to the basic options, standard high school gifted programs provide:

◆ opportunities for discipline-specific study in at least one math or science field and one field in the humanities
◆ consistent technology use
◆ comprehensive honors course offerings
◆ options for extremely gifted learners

The very best gifted programs are multifaceted and include:

◆ options for interdisciplinary study
◆ options for early subject specialization
◆ contact with domain-specific mentors
◆ direct instruction in epistemology (such as the IB Theory of Knowledge course)
◆ required use of discipline-specific advanced technology

The Best Options for Gifted Learners

While academics may propose best practices for the gifted population in general, it's also important to align alternatives to the specific needs of individual students. Some seek immediate change, while others want to investigate possibilities for the future. Based on my workshop survey responses, students' desires for change most frequently fall into one of four categories.

1. Finding Appropriately Challenging Academic Work

This can happen both inside and outside the regular school setting.

◆ Options within the regular classroom include alternative assignments, curriculum compacting using pretesting, and within-class cluster grouping.
◆ Alternatives to the heterogeneous classroom may be AP, IB, honors, "college in high school" classes, online learning, independent study, mentorships,

subject acceleration, concurrent enrollment in both middle and high school, and full grade acceleration.

◆ Alternatives to the conventional school could be post-secondary options, summer programs, semester schools, magnet or charter schools, residential schools, and early college admission.

2. Exploring an Interest

There are several ways for students to delve into areas of interest or passion not covered in the typical curriculum: online learning, independent study, mentorships, concurrent enrollment, post-secondary options, summer programs, semester schools, extracurricular activities, study abroad, and taking a gap year between high school and college.

3. Spending Time with Gifted Peers

The academic, social, and psychological importance of this desire cannot be overstated. Many gifted students have learned to fit into the general school population but still yearn for interaction with like-ability peers. Many opportunities for this exist, such as within-class cluster grouping; AP, IB, and honors classes (although they rightly include students of varying ability levels); post-secondary options; summer programs, especially those affiliated with Academic Talent Searches; specific semester, magnet, charter, or residential schools; early college admission to institutions that cater to gifted students; academic and creative extracurricular activities; and counselor-led discussion and book groups.

4. Adjusting School/Home Practices to Accommodate Personal Needs

For some students, this step is more critical to personal contentment and academic success than changes to their curriculum. Students need to know that, with good reason, they can adjust their daily class schedule, request specific seating in the classroom, create their own study environment, and work with staff to coordinate project deadlines, assignment due dates, and, to some extent, testing timetables.

How Do Students Learn About Options and Opportunities?

Several years ago, I initiated the "Senior Honors Panel" in my district. Each spring we asked six of our top

seniors to reflect on their K–12 education. Invited guests included secondary school department heads, teachers, principals, the superintendent and other administrators, school board members, and members of our gifted education parent advisory. The conversation included questions such as:

◆ Did you find school academically challenging?

◆ What have been your best educational experiences in this district?

◆ What unique educational options have you taken advantage of? (mentorships, accelerated classes, independent study, school-to-work, technology, travel, etc.)

The students spoke candidly and we learned a great deal from them that helped us evaluate our programming. But the first year, I was surprised and somewhat disappointed to hear a student ask, "Why didn't anyone ever tell me *I* could do that?" upon hearing what someone else had experienced. I realized that, despite our sharing course information, gifted students sometimes failed to think outside the box when it came to their school schedules. They don't always hear about, don't actively seek out, and sometimes aren't interested in exploring new options, even when they feel that what they're doing isn't working for them. When they *are* ready for a change, they want to know precisely what is involved and, perhaps more importantly, how they will benefit. I learned that we must be intentional in relaying this information to all gifted students periodically and to individual students as their specific needs dictate. It is also important for them to have real-life examples of kids like themselves who have created their own unique routes and flourished.

We learned a lot that first year. With those seniors' words to guide us, we began inviting gifted eighth graders to the panels, as well, to reflect on their middle school education and to hear the seniors' stories. The next year we added visits to the middle schools where the soon-to-be graduates shared their individual experiences, answered questions, and interacted informally with large groups of younger gifted students who ate up the stories about changing the system.

> **Chapter 7: Paths and Plans** details many students' personal successes in creating alternative routes through secondary school.

Sharing Academic Options with Students

Following are some of the best ways to communicate with students about gifted programming options.

District and School Websites

- The most obvious way to inform all students of the options available to them is to post the secondary schools' course catalogs on the district and individual school websites, making sure each alternative is clearly described for both middle and high school students. Academically challenging courses should be so designated, as well as opportunities for independent study, mentorships, online learning, and acceleration.

- Often, course catalogs divide offerings into "college" and "career" tracks. But every learner needs to feel that any option that's right for them will be made available, assuring that, in addition to acceleration, gifted students also consider the arts, technology classes, and school-to-work opportunities that also may have benefits for them.

- The district website should also contain the district-wide plan for gifted education with all course, extracurricular, and out-of-school alternatives recommended for gifted students clearly listed and explained.

Individual Student Conversations

Any time we have conferences with students, we can relay the steps to self-advocacy and share a basic list of options. Some examples include:

- Gifted coordinators and resource teachers should be available with gifted programming information in hand during regular student-parent-teacher conferences, registration or scheduling events, orientation days, and school open houses.

- During student-parent-teacher conferences, teachers can share lists of additional possibilities for challenge and enrichment, both in and outside of their classrooms.

- Students who participate in the out-of-level testing of Academic Talent Searches should be invited to meet with the program coordinator after the results are reported to discuss the testing experience and recommended paths and plans based on the test scores.

- Students with differentiated education plans (DEPs) should meet at least annually to reevaluate their plan and learn of new options.

- Any time students with recognized gifts meet with a school counselor or building consultation team regarding academic or social-emotional concerns, they should be made aware of the alternatives available to them.

> More detailed ways for educators to spread the word about options can be found in **Chapter 6: Advocates and Advisors** and **Chapter 8: Workshops and Ways Forward**.

The Value of Understanding One's Options

Survey responses from students at my GT Carpe Diem Workshops help underscore the value of talking with students directly about their educational alternatives.

At the beginning of the workshop, participants were asked, "Have you created your own unique route to graduation that may be different from the norm? If so, please describe what you are doing differently" (see **Figure 5.1** on page 78).

- 30 percent of the students (97 out of 323) reported that they did indeed have a unique route to graduation.
  - 25 percent of these unique routes included advanced mathematics; only a few students mentioned another academic area.
  - 23 percent of students with a unique route were taking or planning to take AP/IB/honors/advanced classes.

FIGURE 5.1
Survey Responses: Unique Routes to Graduation

Number of respondents = 323	Pre-Workshop Already Had Unique Route		Post-Workshop Wanted Unique Route	
	Number	Percent	Number	Percent
	97	30% of total students	300	93% of total students
Elements Involved in Unique Route	Number	Percent out of 97	Number	Percent out of 300
Subject Areas				
Arts	1	1%	17	6%
Business	1	1%	0	0%
Language Arts/English	1	1%	29	10%
Mathematics	24	25%	36	12%
Science	3	3%	24	8%
Social Studies	0	0%	11	4%
Technology	1	1%	12	4%
World Languages	2	2%	16	5%
Other Academic Options				
Acceleration	0	0%	5	1.5%
AP/IB/honors/advanced	23	24%	8	2%
Differentiation	0	0%	8	2%
Electives (nonspecific)	0	0%	4	1%
Extracurricular activities	1	1%	22	7%
Online learning	4	4%	4	1%
Special school	3	3%	2	.5%
Summer program	0	0%	1	.3%
Study abroad	2	2%	2	.5%
Specific Personal Needs				
Change scheduling	0	0%	11	4%
Get organized	0	0%	5	1.5%
Improve grades	0	0%	7	2%
Meet peers	0	0%	2	.5%
Minimize perfectionism	0	0%	3	1%
Reduce procrastination	0	0%	2	.5%
Reduce stress	0	0%	3	1%
Future Plans				
Career plans	2	2%	19	6%
College plans	8	8%	8	2%
Early graduation	5	5%	4	1%
Vague Generalizations	12	13%	36	12%

- 15 percent mentioned graduating early and future career or college plans.
- 13 percent offered vague generalizations about working hard, getting good grades, and taking more difficult classes.
- None of the students' plans mentioned adjustments to accommodate specific personal needs.

At the end of the workshop, following an exploration of specific options, opportunities, paths, and plans, participants were asked, "Do you feel you need or want to create a unique route to graduation? What is the goal you have set for yourself?"

◆ 93 percent of the students (300 out of 323) reported that they wanted to create a unique route. The options they selected to explore were far more diverse, specific, and personalized than those mentioned at the beginning of the workshop.
  - Only 12 percent of the students' unique route goals mentioned mathematics, while interest in other academic areas rose significantly, especially in language arts and science.
  - Only 2 percent of the goals included AP/IB/honors/advanced classes, while interest in a variety of other academic options increased.
  - 7 percent of the students included extracurricular activities in their plan.
  - Over 10 percent of the students incorporated alternatives to address specific personal needs.
  - Interestingly, a similar percentage of the students' goals (12 percent) were still vague generalizations. Thirty-six students didn't select a specific objective and my best guess is that they felt no immediate need to self-advocate. Still, equipping them with the information that empowers self-advocacy (and reminding them of it periodically throughout their school years) should help ensure that they will use the skills when necessary.

When gifted students are provided with information about alternatives, they become more productive problem-solvers, discovering paths never before imagined. After reviewing seventh grader Liam's Academic Talent Search results with him (his composite ACT score was 32), I handed him a paper copy of the high school course catalog and said, "See anything that interests you?" He couldn't contain his excitement, quickly flipping through the fifty-five pages. Then, grabbing a highlighter from his backpack, he started again from the beginning of the packet, marking course after course. Finally, he looked up with a smile and said, "I didn't know about any of this. I can't wait to get to high school." To which I gladly replied, "Oh, but you don't have to wait. You can begin taking advantage of these classes next semester. We just have to create your plan."

Matching Options to Individuals

The second part of Self-Advocacy Step 3 is matching options to individuals. This is where it starts to get tricky. Gifted students who are aware of the possibilities need to decide if they are *ready*, *willing*, and *able* to take the plunge. I've heard many students say, "I'm ready for a change," but just how ready are they and what specifically are they ready for? A lot of factors come into play, because there are different ways to be "ready" that impact being "willing" and "able." Students must decide if they are intellectually ready, academically ready, developmentally ready, as well as emotionally and psychologically ready to face a new challenge.

Being *Ready* for Change

According to Carol Ann Tomlinson, "*readiness* is the capacity to learn new material as determined by the student's proximity to specified learning goals."[48] *Readiness is* fluid, not fixed. And it is *more than a high IQ, high test scores, or good grades.* It's clear that a five-year-old who begins school reading at the third-grade level has already exceeded the kindergarten reading goals and is ready to move on. Likewise, a mathematically talented student may be ready for an accelerated pace in algebra but need to take it more slowly in geometry. Readiness also depends on the task at hand. A gifted writer may produce amazing short stories but need more assistance with expository writing. Working at their readiness level should stretch students and may even take them out of their comfort zone. Despite the myths, even gifted students often need academic support and encouragement when taking on a challenging task.

Elijah was ready for calculus, even though he was only in eighth grade. He'd been accelerated in math throughout elementary school and finished compacted algebra, geometry, and trigonometry in middle school. Everything had come easily for him. Before the school year began, we visited the high school together where he met the calculus teacher, an experienced educator who was not convinced, however, that a thirteen-year-old should be in his class. I sensed Elijah was feeling a bit intimidated but felt assured he was academically ready for the challenge. The first few weeks I checked in with him regularly when he arrived from the middle school each day and he said all was going well. So I was truly surprised when I got a call from his father during the middle of the first quarter. "Elijah's failing calc," he said. "He won't come out of his room at night, he won't talk about it, and he says he wants to quit school." I pulled Elijah out of his first hour class the next day. It didn't take me long to guess the truth. For the first time in his life, math was finally challenging. He was afraid to ask the teacher for help, embarrassed to turn to his older classmates, and he lacked the study skills to dig in and figure it out for himself. In other words, Elijah was in his zone of proximal development, but without the support he needed to be successful.

FIGURE 5.2
Zone of Proximal Development

- Learner cannot do
- Learner can do unaided
- **Zone of Proximal Development** Learner can do with guidance

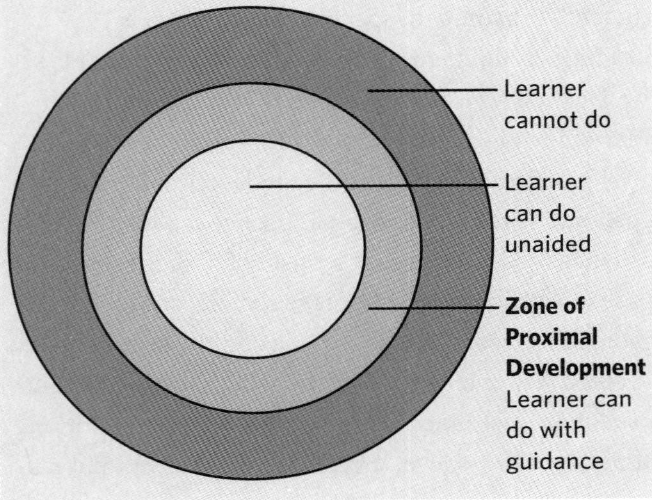

As defined by psychologist Lev Vygotsky, the zone of proximal development (ZPD) is the area of learning in which growth toward attaining skills or knowledge can only occur when a teacher or an advanced peer assists a person. Elijah needed to understand that struggle does not equal failure. Rather, it's where real growth begins. He also needed a nonjudgmental tutor, which turned out to be easy to find. Transportation to the high school meant Elijah always arrived thirty minutes early for class. That coincided with the math department head's office hours, and she was more than willing to spend time helping a brilliant young mathematician. Elijah *was* ready. He just had to learn how to tackle something difficult with assistance. He caught on and caught up in no time and successfully finished the year, readily asking for help when needed.

Some intellectually or academically gifted learners let us know they are ready for a challenge when they say, "I'm bored." But what's behind that boredom? Is the pace too slow or is it lack of depth? Or is it caused by previous mastery of the skill or concept? Students must search for these answers to help us understand specifically what needs to be changed and supported. Are they ready to pick up the pace? To move from concrete to more abstract? From simple to more complex? From structured to more open? From less to greater independence? Our students must have the information that will allow them to zero in on their readiness levels. Following are four helpful concepts we can share with students: Bloom's Taxonomy, grade-level learner outcomes, the Pyramid Model, and changing education initiatives.

Bloom's Taxonomy

Sometimes, to be challenged in a lesson or unit, gifted students need to choose to move to higher levels of critical or creative thinking than the assignment requires. How do they recognize their readiness level? Bloom's Taxonomy of the Cognitive Domain, devised in the 1950s by Benjamin Bloom and colleagues, provides an important way to determine readiness level. Bloom described a hierarchy of thinking skills ranging from less to more complex, ordered as follows: knowledge, comprehension, application, analysis, synthesis, and evaluation. (*Note:* Synthesis and evaluation are often considered to be at the same level of complexity and synthesis is now sometimes referred to as creating.) The taxonomy is a crucial tool for teachers in designing learning tasks, creating discussion questions, and providing feedback on student work. Students need to

be aware of the level at which they are being asked to work and compare it with the level of critical or creative thinking they are ready to use. A brief explanation, as in the cookie chart in **Figure 5.3,** may be all they require to assess their readiness. Have them read the chart from the bottom up to better understand the increasingly complex levels of critical and creative thinking.

For example, during a fifth-grade enrichment class, students selected topics for their independent projects. When we met for their first check-ins, many of the students seemed uninspired. But a quick look at their initial plans revealed the cause: most were proposing to work at the knowledge and comprehension levels of thinking. After we talked about Bloom's Taxonomy, the students eagerly matched their projects to their thinking readiness levels and found increased excitement, motivation, and creativity. A few anecdotes:

- ◆ Tim loved chemistry and at first proposed memorizing the periodic table and enhancing it with pictures of the elements' real-world uses. An online search revealed that several illustrated tables already existed. After considering Bloom's, Tim chose to instead research fictional chemical elements that play roles in Marvel and DC comics. Then he redesigned the periodic table, inserting each fictional element in the appropriate place based on its characteristics. He still used knowledge and comprehension processes, but they were in support of additional higher levels of thinking: application, analysis, synthesis, and evaluation.

- ◆ Because she had adopted a puppy from the animal shelter where she volunteered, Vonda selected the proper care and feeding of dogs as her project. It, too, was at the knowledge and comprehension levels of Bloom's. However, after a lively discussion of her puppy experiences, she decided on something more exciting. Her new project required analysis, synthesis, and evaluation as she investigated ways to keep a dog from gobbling its food too quickly and conducted original research with her puppy. "That was a whole lot more fun than just writing a report," said Vonda. (And yes, a dog does eat more slowly

FIGURE 5.3
Thinking About Cookies with Bloom's Taxonomy

Creating
Create a new cookie recipe that combines the best characteristics of the two cookies.

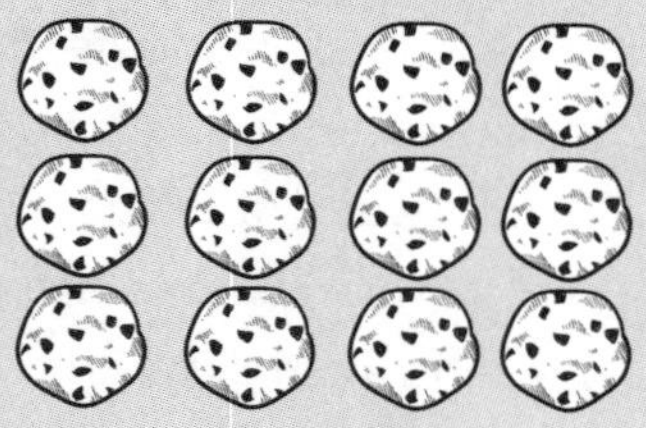

Evaluating
Judge which characteristics of the two cookies are best.

Analyzing
Determine the characteristics of each type of cookie by examining and tasting.

Applying
Make the two types of cookies.

Understanding
Understand the directions.
(For example, What's the difference between baking powder and baking soda?)

Remembering
Read two different chocolate chip cookie recipes in a cookbook.

when it must hunt for its dinner, hidden in small bowls around the house.)

◆ Kahlil and his family spent their summer vacation visiting the national monuments in Washington, D.C. He could have written a simple travelogue, but he looked to Bloom's and instead chose to create a database comparing the physical characteristics of the memorials and their relevance to the individuals being memorialized. He then selected a historical event in his Wisconsin hometown: the marshalling of local soldiers for the Civil War on land that became known as Union Park. Using his analysis of the national monuments, he designed a scale model of a memorial to commemorate the 2,467 volunteer soldiers who left for the Civil War from that site. After presenting his idea to his local parks department, the project took off, an architect got involved, and construction began the following summer. Kahlil's application, analysis, synthesis, and evaluation led to change in his community.

Like these students, all learners will find greater, more interesting challenges the higher they reach on Bloom's Taxonomy. Gifted students can learn to recognize the thinking level required for an assignment, and, when necessary, seek alternatives that better match their readiness. On the contrary, this could also mean that a student might recognize he is in over his head because he doesn't have the basic background knowledge and comprehension that's required, and he may need to step back and get caught up. No stigma should be placed on this remediation. It is not unusual for learners who have accelerated through a subject or grade level to miss something—in most cases, they can pick it up in record time.

Grade-Level Learner Outcomes

To assess their readiness within the curriculum, gifted students need to be aware of mandated standardized learner outcomes. What does that mean? Students are assessed according to their progress on predetermined learning outcomes for each grade level in a subject—statements of what students will learn, what they will be able to do, and how they will apply that skill or knowledge. (See the geometry example in the following paragraph.) These learner outcomes vary depending on district, state/provincial, and/or federal requirements and can shift over time. Teachers are familiar with these learner outcomes because teachers are often evaluated based on their students' progress. Parents may be aware of learner outcomes but may not easily relate them to the day-to-day work their child is doing. Students, however, tell me it's rare that either a teacher or a parent shares specific learner outcomes with them, even though that information is necessary for students to make wise decisions about their options. One simple way to share learner outcomes is by posting them on the classroom board at the beginning of each curricular unit.

While these educational standards in core subjects like math and language arts are similar throughout all grade levels, the difficulty of the content and the complexity of student work changes and the outcome statements become more complex for each grade. For example, a geometry standard for all middle school grades may be: *Students will be able to solve real-life and mathematical problems involving angle measure, area, surface area, and volume.* But the specific grade-level expectations will be different, such as:[49]

Grade 6: Students will solve real-world and mathematical problems involving area, surface area, and volume. They will find the area of right triangles, other triangles, special quadrilaterals, and polygons by composing into rectangles or decomposing into triangles and other shapes.

Grade 7: Students will solve real-world and mathematical problems involving angle measure, area, surface area, and volume. They will know the formulas for the area and circumference of a circle and use them to solve problems.

Grade 8: Students will solve real-world and mathematical problems involving volume of cylinders, cones, and spheres. They will know the formulas for the volumes of cones, cylinders, and spheres and use them to solve real-world and mathematical problems.

When we help gifted students sift through these outcome statements for their own grade level as well as look ahead to higher grade levels, we allow them to more fully understand the depth and breadth of their academic strength areas, assess their own progress, and discover advanced skills and concepts they have yet to encounter. Admittedly, this may be a bit complicated. But students can't take charge of their education if they can't see how they fit into the system's big picture: the academic goals they've accomplished, the ones they should reach for, and what lies ahead. In addition, understanding this spiraling nature of the curriculum answers many common student questions such as, "Why are we studying this?" and "Didn't we do this last year?"

Standards and learning outcomes can also lend structure to individualized instruction, assuring that students are still progressing even when diverging from the regular curriculum. For instance, together with a master English teacher, I created a nine-week independent investigation for her freshman accelerated class using the ninth- through twelfth-grade reading, writing, language, speaking, and listening standards as a starting point. The students began with an honest self-assessment of their progress on the learner outcomes, identifying the areas they were confident about and the areas that required more work. Then, in crafting independent learning plans and creating their own learning experiences, students delved into a passion project that also provided growth in the state-mandated learner outcomes.

The Pyramid Model of Gifted Programming

Many school districts, states, and provinces use the three-tier pyramid model of gifted programming originally conceived by the Richardson Foundation of Texas in the early 1980s. The Pyramid Model specifies three levels of programming options matched to individual students' needs. Services become more specialized as the needs become greater. For example, Tier 3 students will require more specialized services than the Tier 2 or Tier 1 students. In matching their profiles to appropriate alternatives, students can ask themselves several questions: What does my learner profile indicate I need? What do I want? Which of my strengths are at which tier? In what areas am I willing to accept greater challenge? Do I need an all-inclusive

Tier 3 differentiated education plan to address all my needs across the board? (See **Figure 5.4**.) Following are descriptions of each tier of the pyramid.

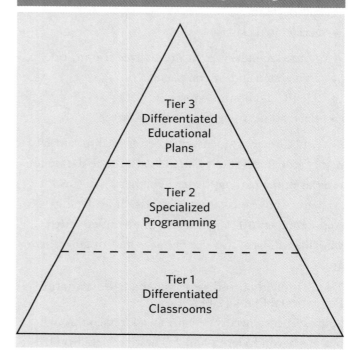

FIGURE 5.4
The Pyramid Model of Gifted Programming

Tier 3
Differentiated
Educational
Plans

Tier 2
Specialized
Programming

Tier 1
Differentiated
Classrooms

Tier 1: Differentiated Learning Options Within the Classroom

This tier includes programming options for students whose needs can be met through regular classroom differentiation. Teachers need training, practice, and administrative support to provide effective differentiation. This level generally includes 60 to 70 percent of identified gifted children. Students should be able to work at an appropriate pace and depth using differentiated curriculum and instructional strategies, such as:

◆ pretesting and compacting
◆ learning contracts
◆ flexible ability grouping
◆ independent projects
◆ tiered assignments
◆ learning centers
◆ interest centers and groups
◆ adjusted questions

Tier 2: Special Programming

This tier consists of options for students who require programs beyond the regular classroom. Options may incorporate:

- full-time cluster grouping
- independent study
- online learning
- accelerated classrooms

At the secondary level, alternatives also include:

- accelerated and/or compacted core classes
- AP, IB, and honors courses
- electives in strength and interest areas

Additionally, students may be referred for enrichment through co-curricular and extracurricular opportunities in their strength area, whether it is a specific academic subject, creativity, the arts, or leadership. Approximately 20 to 30 percent of identified gifted students will be at this tier in one, some, or all academic areas.

Tier 3: Individualized Services and Differentiated Educational Plans (DEPs)

Some students' needs will only be addressed through options beyond Tiers 1 and 2. These services would benefit approximately 5 to 10 percent of identified gifted students. In the best-case scenario, a team consisting of the student, parents or guardians, teachers, school counselor, school psychologist, administrator, and gifted education staff develops a differentiated education plan (DEP). The plan may recommend any of several options including, but not limited to, the following:

- concurrent enrollment
- continuous progress curriculum
- credit by exam
- online courses
- early entrance
- early graduation
- grade acceleration
- independent study
- mentorships
- subject acceleration

There are no actual barriers between these three tiers. Rather, they indicate a continuum of services. And

because gifted students' needs for greater challenges can vary over time, topic, and teaching, their self-advocacy needs will vary as well.

Changing Educational Initiatives

Most often, new educational initiatives and innovations aren't specifically aimed at addressing the needs of gifted students. Sometimes, the education system even uses them as an excuse to deny services. For instance, I've heard administrators remark, "We can't group gifted children because we are following the Heterogeneous Classroom model." But such barriers shouldn't stop us from helping students find ways, in the name of equity, to use these initiatives to their advantage.

For example, consider Response to Intervention (RTI). The gifted education Pyramid Model has taken on new relevance since the RTI framework was introduced in 2004, with reauthorization of the Individuals with Disabilities Education Act (IDEA). According to the RTI Action Network, RTI is a "multi-tier approach to the early identification and support of students with learning and behavior needs. Struggling learners are provided with interventions at three increasing levels of intensity to accelerate their rate of learning."[50] The parallel to the Pyramid Model of gifted programming is striking:

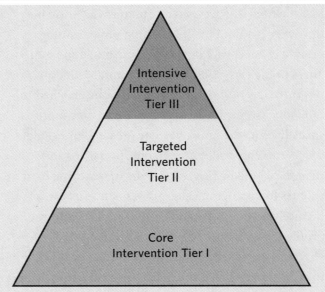

**FIGURE 5.5
RTI Framework**

Intensive Intervention Tier III

Targeted Intervention Tier II

Core Intervention Tier I

RTI Tier I: Core Interventions

At this tier, all students receive high quality, scientifically based instruction provided by qualified personnel to ensure that their difficulties are not due to inadequate instruction. Tier I includes screening and group interventions. This classroom setting is appropriate for 80 to 85 percent of students with differing abilities.

RTI Tier II: Targeted Interventions

Students not making adequate progress in the regular classroom in Tier I are provided with increasingly intensive instruction matched to their needs, based on levels of performance and rates of progress. Tier II may include 15 to 20 percent of the students.

RTI Tier III: Intensive Interventions

At this tier, students receive comprehensive evaluations that lead to individualized, intensive interventions targeting their skill deficits. From 1 to 5 percent of students with differing abilities may need Tier III specialized programming.

With a slight change in their orientation, the Pyramid Model of gifted programming and the RTI framework begin to look remarkably like the bell curve (see **Figure**

5.6). In fact, several states have expanded the RTI framework to include services for high ability and high potential students, assuring that options and opportunities are available to *all* students along the continuum based on their readiness. **Figure 5.7** on page 86, developed by the Oregon (WI) School District, takes it one step further, clarifying the way RTI should be used to address student needs across the continuum.

As outliers, gifted students can use RTI as another means of matching their learner profile to their most challenging alternatives and best personal level of support. RTI also helps them believe that when they self-advocate, they are simply asking for the opportunities that every student deserves. This belief is of utmost importance for our brightest students who have been fed the myth that others may need a boost, but gifted kids will make it on their own.

As we know, educational initiatives and the accompanying jargon come and go: authentic learning, constructivism, multiple intelligences, inclusive classrooms, brain-based learning, whole child, integrated curriculum,

FIGURE 5.6
Gifted and RTI Pyramids Combined

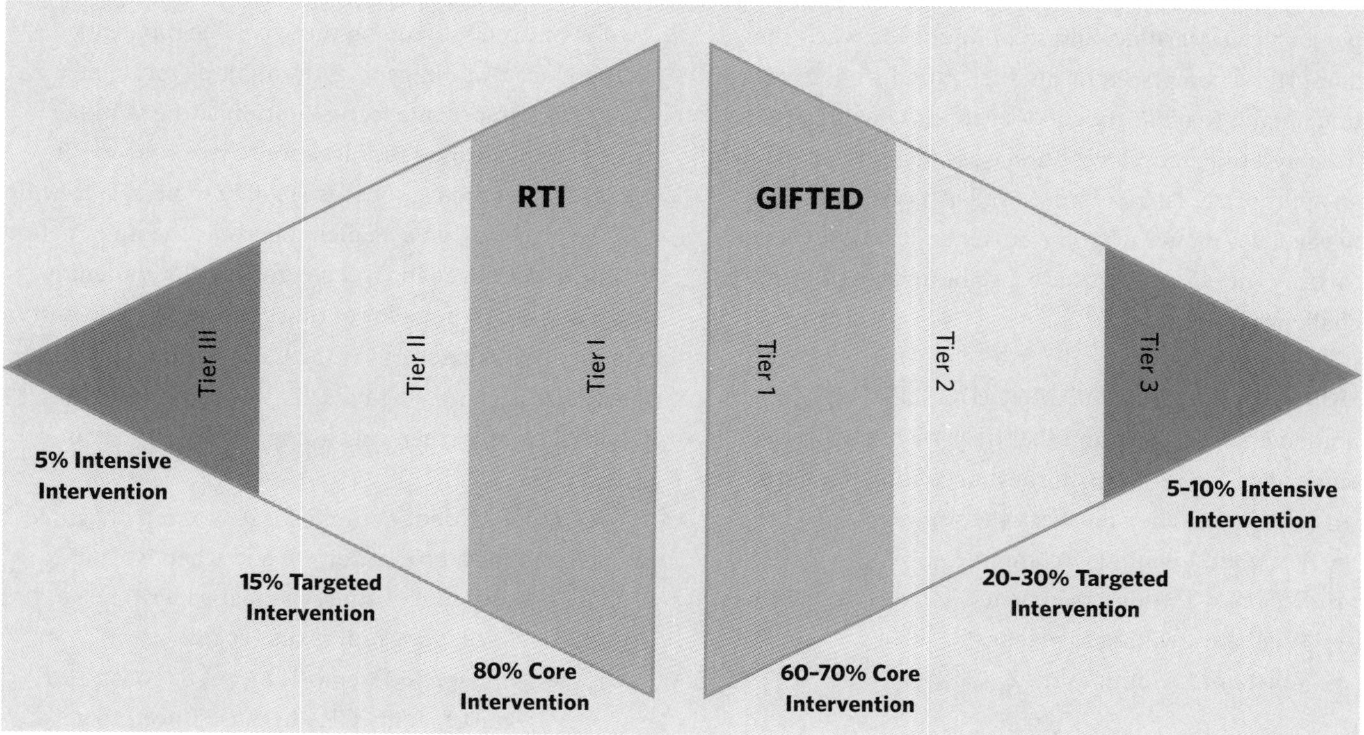

RTI

Tier III — 5% Intensive Intervention
Tier II — 15% Targeted Intervention
Tier I — 80% Core Intervention

GIFTED

Tier 1 — 60–70% Core Intervention
Tier 2 — 20–30% Targeted Intervention
Tier 3 — 5–10% Intensive Intervention

FIGURE 5.7
Response to Intervention for All Students

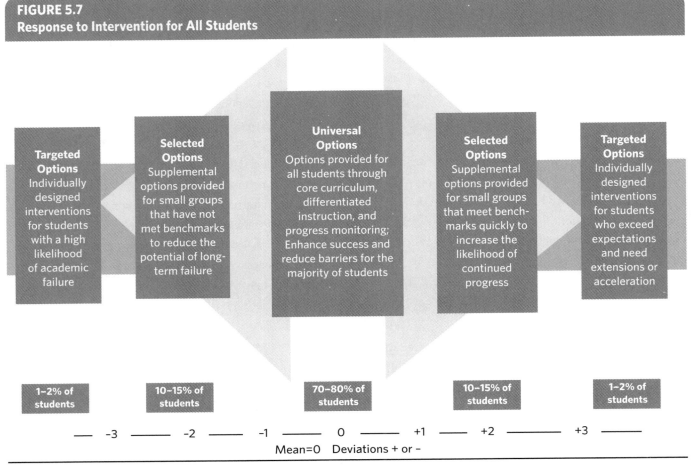

Targeted Options
Individually designed interventions for students with a high likelihood of academic failure

Selected Options
Supplemental options provided for small groups that have not met benchmarks to reduce the potential of long-term failure

Universal Options
Options provided for all students through core curriculum, differentiated instruction, and progress monitoring; Enhance success and reduce barriers for the majority of students

Selected Options
Supplemental options provided for small groups that meet benchmarks quickly to increase the likelihood of continued progress

Targeted Options
Individually designed interventions for students who exceed expectations and need extensions or acceleration

1–2% of students   **10–15% of students**   **70–80% of students**   **10–15% of students**   **1–2% of students**

— -3 —— -2 —— -1 —— 0 —— +1 — +2 —— +3 ——

Mean=0   Deviations + or –

Used by permission, Oregon (WI) School District

personalized learning, and so on. But even when the latest trend is replaced by another, gifted students must understand that *all* students—even those who have mastered the grade-level standards—deserve access to an appropriate curriculum as well as assistance when needed. No matter what the current education system focus is, gifted students have a right to an appropriately challenging education.

Being *Willing* to Accept the Challenge

Students who understand that they are ready for a challenge need to also assess if they are willing to take on that challenge. They must ask themselves:

◆ What am I willing to commit to?

◆ What am I willing to expend?

◆ What am I willing to give up?

◆ What am I willing to risk?

Beyond a doubt, doing more challenging work means more work in general. It might be more interesting work, more intellectually stimulating work, or more creative work, but it is definitely *more* work. It means that a gifted student isn't going to be able to whip together an essay on a challenging topic the night before it's due and still get an A. It means that the student is going to need to put a lot of time, effort, thought, and integrity into whatever it is she has committed to doing. It may also mean giving up activities that other kids are doing, and, perhaps most importantly, it may mean taking a risk.

A former student of mine, Jorge, was a truly gifted poet. Here's the conversation we had when we met to design his independent study in creative writing:

Me: "What are your goals for this class?"

Jorge: "First and foremost, I want to get an A. I can't risk my GPA because I need to get a scholarship to get into a good college. My parents said if this is too hard or too much work and I can't earn an A, then I'll have to drop it."

Me: "Okay, let's say you're assured an A. *Now* what are your goals?"

Jorge: "Oh, well I want to explore the connections between math and poetry. You know, symbols and patterns and symmetry. And I want to show how mathematical concepts can deepen the imagery of a poem. And I want to write some mathematical poems that reflect the complexity of life itself."

Me: "Wow!"

I have found repeatedly that a motivated, self-directed gifted student in a well-structured independent study will do high quality work. And once released from the pressures of the typical grade/reward system, Jorge and others like him feel free to pursue their unique passions without that weight hanging over their heads.

Parents and students, however, often need to be convinced that accepting academic challenges, sometimes at the cost of an A, can be a good decision. As mentioned in Chapter 2, the members of the National Association of College Admission Counselors are surveyed regularly on college admission trends. The chart in **Figure 5.8** summarizes the 2014 results; they have remained generally unchanged for years. Note that grades in college prep courses are of greatest importance in the admission decision with more than 79 percent of college counselors saying they are of "considerable importance." GPA, or "grades in all courses," ranks second with 60 percent of counselors reporting that it is considerably important. Equally important is the strength of the curriculum the student has pursued. Class rank is lower with only 14 percent of counselors saying it is of "considerable importance" to the selection process, and nearly 50 percent of counselors report that it is of "limited" or "no" importance.

FIGURE 5.8
College Admission Trends Survey

Factor	N	Considerable Importance	Moderate Importance	Limited Importance	No Importance
Grades in College Prep Courses	231	79.2%	13.0%	6.9%	0.9%
Grades in All Courses	229	60.3	31.0	8.7	
Strength of Curriculum	231	60.2	26.8	10.0	3.0
Admission Test Scores (SAT, ACT)	228	55.7	32.5	7.9	3.9
Essay or Writing Sample	231	22.1	39.0	21.6	17.3
Counselor Recommendation	231	17.3	42.4	27.3	13.0
Student's Demonstrated Interest	231	16.9	33.3	26.8	22.9
Teacher Recommendation	230	15.2	43.5	27.8	13.5
Class Rank	228	14.0	37.7	32.0	16.2
Subject Test Scores (AP, IB)	227	7.0	35.2	32.6	25.1
Portfolio	229	6.6	10.0	30.6	52.8
Extracurricular Activities	231	5.6	43.3	34.6	16.5
SAT II Scores	226	5.3	8.4	23.0	63.3
Interview	229	3.5	23.1	28.4	45.0
State Graduation Exam Scores	228	3.5	11.0	25.4	60.1
Work	230	0.9	21.3	44.8	33.0

"Table 7: Percentage of Colleges Attributing Different Levels of Importance to Factors in Admission Decisions: First-Time Freshmen," *NACAC 2015 State of College Admission*, National Association of College Admission Counseling, Arlington, VA (2015). Used with permission.

When we counsel gifted students, we cannot overemphasize the importance of taking a risk on a task that may be difficult and might not warrant an A. Sadly, it's not unusual for bright kids who have never had to stretch themselves intellectually or academically to wind up at selective universities, only to be recommended for remedial study skills support. If everything has always been easy and they've never had to learn perseverance, they may give up when the going gets tough.

Every option that we help gifted students design for themselves should have both structure and flexibility. The structure ensures an appropriate challenge and the flexibility enables them to determine the scope of the plan, matching it to their wants and needs. Over time, students who find success in educational risk-taking become motivated to accept and create other demanding options, grow more adept at directing and monitoring their work, and are better equipped to succeed when they encounter poorly structured ventures throughout their lives.

Ready and Willing: Zeroing In on the Best Enrichment Options

In *Re-Forming Gifted Education*, Karen Rogers shares twenty-one tables containing specific readiness and willingness characteristics that are required for students to be successful at many of the most frequently recommended enrichment options. Used in conjunction with a student's self-assessed learner profile, these characteristics help kids zero in on the best choices for them. For example, **Figure 5.9**, based on one of Rogers's tables, lists the characteristics generally required for a student to be successful in a distance learning program.

I include a three-page assessment on pages 169–171, also based on Rogers's tables, in my GT Carpe Diem Workshops. To self-assess, students read through the option descriptions and highlight all that sound interesting. Then, based on their learner profile assessments, they compare what they know about themselves with the characteristics required for each option. Students choose the alternative they are best suited for and create a corresponding goal and action plan to pursue.

FIGURE 5.9
Characteristics Required for Distance/Independent Learning Options

Cognitive Functioning	Personal Characteristics	Learning Preferences	Interests
❖ Is processing and achieving well beyond grade-level peers in a specific academic area ❖ Has above-average ability ❖ Is achieving beyond current grade in specific subject area ❖ Possesses strong need for achievement ❖ Shows strength in planning and precise communication	❖ Self-directed, independent, and motivated to learn ❖ Shows independence in thought and action ❖ Is persistent in own interests, assigned tasks ❖ Enjoys learning ❖ Is good at structuring and organizing tasks and own time ❖ Is socially mature, emotionally stable	❖ Enjoys a variety of instructional delivery methods and challenge in learning experiences ❖ Strongly prefers independent study and self-instructional materials ❖ Prefers challenging, fast-paced instruction	❖ Has strong interest in specific academic areas and time to supplement learning outside of school ❖ Has intense interest in specific topic ❖ Has wide-ranging academic interests ❖ Is involved in a variety of out-of-school activities ❖ Does not find the general extracurricular offerings in school very interesting

Adapted with permission of Great Potential Press from *Re-Forming Gifted Education: How Parents and Teachers Can Match the Program to the Child* by Karen B. Rogers (2002).

Being *Able* to Access Appropriate Enrichment Options

Use of the term *able* here is not to denote intellectual ability since gifted learners have greater capabilities in their talent areas than their peers. *Able* in this context refers instead to students' ability to access the enrichment options that match their learner profiles. Possible concerns to consider include:

◆ **Time.** Does the student have time to take on the challenge? School schedules are sometimes inflexible, homework and after-school activities are time consuming, and part-time jobs may interfere.

◆ **Finances.** Most public school options are provided at no cost, but if there are additional fees for the chosen option (such as an online course, summer program, or residential school), can the student or family afford it? If not, are grants or scholarships available?

◆ **Materials.** In the same vein, does the option require additional books, lab equipment, or computer software? Are the materials readily available? Who will pay for them?

◆ **Technology.** What technology is required? Does it need to be available both in school and at home? And again, who will pay for it?

◆ **Transportation.** If an option requires traveling to another location near or far, does the student have reliable, consistent, and affordable transportation?

◆ **Communication skills.** Has the student developed sufficient writing, speaking, and listening skills to effectively communicate his plan to those who must endorse it and advocate for him?

◆ **Family support.** Is the student's immediate family committed to supporting her efforts, providing assistance when needed, and celebrating her successes? At the very least, will they agree to not get in her way?

◆ **Peer support.** Does the student have friends and classmates who are interested in his work and value his effort? A peer group that doesn't understand and isn't supportive could undermine his success.

Ari's Story, Revisited

I began this chapter with Ari's story. I admit that he and I ran into several obstacles before we finally matched an option to his learner profile. Both of us had to accept what would or would not work for him personally, and that meant facing some hard truths. We tried pretesting and compacting, but Ari wasn't persistent, independent, or self-directed enough. He did not demonstrate confidence, nor was he intense and focused in his learning. Each of those characteristics was essential to his success with compacting, according to Rogers's criteria.

Next we tried an online math program, but in addition to the deficits above, Ari was not highly motivated to learn in the subject, nor was he good at structuring and organizing tasks or his own time. He was socially immature and emotionally unstable. In short, he was ready for the challenge, but neither willing nor able.

For sound advice, I turned to Maureen Neihart via a YouTube video of a presentation she gave in the Netherlands. I was reminded that as an At-Risk gifted learner, Ari would work for a *person*, not a grade, and that we needed to be empathetic and supportive, while holding him accountable and maintaining high expectations. As Neihart explains, "lowering expectations can backfire as it may be interpreted by the child as a loss of confidence in their abilities."[51]

So, what eventually did work? First, we searched for a tutor that Ari could relate to and who could commit to working with him weekly for the rest of the current school year. Dan was a perfect fit: a recently retired middle school teacher with loads of patience, depth and breadth of knowledge, a great sense of humor, and kid-friendly skills from raising his own gifted son. Together, he and Ari crafted a plan of action. It began simply with getting Ari to school each day. In the beginning, Dan picked him up at home and they had a healthy working breakfast in the school conference room. Once the attendance and work patterns were firmly set, they met only two mornings a week; every Monday they checked homework, worked on compacted math units, and chatted over bagels and cream cheese; on Fridays they met to evaluate progress and revise their plan as necessary. If Ari was making good progress, it was breakfast at McDonald's versus bagels. On the other three days, Ari began his morning with the school librarian, who microwaved a breakfast burrito for him and watched over his shoulder as he worked on the assignments he and Dan had agreed on. It was she who called Dan on Thursdays to let him know if it would be McDonald's or bagels the following morning!

With increased motivation, first extrinsic and eventually intrinsic, Ari turned his habits around, but he continued to need aggressive advocacy. His middle and high school teachers and counselors were made aware of his story and maintained high expectations, while giving him direction and helping him create achievable short-term goals.

It's clear that At-Risk students take up a lot of time and resources. And while kids like Ari may make up a small percentage of the gifted students we work with, we must assume there are many more At-Risk gifted learners who remain unidentified and therefore underserved. We need to find them, support them, and give them the information that will allow them to advocate for themselves as special needs learners. And lest we forget, Successful, Creative, 2E, Underground, and even Autonomous gifted students sometimes remain unidentified and they, too, need to be recognized and to find their own unique way to self-advocate.

What to Do When Options Don't Exist

With help from advocates, all gifted learners should be able to take on the new challenges they choose. However, it's possible that in some schools, districts, and communities, there are no clear choices for acceleration or enrichment that fit a particular student's needs. If that is the case, the student has three options:

1. **Choose alternatives outside the general public school parameters.**
   - **Homeschooling.** This is a first response for some students, and for others it may be a last resort. No matter what the case, it is now easier for families of gifted children to homeschool because some

states and provinces have enacted laws that allow them to create a homeschool/public school hybrid. A wide variety of resources are available through the Hoagies' Gifted Education website (see page 132 in References and Resources).
   - **Residential schools.** Because students at these schools study and live together, they often receive academic and social benefits that students at most traditional secondary schools do not. Again, Hoagies' maintains a list of schools as well as articles on the pros and cons.
   - **Charter schools.** Many larger districts create specialized charter schools that receive public funding but operate independently. Some have a specific academic or artistic focus that can appeal to gifted students.
   - **Online learning.** Online academic options continue to grow, ranging from individual courses to earning a high school diploma or a college degree. Of special interest are the free programs highlighted on the Hoagies' website.
   - **Mentorships.** While some schools offer mentorships as a for-credit course, there is nothing to keep motivated students from setting up their own mentorship with an expert in their passion field.
   - **Early graduation and entrance to college.** There are many obvious trade-offs in graduating early, but for the right student it can be the perfect solution. The advocacy of informed and caring adults is essential.

2. **Create alternatives that fit within the traditional public school parameters.**
   - **Open enrollment.** Some states and provinces have enacted policies that allow students residing in one school district to enroll freely in another district. Also, intradistrict open enrollment may allow students to attend a school in their city that is outside their attendance area. Since policies vary widely, students must verify local, state, and provincial regulations.
   - **Independent study.** This opportunity is often available, but not necessarily intended for gifted

students. However, the option can be used by learners to pursue a passion subject not typically taught in school, and it should be eligible for high school credit. As with a mentorship, independent study must be carefully planned to assure challenge, growth, and accountability.

- **Interest enterprise.** Students can start a club, create a contest or competition, develop a team project, form a local chapter of a national or international group, or initiate a discussion or book group that brings together others with similar unique interests.

- **Online learning.** Courses that aren't available in a school district are usually available online in one form or another. Students should be allowed to take them during the school day for high school credit. Many are free, but some states require districts to pay for online courses they do not offer.

3. **Change the system to affect their own academic lives and also the lives of future students.**

- **Administrative waiver.** Sometimes all it takes is one principal who knows a particular student's ability to say, "We never have done that, but yes, you can [test out of that course] [compact that class] [change your schedule] [do independent study]." With such a waiver, the precedent is set for future students.

- **Policy change.** Some options such as grade acceleration, concurrent enrollment, or early entrance or graduation may require changes to school district policy. This requires students and their advocates to work with the school board and to possibly provide research, expert witnesses, personal student stories, and examples of policies existing elsewhere.

- **State and provincial mandates.** Students may need to ensure that their school board is aware of the law. The NAGC publication *2014–2015 State of the States in Gifted Education, Policy and Practice Data* reports that twenty-three of the forty responding states at that time had some form of legal mandate related to gifted and talented students. But when such mandates are unfunded and unaudited, states and provinces have little accountability and their failure to comply may go unnoticed. There is even the possibility that local districts are unaware of the statutes.

- **Official complaint.** When other options have been exhausted, it may be necessary for students and their advocates to file a formal complaint with their state or provincial department of education, requesting an audit of their school district to determine if it is adhering to the mandate for gifted education.
- **Alliances.** Students can join with others of like mind. A sea change is possible when gifted students come together with their adult advocates, whether local, regional, state, or national.

Chapter 6: Advocates and Advisors lays out the roles of all the people needed to assure that gifted students find the education they need.

Changing the education system requires time, energy, and the support of strong adult advocates. But I have witnessed more than once the power of one persistent, articulate, reasonable student to effect policy changes almost overnight that adults have argued over for years. As fulfilling as it is for gifted learners to make changes that improve their own education, many also find empowerment and real satisfaction in knowing they have changed the world for others . . . or at least their corner of it.

"We tend to think that a qualitative difference has to be large, but that is not correct. What makes the difference may be just a pinch, as between the taste of food without salt and the taste with salt. For the young and bright, many small but significant differences add up to a whole tapestry of more vivid, more nuanced, and more keenly felt experiences."
—Michael M. Piechowski, *"Mellow Out," They Say. If I Only Could*

Conclusion

Ultimately, we must encourage gifted students to ask themselves: "What kind of education do I want?" Then, they can use the following questions as guidelines for setting priorities.

- Does my education provide academic challenge?
- Does it remediate any academic weaknesses I might have?
- Does it enhance my psychological health?
- Does it enable me to socialize with like-ability peers?

If the answer to any of these is "no," students must be encouraged to look for alternatives that better fit their learner profiles.

keyCONCEPTS IN CHAPTER 5

- The third step in self-advocacy is to investigate available enrichment options and opportunities and match them to one's learner profile.
- Students have the greatest chance of succeeding in educational alternatives if they find the right match.
- Not all options are right for all students; not all students are right for all options.
- Student wants and needs generally fall into four categories: finding more challenging work, exploring an interest, spending time with gifted peers, and adjusting their environment to accommodate personal needs.
- Some options already exist in many school districts; others will need to be created by the students and their advocates.
- Students sometimes need to work outside the education system to find the best alternatives.

6 ADVOCATES and ADVISORS

During the first semester of her senior year, Rana was on track to complete all graduation requirements except for one elective credit she would finish during second semester. Then she received the chance of a lifetime: an offer to work as a fashion design apprentice in Italy from January through April. With my help, she proposed a mentorship that would be worth the remaining credit, but she needed the assistance of many other adults for her proposal to work:

◆ Her Italian chaperone (a designer herself) agreed to be her mentor.

◆ The CATE (Career and Technical Education) department chair helped her create assignments to be completed with her mentor.

◆ The principal approved the plan and authorized the elective credit she would receive.

◆ Her parents kept her motivated by regularly checking on her progress.

◆ The director of the local art museum agreed to host her final presentation.

◆ Her family, friends, and teachers formed the audience and critiqued her work.

In essence, it took a village of caring advocates to make her mentorship happen.

Self-Advocacy Step 4: Students Connect with Advocates

While it's key for gifted students to take the lead in determining their path through school, their advocates and advisors—teachers, gifted education specialists, counselors, administrators, coaches, parents, guardians, and other adults—must also play major roles. Frequently, these people are the gatekeepers. Many gifted learners will have access to appropriately challenging educational experiences only if we adults advocate with them, and only if we explain their rights and responsibilities, help them recognize their own learner needs, and point them to the opportunities that match those needs. But informing students is only part of the process; supporting them throughout the process is paramount. We must ask ourselves in what ways we can nurture, guide, and encourage them. Even well-intentioned advocates sometimes advise students to adapt too much to the current system. But if students are to become Autonomous Learners, we must prepare them to use the education system to get what they need, a skill many of us never developed when we were in school. When students, parents, and educators work as advocacy partners, they form a perfect right triangle. The children are the foundation, leading the way, while the adults support on either side.

In asking for this assistance from adults, students are responsible for developing and using their attributes of good character: attentiveness, timeliness, organization, consideration, enthusiasm, gratefulness, humility, and generosity. They must communicate clearly and calmly, relaying their needs with enthusiasm and addressing their frustrations without unnecessary drama. They must be able to articulate their specific goal and the part they would like each person to play. Students may need advocates throughout the problem-solving process to help craft a self-advocacy action plan, authorize the plan, mentor and monitor as the plan progresses, provide feedback, and help evaluate the outcome.

For example, Rana had a long list of people she needed assistance from to successfully complete her study in Italy. First, she had to convince her parents to approve such an unusual decision as missing her last semester of high school. To ease one of their fears, she contacted an admissions counselor at her prospective university to make sure her decision wouldn't affect her acceptance. With that assurance, she worked with me to design the "Careers in the Fashion Industry" independent study proposal that would supply the last high school credit she needed to graduate.

Since I knew little about the fashion industry, our first step was finding Rana a mentor in the field. The best person turned out to be her agency chaperone who agreed to provide guidance, resources, topical discussions, and insights. This mentorship would help Rana create and carry out the meaningful assignments and final project that would turn her fashion design adventure into an educational, credit-worthy experience.

Proposal in hand, Rana went to the head of the CATE department who needed to guarantee her plan fit the criteria for independent study and was rigorous enough to warrant a credit. Next stop was the principal's office. Having never seen a proposal like hers, Rana's principal worried about setting a new precedent and discussed it with the superintendent and school board before giving it his stamp of approval. And finally, before heading off to Milan, Rana needed to decide on a location for her final assessment, a presentation of her completed fashion design project to an invited audience. She chose the local art museum as a fitting venue, and the director approved Rana's use of museum space for the week after her return from Milan. She sent formal invitations to her presentation to friends, family members, teachers, and each person who had helped her through the project approval process. Finally, she created an evaluation rubric to be completed by herself, her mentor, the CATE department chair, and me. At each step of the process, Rana communicated her needs with clarity and consideration. Her enthusiasm, poise, and systematic approach persuaded each of her advocates to be part of the process.

Adults' Roles in Helping Gifted Students Self-Advocate

Adult advocates also need all the information the gifted students themselves must have to follow the four steps of self-advocacy. In addition to becoming informed, however, adults have three major responsibilities:

1. Communicate the concept to others
2. Support the practice
3. Initiate the student's attempts at self-advocacy

Informed advocates should be sharing their understandings with those around them: students, educators, and parents. They also can assist students by insuring that action plans receive authorization. And all advocates can help gifted learners initiate their work toward becoming autonomous.

What Do Gifted Learners Need from Advocates?

What specifically do gifted students need from their advocates? According to Neihart and Betts, if gifted learners of the six profile types (see Chapter 1) are going to increase their autonomy and take charge of their own educations, we must provide support in the following areas:

Successful Learners need opportunities for subject and grade acceleration and other in-depth studies that will push them out of their comfort zones and allow time with like-ability peers. We must give them the freedom to make their own choices while also encouraging them to take and make risks and develop the requisite independent learning skills.

Creative Learners need respect for their personal goals, affirmation of their strengths, and encouragement in pursuing their passions. We must place students with appropriate teachers who not only tolerate but enjoy their nonconformity, as well as counselors who will recognize their psychological vulnerability and provide interventions when needed.

2E Learners need us to provide challenges in their areas of strength along with the skill development, perseverance, and coping strategies they need to be successful. While we continue to offer accommodations for their disabilities, we also must make room in their schedule for enrichment, acceleration, and time with intellectual peers.

Underground Learners need a welcoming learning environment that encourages them to seek challenges. We must find (or become) the role models and cultural brokers who can bridge the gap between a learner's social group and academic setting, and also provide coaching in social skills. We should encourage open discussions with these students about class issues,

racism, sexism, xenophobia, and the cost of success. We must help with short- and long-term goal setting and early college and career planning.

At-Risk Learners need individualized programming and aggressive advocacy, both academic and social-emotional. We need to maintain our high expectations of them but may have to provide the challenging work they need in alternative environments with a supportive mentor. We can help them utilize nontraditional study skills and set short- and long-term goals. In addition to school counseling, these students may also need outside mental health assistance.

Autonomous Learners need ongoing, facilitative relationships with advocates. We should provide information about unique options and opportunities, support for their positive risk-making, and supply feedback at every step of their decision-making process. They may also need cultural brokers to build bridges for them and mentors who can share their own stories of autonomy that led to success.

Within each of these sets of needs, certain groups of advocates can make more specific contributions to every student's successful self-advocacy. The following sections discuss the various types of primary and secondary advocates.

Primary Advocates

Those of us who encounter gifted students every day—parents, classroom teachers, school counselors, and gifted education coordinators—are their primary advocates and our action or inaction has a considerable effect on whether students will speak up for themselves. Our first responsibility is to teach them the hows and whys of self-advocacy as laid out in the preceding chapters. Secondly, we must help students identify the other adults in their lives who will understand their needs and who are necessary to the success of their plans. Thirdly, we must insure that students know how to communicate effectively with those advocates and advisors.

Gifted Education Coordinators

These coordinators, where they exist, are responsible for guiding students through the problem-solving and self-advocacy processes. These coordinators must have a clear understanding of how the education system can be creatively adapted for individual students, what is currently available within their district, what might be initiated, and what might realistically be changed. As they lead the students in creating workable action plans, they must also be knowledgeable about any state or provincial laws or regulations that relate to gifted learners, as well as state/provincial curriculum and graduation requirements.

Gifted education coordinators are also responsible for ensuring that parents, teachers, school counselors, and principals understand the concept of self-advocacy and the student's right to self-advocate. Several years ago, I encouraged eighth grader Rosa to speak with her science teacher, Mr. Schneider, about the frustrations she was experiencing in class. She felt confident about approaching him herself, but too late I realized I hadn't shared the steps of self-advocacy with Mr. Schneider.

Understandably, their first conversation was less than successful. Rosa asked if there were some way for her to move more quickly through the curriculum and work with a lab partner who was as passionate about science as she was. Caught off guard, Mr. Schneider assumed Rosa was questioning his teaching skills, asking for special treatment, and being disrespectful to her less-able classmates. He told her nothing could be changed. Rosa came back to my office in tears. But the conflict was resolved when the three of us met together, calmly discussed each of their concerns, and created an enrichment and acceleration plan. When Mr. Schneider suggested that two other advanced learners would benefit from the same plan, the three students became an inquiry team, going above and beyond the regular science curriculum. And I, too, learned a valuable lesson: for self-advocacy to work, all stakeholders need to be well informed.

Classroom Teachers

Teachers can provide the problem-solving information that will help gifted students understand themselves and their rights and responsibilities, and help students find resources and opportunities inside and outside the education system, as well as help change the system. Students can more easily take charge of their educations when teachers affirm students' differing abilities and let them know that the system can be adjusted to meet their needs. The teacher advocate should seek out giftedness in children—especially those in underrepresented populations who are frequently unidentified—and communicate what they have observed and what students have experienced to parents, coordinators, school counselors, and other teachers. Most importantly, teachers must be proactive in recognizing when students need more depth or breadth in learning and communicating with students about their needs.

The experiences of the students in my self-advocacy workshop indicate that many teachers need to do better as advocates. In the workshop surveys (**see Figure 6.1**), 66 percent of the gifted students said that their teachers have never or only occasionally asked them to do more challenging or interesting work, while 86 percent indicated that they always or occasionally wished their teachers would modify classroom work for them. A teacher advocate's goal is to turn those wishes into reality.

Teachers must solicit and respond to student input and create classrooms where students feel safe to suggest

FIGURE 6.1
Survey Responses: Teachers as Advocates

How often have teachers asked you to do something different from the rest of the class to make your work more challenging or more interesting?			
Number of respondents = 323	# of students	% of students	
Never/Almost never	92	28.4	66.8
Occasionally	124	38.4	
Frequently/Always	107	33.2	
How often have you wished a teacher would modify something for you?			
Number of respondents = 323	# of students	% of students	
Never/Almost never	43	13.3	
Occasionally	110	34.0	86.6
Frequently/Always	170	52.6	

alternatives. We can't assume that students will think to self-advocate without learning how to do so, and we can't assume that they know we welcome their assertiveness. We must say so loudly and clearly.

Two simple ways teachers can be invitational:

◆ Post Galbraith and Delisle's "Ten Tips for Talking to Teachers" in the classroom and discuss it on the first day of class, ensuring that all students know you are open to conversation (see page 173).

◆ Send letters to students and their parents during the first week of school outlining the differentiation that will take place in your classroom during the year to meet students' varying needs. Invite student and parent participation in the process. Letters can be easily customized for individual students, as illustrated by the following fifth-grade teacher's letter:

Sample Parent Letter from a Teacher Advocate

Dear Mr. and Mrs. Mendez,

As Ethan's teacher, my goal is to provide quality instruction tailored to the developmental level of your child. I am constantly monitoring and adjusting my instruction, activities, and assessments to meet the needs of all students in my classroom. During this school year, Ethan will experience challenges at his achievement level in every subject. The following is a list of the strategies I use to encourage academic growth for all students.

◆ *Pretested mathematics units*

◆ *Compacted curriculum for faster-paced instruction*

◆ *Tiered assignments promoting higher-level thinking and depth of knowledge*

◆ *Cooperative learning groups tailored to student interests*

◆ *Literature circles and independent, self-selected reading at students' levels*

◆ *Writer's workshop individualized for pace and interest*

I'm aware that Ethan is in the Gifted Programming Talent Pool and that in the past he has received enrichment and acceleration in math. I plan to offer him a compacted unit with additional enrichment whenever he demonstrates mastery on the chapter pretest. Please

encourage Ethan to let me know if this is providing an appropriate challenge in math. If you and Ethan have other ideas about how his needs could be better met this year, please contact me by phone or email.

Happy learning!

Mrs. Churchill

Beyond a doubt, teachers want all kids to learn. But since many teacher training programs include only a passing glance at the needs of gifted learners, educators may not realize how to create and maintain a gifted-friendly classroom. When I first began exploring giftedness, Dorothy Kennedy was the director of the Network for Gifted Education at the University of Wisconsin–Stevens Point. I learned much from her years of experience. Several of her valuable suggestions have been included on the form on page 104. The suggestions are as relevant for teachers of gifted students today as they were years ago.[52]

The Rights of Teachers of Gifted Students

It is unfair to expect classroom teachers to address the varying needs of students in their classrooms all by themselves. They need support from parents and administrators. In addition to teachers' responsibilities, they also have the right to:

◆ Professional development concerning the characteristics of gifted children and ways to address their needs in the classroom.

◆ Access to a wide variety of curriculum resources and instructional techniques.

◆ Time and compensation for producing differentiated lessons.

◆ Collaboration with other teachers (including special education and ELL), school counselors, school psychologists, and gifted education personnel.

◆ Respectful behavior from self-advocating students and their parents.

School Counselors

Counselors are trained to help every student with academic achievement, personal and social development, and career planning. This is practically impossible, however, when many counselors are responsible for hundreds of students. One large urban school district counselor recently told me that she is the lone person serving four middle schools with a total population of 2,000 students. Therefore, self-advocacy needs to be in every school counselor's toolbox. Instead of seeking out gifted students who need assistance, counselors can encourage students to come to them. Even though parents, coordinators, and teachers are also part of the advocacy team, counselors are the ones who have the training and experience to understand students' social and emotional needs, as well as the guidance information needed to support students' unique paths from the early grades to graduation and on to college and careers.

In empowering students to self-advocate, school counselors provide guidance services beyond course registration and long-range planning. Their assistance may include assessing students' learner profiles through test score interpretation and inventories of interests, preferences, attributes, and attitudes; helping students set goals and develop assertiveness; and guiding students' college and career decision-making through online programs, field trips, and mentor relationships.

Unfortunately, professional training for school counselors frequently doesn't include information on the specific social and emotional needs of gifted learners. I value the honest reflection of this school counselor: "I didn't know anything about gifted kids in the beginning, but the more I work with them the greater I understand their differing needs. I'm kind of embarrassed to admit that early on in my career when a very quiet intellectually gifted student told me she didn't fit in anywhere, I gave her my standard advice, 'Join a sports team.' So, she obediently went to cross-country practice where her lack of athletic ability and introverted discomfort made her feel like even more of an outsider. Fortunately, we continued working together and she eventually found her niche creating and editing the school literary journal."

Counseling services are especially valuable to gifted students who are experiencing some of the common concerns that can get in the way of self-advocacy: perfectionism, introversion, anxiety, existential angst, depression, lack of motivation, academic underachievement, impostor syndrome, and low self-efficacy. School counselors can work with the students and their families to mediate or overcome the obstacles through individual counseling, academic intervention planning, bibliotherapy, support groups, peer mentors, culture brokers, and community resource referrals and consultations.

School counselors are adept at reading the often subtle yet telltale signs that a student wants or needs things to change. By recognizing, discussing, and encouraging that change, they become part of the team of advocates who help gifted students grow toward autonomy.

Parents and Guardians

Parents and guardians are also on the front line of support for their children's self-advocacy, especially in the absence of gifted education coordinators. To be effective advocates, however, parents must be knowledgeable. They should have a clear understanding of the nature of giftedness, their own child's learner profile, the rights and responsibilities of parents and students within the education system, and possible resources both inside and outside of it (the topics of the first five chapters of this book). They also need to develop and maintain amicable working relationships with other advocates, especially classroom teachers who are their partners in supporting their children's self-advocacy.

It helps if everyone in the family is on the same page. As stated earlier, a good first step is sharing Judy Galbraith and Jim Delisle's *The Gifted Teen Survival Guide* with students. In my opinion, it is the most inclusive resource on giftedness written *for* gifted students. It is also a valuable read for parents and a great starting point for family discussions.

One concern for parents, especially those with gifted teenagers, is whether their child wants them to be part of the self-advocacy process. The good news is that 71 percent of the students surveyed at the beginning of the GT Carpe Diem Workshops did indeed feel comfortable having their parents advocate for them with their teachers. That number rose to 82 percent following the workshop, indicating that with increased understanding of their rights, needs, and possibilities, students were even more willing to see their parents as partners in self-advocacy.

FIGURE 6.2
Survey Responses: Parents as Advocates

Number of respondents = 232

How comfortable are you having your parent ask a teacher to modify something for you?

	Very uncomfortable				Okay			Very comfortable		
	0	1	2	3	4	5	6	7	8	9	10
Pre-Workshop	13	24	22	35	34	43	39	56	21	15	21
	94 29%				229 71%						
Post-Workshop	11	5	15	27	31	44	35	45	40	31	39
	58 18%				265 82%						

WORDS OF WISDOM FOR PARENT ADVOCATES

One of the great joys of my professional life is hearing from former students like the multitalented Sandy, now with a family of her own. She emailed me asking for advice on the best way to advocate for her daughter who had just begun kindergarten. I'm not an expert on the early years, so I turned to someone who is: Gay Eastman, an early childhood education specialist and parent of gifted children. Following is Dr. Eastman's response to me—good advice for all parents, not just those with five-year-olds:[53]

"Sara Lawrence-Lightfoot wrote *Worlds Apart: Relationships Between Families and School* based on her Harvard research on mothers and teachers. In it, she posits that there will always be some conflict between parents and teachers simply because they have different roles in relation to children. That is, the parent wants what's best for their individual child while the teacher (and principal, etc.) must look out for the best interest of all the children in a class (or the school). These different perspectives are actually healthy for children—it's good for them to have adults looking out just for them, but also to have adults reminding them that they're not the only person in their universe. Lightfoot goes on to suggest that whether these differences in perspectives lead to 'creative conflict' or 'negative dissonance' depends upon the nature of the interactions between the parents and the school.

"Simply understanding that teachers and schools must, because of their roles, look out for the good of *all* children can go a long way in helping a parent see where the school is coming from and refraining from being defensive or adversarial. When parents acknowledge and even offer to help with these roles, it helps school personnel see that the parent is someone they can work with. And, if parents keep in mind that they, too, have an important role—to advocate as best they can for and with their child—it may help them to have the calm persistence necessary to find good solutions."

The summer before my first son entered kindergarten, I knew beyond a doubt that no school would ever fit the perfect vision of what I wanted for my little boy—not even in the district I'd taught in for six years and knew to be highly regarded. A wise friend and colleague spoke truth to me that has remained with me for decades: "Consider the school your partner. Take advantage of everything it offers. But it is secondary; you are still his primary advocate and educator in the things of this world." What was the main thing I wanted from a school? What every parent wants. I wanted my children's teachers to see my kids as individuals, to recognize their unique abilities (and sometimes lack of ability), and to be interested in working with us to ensure our kids have engaging, appropriate challenges. It turns out, of course, that our family's favorite teachers were the ones who celebrated everyone's talents, loved connecting personally with each of their students, and weren't intimidated by giftedness or overwhelmed by differing abilities. I'm happy to say we partnered well with many of those teachers.

All parents want assurance that those in charge of their children's educations are aware of, understand, and value the individual child's unique needs and will work with that child to create the most appropriate curriculum, instruction, and classroom environment. Sadly, not all children have parents who are able to serve as their advocates and that is one important reason why regular classroom teachers are also primary support providers for gifted students' self-advocacy.

Secondary Advocates

A host of other educational professionals also play important roles, including principals, superintendents and other administrators, and school board members. Those in charge of running the education system must be willing to adjust it to accommodate students' needs. There are many ways, large and small, that these stakeholders can show their support for student self-advocacy.

> "An advocate supports and promotes the interests of gifted students and helps them address academic, social, and emotional issues. Instead of focusing on one child, advocates work so that all gifted children benefit."
> —Kathy Marks, "From Teacher to Advocate"

Here are some examples of secondary advocates who have contributed to the success of self-advocacy in their districts:

- A middle school principal provided release time and transportation for gifted students and staff members to attend self-advocacy workshops.

- A science department chair offered a means for enrichment and acceleration in her subject area for every grade level. Other department chairs followed suit.
- A curriculum and instruction director sought and gained board approval for credited independent study in any subject area.
- A pupil services director provided time for collaboration between gifted education personnel, school counselors, social workers, and school psychologists.
- A special education director facilitated gifted education training for the teachers in her department and invited English language learner teachers to attend as well.
- A chief diversity officer led her staff in building bridges between gifted students' families and their district schools.
- A director of finance authorized the transportation account to cover the cost of transporting students between schools when needed.
- A superintendent used her monthly newsletter to highlight student and staff self-advocacy collaborations and to publicize the variety of opportunities available within the district.
- A school board president invited students to present their self-advocacy successes during public input time at board meetings.
- An entire school board passed policies covering acceleration, early graduation, and alternative educational options.

Advocates' Roles and Responsibilities

Just as gifted students have rights and responsibilities, so do the individuals who are able to support their self-advocacy. When I coordinated gifted education in my school district, parents and educators often referred to it as "your program." So, to show the breadth of support needed to effectively provide for gifted students, my colleagues and I described the roles and responsibilities of all stakeholders in "our" programming, and included the list in our official district plan. **Figure 6.3** shows examples of these roles in relation to student self-advocacy.

FIGURE 6.3
Roles and Responsibilities of Advocates for Gifted Students

Role of the Student	Role of the Parent	Role of the Regular Classroom Teacher	Role of the District Gifted Coordinator
Students are responsible for reflecting on themselves as learners and choosing the path toward graduation that best meets their needs. In relation to their self-advocacy, students' responsibilities include, but are not limited to: • Coming to school ready to learn. • Understanding the characteristics of giftedness. • Assessing and reflecting on their individual learner profiles. • Seeking out and accepting appropriate challenges. • Communicating their wants and needs to parents, teachers, school counselors, gifted education personnel, and other advocates without compromising the dignity of themselves or others. • Developing the attributes of good character expected of all students.	Parents are responsible for working together with their child and school personnel to understand and address the child's specific academic and social-emotional needs. As partners in their gifted child's self-advocacy, parents' responsibilities include, but are not limited to: • Understanding the characteristics of giftedness. • Working with child and school personnel to identify child's specific needs. • Encouraging child to accept appropriate challenges and engage in positive risk-taking. • Together with child, communicating the child's wants and needs to school personnel without compromising the dignity of themselves or others. • Assisting child in developing skills in communicating needs clearly and appropriately. • Assisting child in developing the attributes of good character. • Networking with educators and other parents to support and advance the district's program options and opportunities.	The classroom teacher has primary responsibility for the instruction of gifted students. Because student abilities vary greatly within each classroom, teachers must encourage all students to ask for the enrichment and acceleration they need and want. As partners in gifted students' self-advocacy, teachers' responsibilities include, but are not limited to: • Knowing each student's strengths and needs and applying this information to delivering appropriate learning experiences. • Providing regular classroom differentiation of content, process, and product based on ongoing assessment of student readiness. • Encouraging students to accept appropriate challenges and engage in positive risk-taking. • Reporting student progress to students and parents. • Recognizing individual social and emotional needs and arranging for appropriate in-school consultation.	The district gifted education coordinator oversees the implementation and evaluation of the district plan for gifted education. As partners in gifted students' self-advocacy, coordinators' responsibilities include, but are not limited to: • Instructing all gifted students in the steps of self-advocacy. • Communicating the concept of self-advocacy to parents and educators. • Assisting students in creating, implementing, and evaluating action plans for change. • Assisting classroom teachers in differentiating curriculum by providing model lessons, team teaching, and assistance in creating and using differentiation strategies. • Assisting principals in aligning, implementing, and evaluating each school's plan for student self-advocacy. • Coordinating professional development across the district regarding the needs of gifted students and their self-advocacy. • Coordinating student, parent, staff, and community communications.

continued

Figure 6.3 Roles and Responsibilities of Advocates for Gifted Students (continued)

Role of Gifted Support Staff	Role of the School Counselor	Role of the Principal	Role of the Administration
The gifted support staff serve in their schools as representatives of and support for gifted programming. As partners in gifted students' self-advocacy, support staff responsibilities include, but are not limited to: - Serving as liaison between students, parents, classroom teachers, school counselors, gifted coordinators, and building administrators. - Assisting in instructing all gifted students in the steps of self-advocacy. - Assisting in communicating the concept of self-advocacy to parents and other educators. - Assisting students in creating, implementing, and evaluating action plans for change. - Assisting with coordination of social-emotional support for students.	School counselors assist staff and students in recognizing and nurturing the unique social and emotional development of gifted learners. As partners in gifted students' self-advocacy, school counselors' responsibilities include, but are not limited to: - Assisting students in creating, implementing, and evaluating action plans for change. - Advocating for activities that address the personal, social, academic, and career development needs of gifted students. - Promoting awareness of the special issues that may affect gifted students. - Providing individual and group guidance services as needed. - Providing individual and group counseling services as needed.	Each principal is responsible for ensuring that the needs of gifted students in his or her building are addressed. As partners in gifted students' self-advocacy, principals' responsibilities include, but are not limited to: - Overseeing the implementation and evaluation of the district's gifted programming plan for his or her school. - Insuring that all gifted students receive instruction in self-advocacy. - Insuring that the concept of self-advocacy is clearly communicated to parents and educators. - Providing professional development for all staff on the characteristics of gifted individuals. - Providing professional development for all staff on addressing academic and social-emotional needs through differentiation, enrichment, acceleration, and counseling services.	The district administrators are responsible for ensuring that the needs of gifted students in the school district are addressed. As partners in gifted students' self-advocacy, the administration's responsibilities include, but are not limited to: - Insuring that the district's vision and/or mission statements address the needs of all students. - Insuring the district complies with state or provincial statutes regarding gifted education. - Recognizing the NAGC PreK–Grade 12 Gifted Programming Standards. - Overseeing the implementation and evaluation of the district's gifted education programming, including gifted students' self-advocacy. - Providing funding to adequately support all aspects of the plan: identification, programming, staffing, transportation, professional development, materials, services, etc. - Insuring that students, parents, and educators are encouraged to be partners in the process of student self-advocacy.

Conclusion

As a mother and an educator, I did a lot of hand-holding, and I was never sure when I was gripping too hard or letting go too early. That became less of a concern when I began intentionally communicating the information that my children and students needed to hear. As advocates, we must: *ask, listen, share,* and *act*. And it is also good to remember that there is great power in collaborative advocacy. Too often one voice sounds like whining, but many voices sound like a cause. Together we can and do make a difference in the lives of the gifted students we know and love.

> "I would wish for each child at least one adult who helps the child find the voice of self-advocacy and the courage to use it."
> —*Carol Ann Tomlinson, "Sharing Responsibility for Differentiating Instruction"*

key CONCEPTS IN CHAPTER 6

❖ The fourth step in self-advocacy is for students to connect with the advocates who can help them accomplish what needs to be done.

❖ Communication between students and their advocates must be open, clear, concise, and diplomatic.

❖ Advocates can help students learn to articulate their needs and craft their plans.

❖ Parents, teachers, gifted education coordinators, and counselors are the primary advocates, but other adults also have important roles to play.

Suggestions for Creating a Gifted-Friendly Classroom

◆ Use curriculum compacting regularly to ensure that students are working at the levels of depth, complexity, and abstraction that will challenge them. Don't simply assign more work to those who are first to finish assignments.

◆ Find or create differentiated supplemental materials, such as learning centers or interdisciplinary units, that extend the regular curriculum and require learners to use higher-level thinking skills (refer to Bloom's Taxonomy).

◆ Establish a classroom atmosphere that encourages intellectual curiosity and learning for the sake of learning. Move students from extrinsic to intrinsic motivation by minimizing the focus on grades and emphasizing effort and growth.

◆ Dismiss both elitism and anti-gifted discrimination. Assist all students in acquiring skills in interaction and communication, which will help decrease bullying and increase acceptance of others and their varying viewpoints.

◆ Remember that gifted students often are creatively divergent thinkers whose comments or responses may seem peculiar at first. Letting them explain their ideas can inform and expand the thinking of all class members.

◆ Include independent study on self-selected topics that allow students to explore their passions in depth and relate them to the general curriculum. Teach research skills (including appropriate internet use) and selection of products that best demonstrate what the student has learned.

◆ Recognize the special needs of underrepresented students. Help them find peers and mentors. Encourage them to set goals—both academic and career—that reflect their gifts and talents.

7 PATHS and PLANS

Freshman Mandy had a passion for math and felt frustrated with the slow pace of her pre-calculus class. Although the teacher pretested and compacted each of the units, she still felt like she was spending too much time waiting to learn something new. So, Mandy took the matter into her own hands by following the four steps for self-advocacy. She understood her right to an appropriate challenge in her talent area and knew she was responsible for initiating the change she wanted. The characteristics of her learner profile—strong interest in the subject area, high motivation, self-reliance, and preference for working alone—helped her choose independent study as the right option for her. When she brought her idea to me, her longtime advocate, we worked together to write a specific goal and to craft an action plan for change.

Using Mandy and other gifted self-advocates as examples, this chapter provides detailed information on forming a goal and creating an action plan, the culminating activity in the self-advocacy process.

Devising Goals

As discussed in Chapter 5, student goals most frequently fall into one of these four categories:

1. Finding appropriately challenging academic work
2. Exploring an interest
3. Spending more time with other gifted peers
4. Adjusting school or home life to better accommodate personal needs

Goals can be big, long-range goals, such as getting into a specific college or pursuing a certain career. Or goals can be more immediate, like setting up an efficient home study space, and require smaller steps. And a myriad of possibilities exists in between. The most productive place to begin is to select one educational goal and design a plan to accomplish it. Mandy expressed her goal of finding appropriately challenging academic work this way: "I want to finish precalculus in one semester instead of two and take statistics second semester." With her goal clearly in mind, she was ready to craft her plan.

Creating Action Plans

As the adage goes, failing to plan is planning to fail. Wishing for change won't make it happen, but careful and thoughtful planning will help ensure success. An action plan is a relatively short and simple outline of specific steps, people who need to be involved, responsibilities, and deadlines that keep the plan moving along. A plan helps change seem possible. Experienced gifted program coordinators, with their knowledge of the community, are invaluable to helping students create and execute action plans. They can also help learners consider how other adults (who may or may not already be advocates) can be brought in on the plan.

As they craft their plans, students and their advocates should consider the questions on the handout on pages 174–175. These important questions relate to the four steps of self-advocacy.

With the answers to these questions in mind, Mandy and I created an action plan to compact her precalculus curriculum into one semester, freeing up time during her second semester to study statistics.

FIGURE 7.1
Sample Self-Advocacy Action Plan

ACTION PLAN		
Goal Statement: I want to finish precalculus in one semester instead of two and take statistics second semester.		
Implementation: **Action Steps**	**Person(s) Responsible**	**Date Completed**

1. Talk to counselor:
   a. Would this have any effect on graduation, college acceptance, ACT/SAT?
   b. What sort of signed approval do I need?
	Mandy and Ms. Douglas	Aug 28

2. Get recommendation from last year's math teacher.	Mandy	Sept 1
3. Get approval from math department head.	Mandy	Sept 2
4. Get approval from principal. a. What credit will I get?	Mandy	Sept 3
5. Find math mentor/independent study teacher.	Ms. Douglas	Sept 7

6. Meet with mentor.
   a. What textbook?
   b. What timeline?
   c. What forms of assessment?
   d. How often will we meet?
   e. Where will we meet?
	Mandy and Ms. Douglas	Sept 10

7. Check-ins for progress report.	Mandy, Ms. Douglas, and mentor	Oct 10 Nov 10 Dec 10 Jan 10
8. Turn in the grade to the principal's office.	Ms. Douglas	end of semester

Mandy and I took into consideration several important factors. Our plan worked out in this way:

1. First we created a contract for compacted pre-calculus, stating Mandy's intentions, listing her responsibilities, and suggesting a timeline. Mandy, her parents, her previous math teacher, the department chair, her school counselor, the principal, and I all needed to agree to the contract and add our signatures, since each of us would play a role in the success of the plan.

2. Working with the school counselor, Mandy determined that neither her College Board exams nor college admission would be affected by her compacting plan. The counselor looked up Mandy's report card, noted her exemplary GPA, and signed on.

3. Mandy returned to my office the next day with her parents' signatures on the contract.

4. The next step was getting a written recommendation from Mandy's Algebra II teacher who was well aware of her interest and abilities in math, as well as her work ethic, motivation and self-direction.

5. With that recommendation in hand, Mandy approached the math department head who, relying on his staff member's recommendation, signed on, as well. He even gave her suggestions for possible mentors.

6. Her next stop was the principal. To her surprise, the principal had approved a similar plan a few years earlier and was easily convinced that the challenge was appropriate for Mandy. The principal also agreed that on successfully completing the compacted precalculus course, Mandy was entitled to the credit associated with the full-year course.

7. During this time, I was meeting with the school's three precalculus teachers to get their input on the compacted curriculum. Knowing that they might have reservations, I wanted to have a conversation with them before they were approached by Mandy. As it turned out, one of the teachers was so excited by the project that he volunteered to mentor Mandy during his prep period.

8. Mandy and I met with the math teacher/mentor and laid out the specifics: textbook, timeline, projects, assessments, and meeting dates.

9. During the second week of the semester, the teacher/mentor asked if two other students who also had great interest and ability could work with Mandy independently. The principal gave her approval. The school counselor rearranged their schedules to make it work.

10. Once a month, Mandy and the two other students, their teacher/mentor, and I touched base to make sure everything was going as planned.

Mandy's successful completion of her compacted precalculus action plan was instrumental in reassuring all stakeholders that this was a workable option. Additionally, bringing all the various advocates into the picture early on helped shine a light on the possibilities for differentiation, compacted courses, and acceleration. The following year, more students were able to carry out similar plans in multiple disciplines. So often success breeds success—for oneself and those following behind!

Following are more examples of students who became self-advocates and made the changes they wanted and needed by following each of the four steps.

Examples of Students Seeking More Challenging Work

Gifted students whose classes move too slowly or whose assignments are too easy may choose to compact a class, test out of a class, replace a class with independent study, alternate a required class with an elective, or accelerate a subject or grade. For example:

◆ Pa Nhia showed exceptional ability in language arts. Having experienced an accelerated seventh-grade English class, she worried that the curriculum in a heterogeneous class the next year wouldn't meet her needs. So, she created a portfolio of her writing that she presented to her eighth-grade teacher. Upon review, Pa Nhia's teacher agreed to help her set up an independent study and ensured that all state standards for eighth-grade English language arts would be met through her work. The four quarters of the year were used to explore:

- A grammar curriculum developed by the Center for Gifted Education at the College of William and Mary
- An extensive comparison study of *Harry Potter, The Lord of the Rings,* and the King Arthur legend
- Writing research papers on career possibilities
- Individual creative writing projects and publication of a student anthology involving the whole school

◆ Max's family heritage was northern European, but many of his closest friends and their families were recent immigrants from Mexico. Understandably, Max's fluency in Spanish was more advanced than the other students in his high school Spanish class. To increase his communication skills with native Spanish speakers (and as a service project and preview of his future career in education), Max worked with his language arts teacher to design and run an after-school English language acquisition club for his friends' Spanish-speaking parents and grandparents.

◆ Within the first week of fifth grade, following a unit pretest, Jeff realized that he had already mastered much of the material in his math class. So, Jeff, his parents, and his gifted coordinator met with his math teacher who suggested they compact the curriculum. She gave Jeff alternative assignments and encouraged him to do his own research. This allowed Jeff to investigate topics that excited and challenged him such as the origin of zero, Fibonacci numbers, the lives of famous mathematicians, and the relationship between music and math. Instead of waiting to learn something new, he extended the breadth and the depth of his mathematical knowledge.

◆ Sophomore Tyrell played trumpet in the high school concert band and viola in the symphony orchestra. He also wanted to study honors-level physics, but the only two sections met during the same periods as his music classes. Tyrell's counselor said his only option was to switch to the less challenging regular physics class or the less advanced band or orchestra courses. But Tyrell devised the following schedule (**see Figure 7.2**) and received permission from his teachers to alternate between the three more demanding courses, attending physics every day and his two music classes every other day. The schedule and the staff were flexible enough to accommodate exams, special labs, and concert preparation.

Examples of Students Seeking to Explore an Interest

Gifted learners who want to explore an interest not offered in their school have many options, including online courses, college or university classes, independent studies, out-of-school mentorships, and community volunteer opportunities. For example:

◆ Marissa's passion for architecture inspired her to apply for a summer teen internship program with the Frank Lloyd Wright Fellowship. Her impressive

FIGURE 7.2
Tyrell's New Schedule

		Monday	Tuesday	Wednesday	Thursday	Friday
A Week	Period 4	Symphony Orchestra	Honors Physics	Symphony Orchestra	Honors Physics	Symphony Orchestra
	Period 5	Honors Physics	HS Concert Band	Honors Physics	HS Concert Band	Honors Physics
B Week	Period 4	Honors Physics	Symphony Orchestra	Honors Physics	Symphony Orchestra	Honors Physics
	Period 5	HS Concert Band	Honors Physics	HS Concert Band	Honors Physics	HS Concert Band

art portfolio got her through the highly selective acceptance process. But knowing that her family would not be able to cover the cost, Marissa took her portfolio to local, regional, and state architectural businesses, from whom she received enough scholarship money to pay for the internship.

◆ Alan was determined to develop his own website, so he arranged to do his study hall in the computer lab and took online courses in HTML. By the end of the year, he gained certification in several areas of computer programming.

◆ Wondering if he was cut out for a medical career, Sacha designed a mentorship/independent study that was approved by the local hospital administration. Every day after school he volunteered in the hospital's pathology lab, observing and assisting in whatever ways were legal and ethical. The physicians were so impressed with his work, they received permission for him to attend an autopsy—a thrill for Sacha!

◆ From the time she was very young, Liv loved tinkering with computers. She attended summer technology camps in middle school but couldn't subject accelerate into her high school's tech program without the electrical systems prerequisite. Working with a local technical college, Liv completed their individually paced program in record time and was the only freshman in her school's senior-level courses.

Examples of Students Seeking More Time with Gifted Peers

Students who spend much of their school time in heterogeneous classes often look for ways to interact more frequently with like-ability peers. Residential and semester schools, study groups, book groups, and extracurricular clubs and teams are just a few of the possibilities. For example:

◆ There were no schools designed specifically for gifted students in her area, so Kylie investigated semester residential schools. During the fall of her junior year, she attended Conserve School in northern Wisconsin so she could spend time with teachers and students who were as passionate about preserving the environment as she was.

◆ Evan was one of only twelve full-time students in the new International Baccalaureate Diploma Program at his school. Preparing for the six exams and writing multiple extended essays required hours and hours of work. For him and many of his IB peers, after-school hours were packed with extracurricular activities and part-time jobs. So, Evan petitioned the staff to create occasional IB study days throughout the year when classes were suspended and the small group of students worked in a quiet space of the library, supervised voluntarily by IB teachers during their prep periods.

◆ After her gifted coordinator gave her a copy of *The Gifted Teen Survival Guide*, Akeesha started an evening book club at the city library where she and her friends could read and discuss it together. They went on to read several other recommended books together over the course of the year, joined by others who heard about the group and were interested in the topics.

◆ Jose discovered Knowledge Master Open, an electronic quiz bowl, and set up team practices during lunch. He even found a community sponsor to pay the team's registration fees for the competition and provide snacks on competition days. Although the team was open to any student, it primarily drew kids who had a wide range of academic knowledge, enjoyed competition, and could hold their own in the fast-paced quiz environment. Not surprisingly, the coordinator who served as the team's advisor identified several gifted students from underrepresented groups who had previously slipped under the radar.

Examples of Students Seeking to Accommodate Personal Needs

With increased understanding of their learner profiles, gifted students become more aware of how their unique combination of personal characteristics affects their lives. Schools are generally willing to make accommodations for gifted students when presented with clear reasons and a well-articulated plan. For example:

◆ Julia was stressed when she had too many exams and term papers due at the same time, so she worked with her teachers to stagger deadlines. She even requested and received "incompletes" at the end of the school year and finished some work during the summer so she could complete it according to her own high standards without feeling rushed.

◆ Ivan couldn't concentrate on schoolwork in the general hubbub of his homeroom and convinced the principal to create a "total quiet" study hall for students who needed a silent environment to get work done during the school day.

◆ Lucia was a night owl by nature and was able to change her schedule so P.E. was her "wake-up" class first thing in the morning, and her most demanding classes were in the afternoon when her mind was more alert.

◆ Ali realized his hypersensitive stomach (possibly part of his sensory overexcitability) couldn't tolerate breakfast early in the morning before he left for school. Although food was banned outside of the lunchroom, he got permission to stop in the gifted coordinator's office to eat a midmorning healthy snack between classes.

Conclusion

Through self-advocacy, gifted students, with the support of advocates, become the initiators of their own action plan, the primary reviewers of its progress, and the final evaluators of its success. Of course, paving new paths to graduation and beyond does not always go smoothly. Modifications and revisions are par for the course. And sometimes (though rarely) the plan may need to be abandoned in favor of a different approach. But as Karen Rogers reminds us: "Even if the educational plan goes no further than modifying a school's attitude or selecting the most appropriate teacher to work with a child, that change will be one very important step toward meeting one child's needs."[54]

keyCONCEPTS IN CHAPTER 7

❖ Designing a goal and action plan for one particular educational goal is often the simplest and most productive place to begin.

❖ Careful and thoughtful planning will help ensure success.

❖ Both short- and long-term ramifications of the plan must be considered.

❖ Students' success with their chosen paths and plans frequently opens doors to other options for themselves and for others.

8 WORKSHOPS and WAYS FORWARD

Once upon a time not so long ago, when I was a district coordinator of gifted education, the stars happened to align. Our district had a little grant money and a truly supportive administration. Our teachers were trained in the needs of gifted kids, while school counselors, psychologists, and social workers willingly volunteered their time. A rustic compound in our school forest was available with overnight accommodations for sixty kids plus adults. And in that magical time, I was able to convince Jim Delisle (who literally helped write the book on gifted kids taking charge of their own lives) to join our gifted teens, their educator advocates, and me on the shores of Lake Michigan for a weekend exploring nature, relationships, and self-advocacy.

Despite the stifling temperatures, hordes of bugs, and lack of potable water, we had a memorable time with some remarkable people. Half of the students were

transitioning into middle school from six different elementary schools. The other half were students two years older who knew the ropes and served as peer mentors. All teens spent two days circulating through activities and discussions led by their prospective teachers, school counselors, and the ever-entertaining Dr. Delisle in which students investigated giftedness, their individual learner profiles, and variations on the typical middle school programming. The first evening brought games, movies, a bonfire, socializing, stargazing, and a moonlit lake walk. At the end of day two, parents arrived for a potluck dinner, an overview of their kids' experiences, and a Q&A with Dr. Delisle.

The gifted students who attended were enchanted by the experience, even though they jokingly referred to the weekend as "nerd camp." I couldn't wait to do it again. But alas, things change, and it turned out to be the first and last forest adventure. Still, it convinced me that gatherings offering direct instruction were the key to developing students' self-advocacy. I just needed to figure out a more expedient, easily replicable model to ensure that amid change, less would be left up to chance and all my students would have the information and support required to ask for what they needed. Hence, the GT Carpe Diem Workshop was born and remains the best model for self-advocacy instruction that I've found.

Direct Instruction in Self-Advocacy

Over the years I have come to believe that the best way to make sure all gifted students know the what, why, how, and when of self-advocacy is to teach them the four steps described in this book directly and specifically. I've tried a variety of possible delivery methods for this instruction with varying success:

◆ Pull-out from one class period per day for a week
◆ Pull-out from one class period each week for 5 to 7 weeks
◆ Homeroom or advisor/advisee time
◆ Before- or after-school weekly sessions
◆ Lunch time weekly sessions
◆ Summer school session
◆ Ongoing group counseling sessions
◆ Ongoing individual counseling sessions
◆ Two half-day introductory workshops
◆ One-day introductory workshop

Each of these options has drawbacks, including time constraints for educators and counselors and a lack of consistent social-emotional programming for gifted students in many school districts (see **Figure 8.1** on page 113 for more details).

No matter which delivery model you choose, direct instruction is the key to jump-starting the self-advocacy process. It empowers gifted students to speak up for themselves through a clearer understanding of their unique needs and their rights to an appropriately challenging education. Following exploration and reflection, students are better able to become ongoing partners in their educations and to lead you in the direction they want to go rather than waiting for you to recognize they need help.

For my students and me, the most beneficial delivery option is a single introductory workshop followed by the continual support of knowledgeable advocates. I call it the GT Carpe Diem Workshop, since its aim is to empower gifted and talented learners to "seize the day" in school and in life. My workshop facilitator's guide and handouts can be found starting on page 135 and are also available to download from this book's digital content. A PDF presentation that goes along with the workshop is also available in the digital content. See page 194 for instructions on how to access the digital content.

The GT Carpe Diem Workshop Model

The GT Carpe Diem Workshop is a one-day event lasting five to seven hours that brings together a group of gifted teens and preteens from several districts and schools along with their adult advocates to network, learn about themselves, and create personal plans for change. The model is based on research and reflects the work of eminent writers and scholars in the fields of giftedness, creativity, and differentiation, including: Miriam Adderholdt, George Betts, Mihaly Csikszentmihalyi, Jim Delisle, Judy Galbraith, Françoys Gagné, Thomas Greenspon, Jonni Kincher, Maureen Neihart, Michael Piechowski, Karen Rogers, Del Siegle, Linda Silverman, Carol Ann Tomlinson, and Susan Winebrenner.

The workshop is a purposefully designed day that introduces students to the ideas and understandings they need to self-advocate and connects students with like-ability peers and supportive adults. The extended period of time allows for more depth, breadth, and community building than shorter events. Together, students study the theories and definitions of intelligence and then use these concepts to analyze their own strengths. They learn about their rights and responsibilities, coping strategies, and a variety of educational options that match their profiles, as well as tools and procedures for developing skills in

FIGURE 8.1
Delivery Methods for Direct Instruction in Self-Advocacy

Delivery Method	Description	Pros	Cons
1 session/day for a week	Students are pulled from their regular classes to meet with gifted coordinator for approximately 1 hour daily for 1 week.	Time of day can vary so students aren't missing the same class every day. Need only one trained facilitator.	Requires daily reminders to students and staff. Continuity may be lost between sessions.
1 session/week for several weeks	Students are pulled from their regular classes to meet with gifted coordinator for approximately 1 hour weekly for 5 to 7 weeks	Time of day can vary so students aren't missing the same class every week. Need only one trained facilitator.	Requires weekly reminders to students and staff. Continuity may be lost between sessions.
Homeroom or advisor/advisee time throughout year	Self-advocacy curriculum is used for the regularly scheduled meetings.	Spreads ownership of process to additional staff members trained to facilitate sessions. Fits into scheduled programming.	Gifted students must be cluster grouped in homerooms. Staff must be trained. Continuity may be lost between sessions.
Before- or after-school weekly sessions	Students meet before or after school with gifted coordinator for up to 1 hour for 8 to 10 weeks.	Students miss no class time. Need only one trained facilitator.	Students may have transportation issues or extracurricular conflicts. Early morning is difficult for many teens. Continuity may be lost between sessions.
Lunch time weekly sessions	Students meet during lunch with gifted coordinator for 8 to 10 weeks.	Students miss no class time. Need only one trained facilitator.	Lunch periods are often less than 30 minutes. Eating and clean up are disruptive. Continuity may be lost between sessions.
Summer school session	Students attend class taught by gifted coordinator for approximately 1 hour daily for 1 to 2 weeks or all day for 1 to 2 days.	Students miss no class time and have no other homework. Need only one trained facilitator.	Students may have transportation issues or conflicts with other activities. Summer school may be seen as remediation or punishment.
Group counseling sessions	Small student groups meet regularly (weekly or monthly) with school counselor during the school day.	Spreads ownership of process to school counselors.	Counselors may need training. Less opportunity for students to experience firsthand the diversity of a larger group of gifted learners.
Individual counseling sessions	Individual students meet regularly with school counselor.	Greater possibility of differentiating the program to focus on an individual student's needs.	One student at a time. No opportunity for networking with peers or experiencing firsthand the diversity of gifted learners.
2 half-day introductory workshops	Students meet with gifted coordinator for approximately 3 hours per day on 2 days (ideally consecutive).	May include students from various grades, schools, or districts. At end of 2 days, students have a plan for change. Spreads ownership of process to attending staff members who support students over time.	Students miss 2 half days. More difficult to schedule 2 days. Continuity may be lost between sessions, especially if days are not consecutive.
One-day introductory workshop	Students meet with gifted coordinator for 5 to 7 hours on 1 day.	May include students from various grades, schools, or districts. At end of day, students have a plan for change. Spreads ownership of process to attending staff members who support students over time.	Students miss 1 day of school.

self-advocating. Students and adults leave the workshop with these essential understandings:

- Gifted students vary in their talents and interests.
- Gifted students need educational opportunities that match their unique needs.
- Gifted students can and should play a major role in designing their own paths through the educational system and beyond.

The GT Carpe Diem Workshop model also provides excellent professional development opportunities for the advocates and advisors who accompany the students, including gifted education coordinators, classroom teachers, school counselors, psychologists, social workers, and administrators. Advocates are actively engaged during the workshop, interacting with the students and assisting the facilitator. Their understandings of giftedness and of the gifted students they serve increase as they guide the small-group discussions, encourage student participation, take part in all the assessment activities, and keep an eye out for students who are struggling with the day for one reason or another.

Throughout the morning, advocates work with students from all attending schools, and in the afternoon, advocates focus specifically on the students from their own schools as students discuss and write their individual action plans. The adults also have a critical role in supporting their students' plans when they are back in their own districts and schools. Through their workshop attendance, they are privy to the same information as the students and may later need to bring parents and other educators up to speed regarding everyone's roles in student self-advocacy.

The Role of Facilitator

The key to providing a successful GT Carpe Diem Workshop for your students is finding a knowledgeable facilitator. That person could be you. In fact, anyone who has read this book, understands the four steps, and believes that gifted learners need to speak up for themselves could be a GT Carpe Diem Workshop facilitator.

To that end, I've created a workshop facilitator's guide with step-by-step instructions for setting up

and running a workshop. To get you started on your own workshop, I have provided the facilitator's guide, student handouts, and the PDF presentation I use during my workshops (see page 194 for download instructions). For each workshop activity, the guide details learner outcomes, key connections, introductory material, instructions, follow-up questions, concluding material, and a transition to the next activity. The corresponding chapters of related information in this book are provided for each activity. While it may be helpful for a facilitator to gain firsthand experience by attending a GT Carpe Diem Workshop along with her or his students, it is not a prerequisite.

ESSENTIAL ELEMENTS FOR GT CARPE DIEM WORKSHOPS

For the workshop to run efficiently, these elements are essential:

- ❖ Facilitator and copy of the facilitator's guide (see page 135 and digital content)
- ❖ 5 to 7 hours of workshop time
- ❖ 15 to 50 gifted students, often from various districts and schools and at least one adult advocate from each school represented
- ❖ Large room with moveable tables and chairs
- ❖ Student handouts (starting on page 162 and in the digital content)
- ❖ Facilitator PDF presentation (available in the digital content)

GT Carpe Diem Workshop Agenda and Learner Outcomes

Page 136 gives an example of a typical workshop agenda and pages 135–136 list the GT Carpe Diem Workshop learner outcomes and goals. To achieve these goals in just one day, every activity is carefully crafted to contribute to students' understanding of self-advocacy and increase the likelihood that students will self-advocate after their time together. For instance, the day begins with an icebreaker, an activity typically used to get participants involved and interacting. The icebreaker I designed, the Express Yourself Talent Search (see page 179), uses Howard Gardner's theory of multiple intelligences to illustrate that gifted students have differing strengths, preferences, and interests. The goal of the activity is for each student to complete the grid by asking others to perform the simple actions described in the squares. It requires students to get out of their chairs, interact with at least twenty other people, and make a brief comparison of their talents with those of other attendees.

The remainder of the day's activities expose students to the steps of self-advocacy explained in the previous chapters of this book:

◆ In **Gripes of Wrath**, the facilitator encourages participants to verbalize and record any frustrations they have regarding their education and social interactions as gifted students. Later, just before the mid-morning break, students review their gripes, record any others that have come to mind, and then shred or delete their lists, signifying a shift from dwelling on frustrations to finding solutions to their concerns.

◆ During **Defining the "G" Word**, students compare a variety of definitions of giftedness and list the key concepts. Then students examine their state or provincial laws and school district mission statements to determine their rights and responsibilities as gifted individuals.

◆ The **Who Am I?** section of the workshop leads students through several different personal assessments relating to each of the five areas in their learner profiles, creating a composite of their current characteristics. Then by comparing their results with those of other students, they again recognize the differences between gifted individuals.

◆ In **The Match Game**, participants summarize their primary learner characteristics and discover which programming opportunities best fit their profiles. Students who have already experienced some of the recommended options explain the possible pros and cons to their peers. Students identify the educational experiences that most interest them.

◆ In the **Teacher Talk Improv** activity, students act out scenarios that demonstrate right and wrong ways to approach adults when asking for change. By this point, most students recognize the changes they would like to make and are aware that to be successful, they need supportive adults. They list the names of adults in their lives who could help them, read the "Ten Tips for Talking to Teachers" by Delisle and Galbraith (see page 173), and complete the activity.

◆ **Diving In.** With all the preceding information in mind, students select a goal and create an action plan for change. Working with the adult advocate from their school who is also at the workshop, they determine the steps to follow to get the desired results.

◆ **Closing, Sharing, and Reflecting.** Participants end the workshop by sharing their action plans with each other and offering recommendations and encouragement.

> The Express Yourself Talent Search and all other GT Carpe Diem Workshop activities are included in the facilitator's guide (see pages 139–159), along with directions for leading each activity.

The Workshop's Alignment with National Standards

The goals, content, and activities in the GT Carpe Diem Workshop are aligned with the following NAGC PreK–Grade 12 Gifted Education Programming Standards.[55]

Standard 1: Learning and Development

1.1. Self-Understanding. Students with gifts and talents demonstrate self-knowledge with respect to their interests, strengths, identities, and needs in socio-emotional development and in intellectual, academic, creative, leadership, and artistic domains.

1.2. Self-Understanding. Students with gifts and talents possess a developmentally appropriate understanding of how they learn and grow; they recognize the influences of their beliefs, traditions, and values on their learning and behavior.

1.3. Self-Understanding. Students with gifts and talents demonstrate understanding of and respect for similarities and differences between themselves and their peer group and others in the general population.

1.4. Awareness of Needs. Students with gifts and talents access resources from the community to support cognitive and affective needs, including social interactions with others having similar interests and abilities or experiences, including same-age peers and mentors or experts.

1.6. Cognitive and Affective Growth. Students with gifts and talents benefit from meaningful and challenging learning activities addressing their unique characteristics and needs.

1.7. Cognitive and Affective Growth. Students with gifts and talents recognize their preferred approaches to learning and expand their repertoire.

1.8. Cognitive and Affective Growth. Students with gifts and talents identify future career goals that match their talents and abilities and resources needed to meet those goals (e.g., higher education opportunities, mentors, financial support).

Standard 2: Assessment

2.2. Identification. Each student reveals his or her exceptionalities or potential through assessment evidence so that appropriate instructional accommodations and modifications can be provided.

2.6. Evaluation of Programming. Students identified with gifts and talents have increased access and they show significant learning progress as a result of improving components of gifted education programming.

Standard 4: Learning Environments

4.1. Personal Competence. Students with gifts and talents demonstrate growth in personal competence and

dispositions for exceptional academic and creative productivity. These include self-awareness, self-advocacy, self-efficacy, confidence, motivation, resilience, independence, curiosity, and risk-taking.

4.3. Leadership. Students with gifts and talents demonstrate personal and social responsibility and leadership skills.

4.5. Communication Competence. Students with gifts and talents develop competence in interpersonal and technical communication skills. They demonstrate advanced oral and written skills, balanced biliteracy or multi-literacy, and creative expression. They display fluency with technologies that support effective communication.

Standard 5: Programming

5.1. Variety of Programming. Students with gifts and talents participate in a variety of evidence-based programming options that enhance performance in cognitive and affective areas.

5.2. Coordinated Services. Students with gifts and talents demonstrate progress as a result of the shared commitment and coordinated services of gifted education, general education, special education, and related professional services, such as school counselors, school psychologists, and social workers.

5.3. Collaboration. Students' with gifts and talents learning is enhanced by regular collaboration among families, community, and the school.

5.5. Comprehensiveness. Students with gifts and talents develop their potential through comprehensive, aligned programming and services.

5.7. Career Pathways. Students with gifts and talents identify future career goals and the talent development pathways to reach those goals.

Standard 6: Professional Development

6.1. Talent Development. Students develop their talents and gifts as a result of interacting with educators who meet the national teacher preparation standards in gifted education.

6.2. *Socio-Emotional Development.* Students with gifts and talents develop socially and emotionally as a result of educators who have participated in professional development aligned with national standards in gifted education and National Staff Development Standards.

Student and Advocate Assessments of Workshops

Frequently throughout this book I've used the responses from student surveys to reinforce my ideas. Students in grades four through twelve from twenty-five school districts and thirty-eight individual schools, as well as students who are homeschooled, completed surveys at the beginning and end of my GT Carpe Diem Workshops. These students come from varied locales: small, midsize, and large cities and suburbs; and fringe, distant, and remote towns and rural areas, as defined by the National Center for Education Statistics. I revised the surveys following my first few workshops, which is why some of the responses are from all 323 students and some are from only 286 students. Copies of the surveys can be found on pages 188–189. When completed by the workshop participants, these surveys provide important information for understanding students' concerns and addressing their needs back in the classroom. Additional questions in the post-workshop survey allow students to evaluate their workshop experience and contribute suggestions for improvement.

The statistics derived from these pre- and post-workshop surveys indicate the success of the workshop goal: "Students will increase their willingness and comfort level in asking for what they need to take charge of their own educations." The numbers reveal that following the workshop, over 74 percent of the students self-reported an increased comfort level in asking a teacher to modify something for them to make their work more challenging or more interesting. Additionally, 72 percent of the students reported an increase in the likelihood that they would soon talk with someone at their school about better meeting their needs. **Figure 8.2** shows the pre- and post-workshop numbers and percentages.

FIGURE 8.2
Survey Responses: Comfort Asking Teacher Pre- and Post-Workshop

Number of respondents = 323				
How comfortable are you asking a teacher to modify something for you to make your work more challenging or more interesting?				
	Pre-workshop		Post-workshop	
Very uncomfortable	59	18%	16	5%
Comfortable	165	51%	102	32%
Very comfortable	99	31%	205	63%

Number of respondents = 286				
How likely are you to talk with someone at your school in the near future about better meeting your needs?				
	Pre-workshop		Post-workshop	
Not likely	88	31%	28	10%
Likely	124	43%	72	25%
Very likely	74	26%	187	65%

Following the workshop, my survey also asked students if they had a greater understanding of giftedness and of their learner profiles, and whether they would recommend the workshop to other gifted students.

FIGURE 8.3
Survey Responses: Understandings and Recommendations

Number of respondents = 323	**Yes**	**No**
Do you have a greater understanding of what it means to be gifted?	313	10
Do you have a greater understanding of your learner profile?	303	20
Would you recommend this workshop to other gifted students?	313	10

As disappointing as the "no" responses might be, they did not surprise me. The fact is, I could pick out the students who might be negative about the workshop shortly after beginning the activities. In most cases, they are the Creative, Underground, and At-Risk learners who are at odds with the education system and uncomfortable being singled out as gifted by the adults who invited them to the workshop. And yet, despite their unenthusiastic and sometimes surly responses, I believe that for most students the workshop had and will continue to have a profound effect on their self-advocacy.

Consider this feedback from Antoine, a freshman I met in Arizona: "This workshop did nothing for me. In fact, it didn't challenge me at all. Six hours of rambling bores me. How should it be improved? I would just get rid of it. My overall rating for the day is zero. Thanks for wasting my time. Any goal I set would be irrelevant."

Even more telling was his end-of-the-day note to his new high school gifted coordinator, who had planned the day as a way to get to know her incoming ninth graders: "To Whom It May Concern: Just to let you know, I'm really, really, really mad. I moved here last year and no one has a clue who I am or what I want. Nobody ever listens to me and nobody listens to my mom when she tries to talk for me. I don't know who invited me to this thing or what they thought I'd get out of it, but I wish you'd just leave me alone. One day isn't going to fix anything. Yours truly, Antoine J."

After initially being stunned by the poor evaluation and intensity of his words, both the coordinator and I were elated. We had discovered a gifted student who was crying out for help. He was more than ready for self-advocacy, but he needed assistance establishing positive relationships, developing his communication skills, and reflecting on himself as a learner. Of course, his coordinator followed up with him the next day. Their conversation led to Antoine calling a meeting with his parents, teachers, school counselor, and principal. There, he was assured that he had a voice in his own education and that those who oversaw the system were willing and eager to work with him. With the help of those advocates, he began his plan for change immediately. And as his freshman year progressed, he took baby steps toward autonomy including meeting regularly with his coordinator, asking for and receiving differentiated assignments in his

areas of strength, and starting an anime club where he met new friends. His action plan changed his life rather quickly, but who knows how long he might have waited if he hadn't participated in—and hated—the workshop!

Student and Advocate Workshop Reviews

Even more affirming than the statistics on students' comfort level and likelihood to self-advocate are the positive reviews of the workshop from the students and advocates themselves:

"Really fun and inspirational."
—*Xiong, grade 6*

"I don't know where I would have learned these things if I wasn't here today."
—*Micah, grade 8*

"I loved the spark of hope you gave us."
—*Becca, grade 7*

"I now have a plan to make sure my needs are met." —*Jaime, grade 9*

"Keep on doing this. You are changing kids' lives!" —*Nolan, grade 10*

"Both my daughter and I attended the workshop last fall. What a transformation it was for her. She's eliminated frustration and disappointment, and made good use of what was not working to direct it toward a possibility that could work." —*Katherine, parent*

"I wish this workshop had been around when I was a girl! It would have helped me discover that I wasn't alone—that there are other kids out there with learning needs beyond the norm, and that it's okay to be different!"
—*Lorie, gifted education coordinator*

"The workshop provided a first step for many of my students—they began a conversation

with me that they hadn't felt comfortable initiating and are now speaking up for themselves and ensuring their voices are heard!"
—*Janell, gifted education coordinator*

"This workshop empowers students in so many ways. They were truly energized and couldn't wait to implement what they had learned and share their knowledge with peers who were unable to attend. Transformational and highly recommended!"
—*Sharon, gifted education coordinator*

Sustaining Self-Advocacy Following a Workshop

A one-day direct instruction model such as the GT Carpe Diem Workshop is an excellent way to start the self-advocacy process and engage students in pursuing accommodations and options back in their home schools. Most participants leave the workshop feeling empowered and energized. However, one day by itself will not guarantee that students self-advocate. It may be the initial step that opens the door, but it is what happens back in the school and home after the workshop that leads students from understanding to action. Advocates who have accompanied the workshop students need to make sure that their school and district provide access to options, ongoing action plan support and feedback, and continuous encouragement.

Schools that have strong gifted programming or employ any of the curriculum models recommended for gifted students—such as differentiated instruction, personalized learning, schoolwide enrichment, or the Autonomous Learner Model—already provide some opportunities students may want to pursue. But many district leaders may need to open their minds to providing additional options and alternatives. Also, students need to revisit the self-advocacy process over time throughout their school years. Their need to speak up fluctuates as they experience changes in teachers, classes, grade levels, subjects, interests, motivation, and movement toward independence.

As often as it seems appropriate, parents and educators should ask students, "What do you want or need now?" followed by, "Remember that when you want something in the future, here's what you can do." We simply need to remind them of their rights and options and then let them decide if and when they're ready to become more autonomous.

When No Workshop Is Available

The benefits of learning about self-advocacy while networking with like-ability peers is invaluable, however, there may be occasions when a group experience is not possible. In those instances, one-on-one instruction is the best option. Parents, teachers, coordinators, or counselors can work together with individual students to ensure they have the information and skills needed to self-advocate. The following are recommended steps for adults and students to take together:

- Read and discuss *The Gifted Teen Survival Guide* by Judy Galbraith and Jim Delisle.
- Read and discuss the local school district's mission statement and its implications for gifted learners.
- Research, read, and discuss the local school district's policies and plans regarding gifted education.
- Research, read, and discuss state or provincial laws regarding gifted students' education.
- Assess and reflect on the student's learner profile in all five areas (see Chapter 4).
- Obtain and peruse a copy of the school district's course of study bulletin and, for comparison, those of neighboring districts.
- Discuss which options are appropriate for the student.
- Choose a short- or long-term goal in one of these areas: finding appropriately challenging academic work, exploring an interest, spending time with gifted peers, or adjusting school or home life to better accommodate personal needs.
- List possible advocates.
- Create a plan to achieve the goal.
- Communicate the plan to other advocates.

- Put the plan into action.
- Meet regularly to assess progress and make revisions.
- Celebrate the student's success.
- Choose a new goal and begin again.

Conclusion

As I wrote earlier in this chapter, I began writing this book with the goal of teaching others to facilitate self-advocacy workshops for gifted students. And although it has grown into an explanation of gifted self-advocacy in general, my hope remains that the GT Carpe Diem Workshop will be replicated across the country and perhaps even around the world. The students have convinced me repeatedly of the workshop's power and value.

And while the workshop was created to provide intellectually and academically gifted students with the information they need, I'm now considering variations on the content that would address the needs of other groups of gifted kids. Think how exciting it would be to bring together similarly talented outliers with a comparable but more specialized curriculum. Perhaps "Writers Carpe Diem?" Or Artists? Or Leaders? Or Techies? Or Creative Masterminds? They all could increase their self-knowledge and feel empowered to define their own routes through the education system.

There is joy and strength in being with others who "get you," and it's not unusual for workshop students to find a kindred spirit. As fifth grader Cheyenne commented in her review: "I wish that I could stay here forever. I liked that I didn't have to lower my vocabulary because everyone was just as smart as me. This was a great experience because I felt like I have known these people *forever!*"

keyCONCEPTS
IN CHAPTER 8

- ❖ We must be intentional in teaching gifted students to self-advocate.
- ❖ Students need direct, specific instruction in self-advocacy.
- ❖ The GT Carpe Diem Workshop model is one way gifted students can experience instruction in self-advocacy and networking with peers.
- ❖ Encouragement of and support for student self-advocacy must continue over time.

9 CONCLUSIONS and COMMENCEMENTS

I still hear the voices of Tyrell, Ari, Mandy, Ryan, Akeesha, Jose, Jean, and so many other gifted learners who compel me to tell their stories. For over twenty years they have let me know in no uncertain terms that they want change, they need change, and they wish someone would bring about change. But unless we empower them to self-advocate, most are not likely to seek change on their own. My goal of encouraging self-advocacy is not to create a new initiative to be embraced for the moment and discarded with the next trend. Rather, persuading gifted students to take charge of their lives must be our timeless, tireless pursuit as educators. We must encourage students to speak up for themselves from the time their gifts are identified and we must be vigilant in prompting them again and again over time when we sense they need a change.

Finding an appropriate academic path for a student isn't a new concern. Each of us has likely struggled with it at one time or another, as did generations of educators and parents before us. But because the needs of the gifted outliers are seldom a top priority—especially in a time of educational budget cuts, staff reductions, and gifted program elimination—we must imbue our students with the skills to seek for themselves what they want and need. Hopefully, this book has provided you with some of the answers your students seek and you are already determining which strategies and examples detailed in the preceding chapters will help them map their own course.

Ryan's Route: The Four Steps in Review

You remember Ryan, the young man in the introduction whose shrug and quizzical look inspired my quest to help gifted students find their voices. I continue his story here as one last, shining example of what can happen when students have the self-advocacy skills they need. As Ryan saw it, high school was just going to be a continuation of the drudge he'd been experiencing since fifth grade. More and more, his school life seemed tied to academic assessments and preparation for college and career. He felt that the rest of his existence—his feelings, friendships, fears, passions, pains, and dreams—were of much less importance to those who controlled the education system. Ryan's road to achievement needed to be different and to progress he needed to take the four steps to becoming a self-advocate.

Self-Advocacy Step 1: Students Understand Their Rights and Responsibilities

To convince Ryan of his right to speak up, I showed him the district's mission statement, which read, in part: "We believe that learning should give students the tools to make their dreams come true." Ryan just needed to figure out which dream he wanted to turn into a reality and what tools would be required. Before he could proceed, however, he needed to take responsibility for overcoming the frustrations that deterred him. To help articulate exactly what was bothering him, he wrote never-to-be-delivered letters to his teachers, peers, and parents—things he had thought but hadn't said. Some examples:

> Dear Mrs. Bryce and the rest of the English class,
> I kind of like *Romeo and Juliet,* but going around the room and having everyone take turns reading it out loud is driving me crazy. It's slow, boring, and irritating. To be honest, some of you are really bad readers. Can't we do this some other way?

> Dear Mr. White,
> I don't get this sine/cosine/tangent stuff but I'm afraid to ask for help. I don't want you or the other kids to think I'm stupid, but that's how I feel right now.

> Dear Mom and Dad,
> I know you're hoping I'll go into our family car

repair business, but more than anything I want to be a musician.

> Dear Students in Communication Technology Class,
> I took this class because I love animation and computer graphics. It seems like most of you, on the other hand, just want to goof off. No, I don't want to be your project partner.

When Ryan looked at his gripes as possibilities for change and believed that things should and could be different, he was ready to take the second step.

Self-Advocacy Step 2: Students Develop Their Unique Learner Profiles

Referring to the six profiles of gifted learners (see Chapter 1), Ryan described himself this way:

> "In elementary school, I was a Successful Learner who fit into the system, but then in sixth grade my Creative Learner side started to rebel against it all. I didn't want to be one of the teacher pleasers. The neighborhood kids I went to school with weren't like me at all, but they were my friends and I wanted to fit in so I went Underground. They liked me better when I was in trouble for not doing my homework and for talking back to the teacher. At some point a school counselor thought I might have ADHD because I was so squirrely in class (I think I was just bored), so they did a lot of testing and for a while I was kind of unofficially considered 2E. By the time I was going into eighth grade though, I was At-Risk. I didn't see much point in what we were doing and skipped school with my friends whenever I could. That day, Mrs. Douglas talked to me in the hallway. I thought I was going to be in big trouble. Instead, things started getting better."

The more Ryan understood about himself as a student, the easier it was to find the alternatives that started him on his journey toward autonomy.

Self-Advocacy Step 3: Students Investigate Available Options and Opportunities

What options did Ryan discover? First, he learned to relish his role as a creative outlier. Instead of hiding his intellect by acting out as the class clown, he became known as an "original thinker," valued by his teachers and peers for his divergent questioning. He chose advanced academic work in the core areas, but eschewed the usual world languages and learned Cantonese through independent study. He couldn't bring himself to join band (too traditional), but took every elective music class that was offered. His satirical voice found a place as a columnist and an arts critic for the school newspaper. As a senior, he enrolled in calculus and philosophy classes at the local college.

Self-Advocacy Step 4: Students Connect with Advocates

Of course, Ryan didn't do all of this alone. We worked together to create and set his plan in motion and many other people—students and educators alike—played significant support roles. The GT Carpe Diem Workshop united him with other like-minded creative learners from across the district, teens who wound up becoming Ryan's close friends and encouragers. Many days after school he hung out in the band room with the other "alternative musicians" just to jam and talk, but a lot of informal mentoring from the hip band director took place there, too.

Ryan also connected with his philosophy professor at the community college. She encouraged him to enroll at their two-year campus after graduation, a supportive institution where he would find small classes, a devoted faculty, leadership opportunities in the arts, and the added advantage that earning at least a 3.0 GPA during his time there would assure him junior standing at the University of Wisconsin–Madison.

As the first person in his family to attend college, the two-school combination was a good choice for Ryan. He graduated with honors from UW–Madison in four years and is now a creative marketing expert for nonprofit performing arts groups in the Chicago area. Perhaps more importantly, Ryan is a musician, composing and recording with his alternative classical electronic rock band. Recently, they were listed as one of the ten best new indie bands in the Midwest. I think it's safe to say he's gained Autonomous Learner status!

How is your district supporting gifted students' paths to self-advocacy? You can use the district assessment form on pages 125–126 to gauge your progress.

In Closing

Imagine how incredible it would be if the roughly 2.5 million gifted children in school today (5 percent of all students) had wonderfully positive school experiences that lead them to become activists for gifted education. One would think that adults who were in gifted programs as children would be great supporters of gifted education, but that's not always the case. Fiercely negative reader comments on gifted-related media stories are far too common and reveal misguided notions. A typical line is, "I was in the gifted program when I was a kid and it was the worst thing that ever happened to me." It's possible that for those unhappy with their past experiences, self-advocacy would have been a great option, helping them seek and find the programming that satisfied their needs. It is my hope that when we help those millions of bright children understand their giftedness in all its variations and use the education system to their advantage, they will become the politicians, professors, administrators, psychologists, journalists, parents, and voters who will support gifted education in the future.

You no doubt picked up this book because you believe as I do that gifted learners need our help. At this very moment, tens of thousands of gifted students are waiting for a change. No matter what provisions exist or *don't* exist in their school districts or states, no matter what educational initiatives are receiving attention at the moment, the most productive way to ensure that all students receive the challenge and support they deserve is to empower their self-advocacy.

We can't wait for some time in the future when everyone gets on the self-advocacy bandwagon (if ever there is one!). Instead, we can make a difference right now if each of us—parents and educators alike—simply say to one gifted student, "How's it going?" And then add something like, "You have an ability that is unique and because of that you may need some different learning options. I'm here to help if there is anything you'd like to change at school." Think what would happen if we could share that simple message with a different gifted student every day. It's easy. We just need to ask questions, listen to the answers, share information, and then act accordingly.

I believe the value of self-advocacy is not necessarily in propelling students to achieve eminence. It is about empowering students to believe in their own abilities, discover their own aspirations, and seek the path that is right for them. I can't help but wonder if Ryan's taking charge of his own journey will someday lead to eminence. I'm not even sure what eminence means to an alternative classical electronic rock musician. But I do know that the power of self-advocacy allowed Ryan to value his status as an outlier, speak up for himself, and grab onto the opportunities he wanted.

Near the end of his senior year, Ryan's peers chose him as their class representative to deliver their graduation speech. He was funny, cerebral, wise, and sincere. He affirmed our work together by concluding this way:

> "Mrs. Douglas is always telling us to *carpe diem*. But the truth is, it's not enough to just seize the day. We have to get out there and seize *every* day. Seize life, seize all of it, and make it what we want it to be. We can own our futures if we choose to. So, fellow grads, don't just sit back and let life happen around you. *Carpe Diem! Carpe Vita! Carpe Omnia!*"

District Assessment of Support for Self-Advocacy of Gifted Students

		Yes	No	IDK	N/A
Student Rights	Do students receive direct instruction on their specific rights as gifted individuals?				
	Are there state laws or statutes regarding gifted students?				
	Are gifted students included in the district mission/vision statement, either specifically or implicitly?				
	Are there district policies regarding gifted students, i.e., acceleration, early entrance, dual enrollment, or early graduation?				
	Does the district have a mission statement regarding gifted students and/or gifted education?				
	Does the district have a gifted education programming plan?				
	If yes, does the district publish the plan and related materials on its website and communicate about it to all parents and students?				
	Does the district clearly communicate the concept of giftedness to identified students and their parents?				
	Does the district clearly communicate students' specific learner needs to them and their parents?				
	Does the district share resources with students and their parents regarding giftedness?				
	Does the district develop Differentiated Education Plans (DEPs) for gifted students?				
	If yes, do educators collaborate with students and their parents to develop the DEPs?				
Student Responsibilities	Do students receive direct instruction on their specific responsibilities as gifted individuals?				
	Are gifted students given opportunities to assess and reflect on their academic progress?				
	Are students encouraged to speak with educational staff when they experience frustration?				
	Are gifted students encouraged to acquire the attributes of good character expected of all?				
Learner Profiles	Do gifted students receive direct instruction on creating their unique learner profiles?				
	Are gifted students encouraged to assess and reflect on their learner profiles?				

continued ➤

		Yes	No	IDK	N/A
	Are gifted students allowed access to records that indicate their academic and intellectual ability?				
	Are gifted students provided materials to assess their learning preferences and interests?				
	Are gifted students provided materials that assess their personality traits associated with giftedness?				
	Are gifted students guided in assessing and recognizing areas for improvement?				
Options and Opportunities	Are gifted students guided in matching educational options and alternatives to their learner profiles?				
	Do gifted students receive information about available options that address their learner profiles?				
	Are gifted students informed of new alternatives that may address their learner profiles?				
	Are gifted students informed of opportunities outside the school/district that may better address their learner profiles?				
Advocates	Are gifted students introduced to the various adult advocates in the district who can support their needs?				
	Are gifted students given the opportunity to meet one-on-one with the gifted coordinator?				
	Are classroom teachers informed about self-advocacy and their role in supporting it?				
	Are school counselors informed about self-advocacy and their role in supporting it?				
	Are school principals/administrators informed about self-advocacy and their role in supporting it?				
Goal-Setting	Are gifted students encouraged to set short- and long-term personal educational goals?				
	Are gifted students guided in making sure their goals match their learner profiles?				
Action Plans	Are gifted students supported in writing action plans for change?				
	If yes, does the plan list specific steps and deadlines?				
	If yes, are adult advocates given roles in supporting the plan?				
	If yes, does the plan list dates for feedback, review, and revision?				
General Assessment	Do you feel your district is doing a good job encouraging and supporting the self-advocacy of gifted students?				

ENDNOTES

Introduction

1. Loring Brinckerhoff, "Developing Effective Self-Advocacy Skills in College-Bound Students with Learning Disabilities," *Intervention in School and Clinic* 29, no. 4 (1994), 230.

Chapter 1

2. Attributed to John Fischer, as quoted in *The San Francisco Examiner*, 1973.
3. George Betts and Maureen Neihart, "The Revised Profiles of the Gifted & Talented: A Research-Based Approach." Paper presented at the 11th Asia-Pacific Conference on Giftedness, Sydney, Australia (2010).
4. Jim Delisle and Judy Galbraith, *When Gifted Kids Don't Have All the Answers* (Minneapolis: Free Spirit Publishing, 2002), 191.
5. Jean Sunde Peterson, "A Developmental Perspective," in *Models of Counseling Gifted Children, Adolescents, and Young Adults*, eds. Sal Mendaglio and Jean Sunde Peterson (Waco, TX: Prufrock Press, 2007), 108.
6. Karen Rogers, *Re-Forming Gifted Education: Matching the Program to the Child* (Scottsdale, AZ: Great Potential Press, 2002), xvii.
7. F. Richard Olenchak, "Creating a Life: Orchestrating a Symphony of Self," in *Social-Emotional Curriculum with Gifted and Talented Students*, eds. Joyce VanTassel-Baska, Tracy Cross, and F. Richard Olenchak (Waco, TX: Prufrock Press, 2009), 51.

Chapter 2

8. Paul Pintrich and Elisabeth De Groot, "Motivational and Self-Regulated Learning Components of Classroom Academic Performance," *Journal of Educational Psychology* 82, no. 1 (1990), 33–40.
9. Jeanne Nakamura and Mihaly Csikszentmihalyi, "Flow Theory and Research," in *The Oxford Handbook of Positive Psychology*, eds. Shane Lopez and C.R. Snyder (New York: Oxford University Press, 2009), 195–206.
10. Mihaly Csikszentmihalyi, Sami Abuhamdeh, and Jeanne Nakamura, "Flow," in *Handbook of Competence and Motivation*, eds. Andrew Elliot and Carol Dweck (New York: The Guilford Press, 2005).
11. Del Siegle and D. Betsy McCoach, "Making a Difference: Motivating Gifted Students Who Are Not Achieving," *Teaching Exceptional Children* 38, no. 1 (2005), 22–27.
12. Judy Galbraith, *Survival Guide for Gifted Kids: For Ages 10 & Under* (Minneapolis: Free Spirit Publishing, 2013), 24.
13. Sandra Berger, *College Planning for Gifted Students* (Reston, VA: Council for Exceptional Children, 1998).
14. Christopher Ball, Leon Mann, and Cecily Stamm, "Decision-Making Abilities of Intellectually Gifted and Non-Gifted Children," *Australian Journal of Psychology* 46, no. 1 (1994), 13–20.
15. National Association of College Admission Counseling (NACAC), "2015 State of College Admission" (Arlington, VA: NACAC, 2015).

Chapter 3

16. Mark Kunkel et al., "Experience of Giftedness: Eight Great Gripes Six Years Later," *Roeper Review* 15, no. 1 (1992), 10–14.
17. Section 4644 of the ESEA, as amended by the ESSA (20 U.S.C. 7294).
18. "Definitions of Giftedness," National Association for Gifted Children, nagc.org/resources-publications/resources/definitions-giftedness.
19. "The Columbus Group," Gifted Development Center, gifteddevelopment .com/isad/columbus-group.
20. Annemarie Roeper, *The "I" of the Beholder* (Scottsdale, AZ: Great Potential Press, 2007), vi.

21. Michael Piechowski, "Giftedness for All Seasons: Inner Peace in a Time of War," in *Talent Development: Proceedings from the 1991 Henry B. and Jocelyn Wallace National Research Symposium on Talent Development*, eds. Nicholas Colangelo, Susan Assouline, and DeAnn Ambroson (Unionville, NY: Trillium Press, 1992).
22. Stephanie Tolan "What's in a Name?" *The Deep End* (blog), April 30, 2012, welcometothedeepend.com/2012/04/30/whats-in-a-name.
23. Ann Robinson and Pamela Clinkenbeard, "History of Giftedness: Perspectives from the Past Presage Modern Scholarship," in *Handbook of Giftedness in Children*, ed. Steven Pfeiffer (New York: Springer Science+Business Media, 2008), 13–32.
24. Judy Galbraith, "The Eight Great Gripes of Gifted Kids: Responding to Special Needs," *Roeper Review* 8, no. 1 (1985), 15–18.
25. National Association for Gifted Children, *2014–2015 State of the States in Gifted Education* (Washington, DC: NAGC, 2015), nagc.org /resources-publications/gifted-state/2014-2015-state-states-gifted-education.
26. "CPS: Success Starts Here," Chicago Public Schools, cps.edu/Pages /AboutCPS.aspx.
27. Cleveland Metropolitan School District, clevelandmetroschools.org /domain/169.
28. "Mission and Vision," Minneapolis Public Schools, mpls.k12.mn.us /mission_and_vision_2.
29. "Overview," San Francisco Public Schools, sfusd.edu/en/about-sfusd /overview.html.
30. Lauren Camera, "Students' Views on Teachers, Policy Hold Sway in Georgia District," in "Leaders to Learn from 2015," special report, *Education Week* (2015), 4–5.
31. "Gifted Children's Bill of Rights," National Association for Gifted Children, nagc.org/resources-publications/resources-parents/gifted-childrens-bill-rights.
32. James Delisle, "Tips for Parents: Risk-Taking and Risk-Making," Davidson Institute for Talent Development, 2011, www.davidsongifted .org/Search-Database/entry/A10121.
33. David Yeager and Carol Dweck, "Mindsets That Promote Resilience: When Students Believe That Personal Characteristics Can Be Developed," *Educational Psychologist* 47, no. 4 (2012), 302–314.
34. James Borland, "A Landmark Monograph in Gifted Education, and Why I Disagree with Its Major Conclusion," *The Creativity Post* (blog), June 21, 2012, creativitypost.com/education/a_landmark_monograph_in _gifted_education_and_why_i_disagree_with_its_major.
35. Jane Piirto, *Talented Children and Adults* (Upper Saddle River, NJ: Merrill, 1999), 37.
36. Norman Augustine, "Educating the Gifted," *Psychological Science in the Public Interest* 12, no. 1 (2011), 1–2.
37. Chris Hedges, *Empire of Illusion* (New York: Nation Books, 2009), 95.
38. Carol Ann Tomlinson, "Sharing Responsibility for Differentiating Instruction," *Roeper Review* 26, no. 4 (2004), 188–189.
39. Paul Dolan, *Happiness by Design* (New York: Hudson Street Press, 2014).

Chapter 4

40. Karen Rogers, *Re-Forming Gifted Education* (Scottsdale, AZ: Great Potential Press, 2002), 48.
41. Joseph Renzulli et al., Scales for Rating the Behavioral Characteristics of Superior Students (Waco, TX: Prufrock Press, 2013).

42. Del Siegle and D. Betsy McCoach, "Making a Difference: Motivating Gifted Students Who Are Not Achieving," *Teaching Exceptional Children* 38, no. 1 (2005), 22–27.

43. Maureen Neihart, *Peak Performance for Smart Kids* (Waco, TX: Prufrock Press, 2008), 117–138.

44. Thomas Buescher and Sharon Higham, "ED321494 Helping Adolescents Adjust to Giftedness," *ERIC Digest* #E489 (Reston, VA: Council for Exceptional Children, 1990).

45. Michael Piechowski, *"Mellow Out," They Say. If I Only Could* (Madison, WI: Yunasa Books, 2006), 23.

46. Linda Silverman, "What We Have Learned About Gifted Children," Gifted Development Center, 2009.

47. Rogers, 2002.

Chapter 5

48. Carol Ann Tomlinson, "Quality Curriculum and Instruction for Highly Able Students," *Theory into Practice* 44, no. 2 (2005), 160–166.

49. "Wisconsin Standards for Mathematics," Wisconsin Department of Public Instruction, September 2011, dpi.wi.gov/sites/default/files/imce /standards/pdf/common-core-math-standards.pdf.

50. "What Is RTI?" RTI Action Network, rtinetwork.org/learn/what/whatisrti.

51. Maureen Neihart, "Revised Profiles of the Gifted: A Research-Based Approach." Presentation, Conference on Appropriate Education and High Talent, Utrecht, Netherlands (November 2014).

Chapter 6

52. Dorothy Kennedy, "Plain Talk About Creating a Gifted-Friendly Classroom," *Roeper Review* 17, no. 4 (1995), 232–234.

53. From email correspondence between Dr. Gay Eastman and Deb Douglas (March 2014).

Chapter 7

54. Karen Rogers, *Re-Forming Gifted Education* (Scottsdale, AZ: Great Potential Press, 2002), 9.

Chapter 8

55. "Pre-K to Grade 12 Gifted Programming Standards," National Association for Gifted Children, nagc.org/resources-publications /resources/national-standards-gifted-and-talented-education/pre-k-grade-12. Reprinted with permission by the National Association for Gifted Children.

REFERENCES

Augustine, Norman. "Educating the Gifted." *Psychological Science in the Public Interest* 12, no. 1 (2011), 1–2.

Ball, Christopher, Leon Mann, and Cecily Stamm. "Decision-Making Abilities of Intellectually Gifted and Non-Gifted Children." *Australian Journal of Psychology* 46, no. 1 (1994), 13–20.

Berger, Sandra. *College Planning for Gifted Students* (Reston, VA: Council for Exceptional Children, 1998).

Betts, George. "Fostering Autonomous Learners Through Levels of Differentiation." *Roeper Review* 26, no. 4 (2004), 190–191.

———. "Learner-Developed Programming; Listening to the Voice of the Learner." Session presented at the National Association for Gifted Children Conference, Baltimore, MD (November 2014).

Betts, George, and Jolene Kercher. *Autonomous Learner Model: Optimizing Ability* (Greeley, CO: ALPS Publishing, 1999).

Betts, George, and Maureen Neihart. "Profiles of the Gifted and Talented." *Gifted Child Quarterly* 32, no. 2 (1988), 248–253.

Bloom, Benjamin, Max Engelhart, Edward Furst, Walker Hill, and David Krathwohl. *Taxonomy of Educational Objectives: Handbook I, The Cognitive Domain.* New York: Longman, 1956.

Borland, James. "A Landmark Monograph in Gifted Education, and Why I Disagree with Its Major Conclusion." The Creativity Post (June 21, 2012).

Brinckerhoff, Loring. "Developing Effective Self-Advocacy Skills in College-Bound Students with Learning Disabilities." *Intervention in School and Clinic* 29, no. 4 (1994), 229–238.

Buescher, Thomas, and Sharon Higham. "ED321494 Helping Adolescents Adjust to Giftedness." *ERIC Digest* #E489 (Reston, VA: Council for Exceptional Children, 1990).

Camera, Lauren. "Students' Views on Teachers, Policy Hold Sway in Georgia District." In "Leaders to Learn from 2015." Special report, *Education Week* (2015), 4–5.

Casper, Kathleen. "The Ultimate Plan to Help Gifted Education (and Improve Education for All Kids in the Process." *SENGVine* (November 2014).

Clinkenbeard, Pamela. "Motivation and Gifted Students: Implications of Theory and Research." *Psychology in the Schools* 49, no. 7 (2012), 622–630.

"The Columbus Group." Gifted Development Center, gifteddevelopment.com/isad/columbus-group.

Croft, Laurie. "Six Maddening Myths of Gifted Education." Belin-Blank International Center for Gifted Education and Talent Development, University of Iowa (2002).

Csikszentmihalyi, Mihaly, Sami Abuhamdeh, and Jeanne Nakamura. "Flow." In *Handbook of Competence and Motivation*, edited by Andrew Elliot and Carol Dweck (New York: The Guilford Press, 2005).

Delisle, James. "The 'G' Word (Shhh)." *Understanding Our Gifted* 13, no. 3 (2001), 8.

———. "Tips for Parents: Risk-Taking and Risk-Making." Davidson Institute for Talent Development (2011). www.davidsongifted.org /Search-Database/entry/A10121.

Delisle, Jim, and Judy Galbraith. *When Gifted Kids Don't Have All the Answers.* Minneapolis: Free Spirit Publishing, 2002.

Dixon, Felicia, Shelagh Gallagher, and Paula Olszewski-Kubilius. "Part III: A Visionary Statement for the Education of Gifted Students in Secondary Schools." In *Programs and Services for Gifted Secondary Students: A Guide to Recommended Practices*, edited by Felicia Dixon (Waco, TX: Prufrock Press, 2009).

Dolan, Paul. *Happiness by Design: Finding Pleasure and Purpose in Everyday Life* (New York: Hudson Street Press, 2014).

Dweck, Carol. "Boosting Achievement with Messages That Motivate." *Education Canada* 47, no. 2 (2007), 6–10.

Falk, R. Frank, Sharon Lind, Nancy Miller, Michael Piechowski, and Linda Silverman. The Overexcitability Questionnaire-Two (OEQII) (Westminster, CO: Gifted Development Center, 1999).

Feldhusen, John, Steven Hoover, and Michael Sayler. *Identifying and Educating Gifted Students at the Secondary Level* (Unionville, NY: Royal Fireworks Press, 1990).

Finn, Kit. "Self-Advocacy." Session presented at the Beyond IQ: Paradoxes and Oxymorons Conference, Wakefield, MA, May 2002.

Ford, Donna. "Nurturing Resilience in Gifted Black Youth." *Roeper Review* 17, no. 2 (1994), 80–85.

Gagné, Françoys. "Building Gifts into Talents: Brief Overview of the DMGT 2.0." *Gifted* 152 (2008), 5–9.

Galbraith, Judy. "The Eight Great Gripes of Gifted Kids: Responding to Special Needs." *Roeper Review* 8, no. 1 (1985), 15–18.

———. *The Survival Guide for Gifted Kids: For Ages 10 & Under.* Minneapolis: Free Spirit Publishing, 2013.

Galbraith, Judy, and Jim Delisle. *The Gifted Teen Survival Guide.* Minneapolis: Free Spirit Publishing, 1996.

———. *The Gifted Teen Survival Guide: Smart, Sharp, and Ready for (Almost) Anything.* Minneapolis: Free Spirit Publishing, 2011.

———. *When Gifted Kids Don't Have All the Answers: How to Meet Their Social and Emotional Needs.* Minneapolis, MN: Free Spirit Publishing, 2015.

Gentry, Marcia, and Penny Mork Springer. "Secondary Student Perceptions of Their Class Activities Regarding Meaningfulness, Challenge, Choice, and Appeal: An Initial Validation Study." *Journal of Secondary Gifted Education* 13, no. 4 (2002), 192–204.

Greenspon, Thomas. *What to Do When Good Enough Isn't Good Enough: The Real Deal on Perfectionism.* Minneapolis: Free Spirit Publishing, 2007.

Hedges, Chris. *Empire of Illusion: The End of Literacy and the Triumph of Spectacle.* New York: Nation Books, 2009.

Kaplan, Leslie. "ED321493 Helping Gifted Students with Stress Management." *ERIC Digest #E488.* Reston, VA: Council for Exceptional Children, 1990. ericdigests.org/1994/stress.htm.

Kennedy, Dorothy. "Plain Talk About Creating a Gifted-Friendly Classroom." *Roeper Review* 17, no. 4 (1995), 232–234.

Kunkel, Mark, Beatrice Chapa, Greg Patterson, and Derald Walling. "Experience of Giftedness: Eight Great Gripes Six Years Later." *Roeper Review* 15, no. 1 (1992), 10–14.

Lewis, Joan. *The Challenges of Educating the Gifted in Rural Areas.* Waco, TX: Prufrock Press, 2009.

Marks, Kathy. "From Teacher to Advocate." *Teaching for High Potential* (Spring 2015).

Milsom, Amy. "Living Up to Expectations." *ASCA School Counselor* (July 2004).

Nakamura, Jeanne, and Mihaly Csikszentmihalyi. "Flow Theory and Research." In *The Oxford Handbook of Positive Psychology,* edited by Shane Lopez and C. R. Snyder. New York: Oxford University Press, 2009.

National Association for Gifted Children. PreK–Grade 12 Gifted Programming Standards. Washington, DC: NAGC, 2010.

———. "2014–2015 State of the States in Gifted Education: Policy and Practice Data." Washington, DC: NAGC, 2015.

National Association of College Admission Counseling (NACAC). "2015 State of College Admission." Arlington, VA: NACAC, 2015.

Neihart, Maureen. *Peak Performance for Smart Kids: Strategies and Tips for Ensuring School Success.* Waco, TX: Prufrock Press, 2008.

———. "Revised Profiles of the Gifted: A Research Based Approach." Presented at the Conference on Appropriate Education and High Talent, Utrecht, Netherlands, November 2014. youtu.be/1WH8681781E.

———. "Risk and Resilience in Gifted Children: A Conceptual Framework." In *The Social and Emotional Development of Gifted Children: What Do We Know?* edited by Maureen Neihart, Sally Reis, Nancy Robinson, and Sidney Moon. Waco, TX: Prufrock Press, 2002

Neihart, Maureen, and George Betts. "The Revised Profiles of the Gifted and Talented: A Research-Based Approach." Paper presented at the 11th Asia-Pacific Conference on Giftedness, Sydney, Australia, 2010.

Peterson, Jean Sunde. "The Burdens of Capability." *Reclaiming Children and Youth* 6, no. 4 (1998), 194–198.

———. "A Developmental Perspective." In *Models of Counseling Gifted Children, Adolescents, and Young Adults,* edited by Sal Mendaglio and Jean Sunde Peterson. Waco, TX: Prufrock Press, 2007.

Peterson, Jean Sunde, George Betts, and Terry Bradley, "Discussion Groups as a Component of Affective Curriculum for Gifted Students." In *Social-Emotional Curriculum with Gifted Students,* edited by Joyce VanTassel-Baska, Tracy Cross, and F. Richard Olenchak. Waco, Texas: Prufrock Press, 2009.

Piechowski, Michael. "Giftedness for All Seasons: Inner Peace in a Time of War." In *Talent Development: Proceedings from the 1991 Henry B. and Jocelyn Wallace National Research Symposium on Talent Development,* edited by Nicholas Colangelo, Susan Assouline, and DeAnn Ambroson. Unionville, NY: Trillium Press, 1992.

———. *"Mellow Out," They Say. If I Only Could: Intensities and Sensitivities of the Young and Bright.* Madison, WI: Yunasa Books, 2006.

———. *"Mellow Out," They Say. If I Only Could: Intensities and Sensitivities of the Young and Bright.* Unionville, NY: Royal Fireworks Press, 2014.

Piirto, Jane. *Talented Children and Adults: Their Development and Education.* Upper Saddle River, NJ: Merrill, 1999.

Pintrich, Paul, and Elisabeth De Groot. "Motivational and Self-Regulated Learning Components of Classroom Academic Performance." *Journal of Educational Psychology* 82, no. 1 (1990), 33–40.

Renzulli, Joseph. "What Makes Giftedness? Reexamining a Definition." *Phi Delta Kappan* 60, no. 3 (1978), 180–181.

Renzulli, Joseph, Linda Smith, Alan White, Carolyn Callahan, Robert Hartman, Karen Westberg, M. Katherine Gavin, Sally Reis, Del Siegle, and Rachael Sytsma. Scales for Rating the Behavioral Characteristics of Superior Students. Waco, TX: Prufrock Press, 2013.

Rivero, Lisa. *A Parent's Guide to Gifted Teens: Living with Intense and Creative Adolescents.* Scottsdale, AZ: Great Potential Press, 2010.

Robinson, Ann, and Pamela Clinkenbeard. "History of Giftedness: Perspectives from the Past Presage Modern Scholarship." In *Handbook of Giftedness in Children: Psycho-Educational Theory, Research, and Best Practices,* edited by Steven Pfeiffer. New York: Springer Science+Business Media, 2008.

Robinson, Nancy. "Counseling Agendas for Gifted Young People: A Commentary." *Journal for the Education of the Gifted* 20, no. 2 (1996), 128–137.

Rocamora, Mary. "Enhancing Personal Expression." Rocamora School website. rocamora.org/publications/articles/enhancing-personal-expression.

Roeper, Annemarie. *The "I" of the Beholder: A Guided Journey to the Essence of a Child.* Scottsdale, AZ: Great Potential Press, 2007.

Rogers, Karen. *Re-Forming Gifted Education: Matching the Program to the Child.* Scottsdale, AZ: Great Potential Press, 2002.

RTI Action Network. "What Is RTI?" rtinetwork.org/learn/what/whatisrti.

Schultz, Robert. "Understanding Giftedness and Underachievement: At the Edge of Possibility." *Gifted Child Quarterly* 46, no. 3 (2002), 193–208.

Siegle, Del, and D. Betsy McCoach. "Making a Difference: Motivating Gifted Students Who Are Not Achieving." *Teaching Exceptional Children* 38, no. 1 (2005), 22–27.

Silverman, Linda. "The Two-Edged Sword of Compensation: How the Gifted Cope with Learning Disabilities." *Gifted Education International* 25, no. 2 (2009), 115–130.

———. "What We Have Learned About Gifted Children." Gifted Development Center, 2009. gifteddevelopment.com/articles/what-we-have-learned-about-gifted-children.

Tolan, Stephanie. "Is It a Cheetah?" Stephanietolan.com. 1996. stephanietolan.com/is_it_a_cheetah.htm.

———. "What's in a Name?" *The Deep End* (blog). April 30, 2012. welcometothedeepend.com/2012/04/30/whats-in-a-name.

Tomlinson, Carol Ann. *How to Differentiate Instruction in Mixed-Ability Classrooms.* Alexandria, VA: ASCD, 2001.

———. "Instructional Strategies that Invite Differentiation." Session presented at the MAIS Conference, Rome Italy, November 2013. caroltomlinson.com/handouts/Strategies%20for%20Differentiation.pdf.

———. "Quality Curriculum and Instruction for Highly Able Students." *Theory into Practice* 44, no. 2 (2005), 160–166.

———. "Sharing Responsibility for Differentiating Instruction." *Roeper Review* 26, no. 4 (2004), 188–189.

VanTassel-Baska, Joyce, Tracy Cross, and F. Richard Olenchek, eds. *Social-Emotional Curriculum with Gifted and Talented Students.* Waco, TX: Prufrock Press, 2009.

Webb, James, Janet Gore, Edward Amend, and Arlene DeVries. *A Parent's Guide to Gifted Children.* Scottsdale, AZ: Great Potential Press, 2007.

Winebrenner, Susan, with Dina Brulles. *Teaching Gifted Kids in Today's Classroom: Strategies and Techniques Every Teacher Can Use.* Minneapolis: Free Spirit Publishing, 2012.

Yeager, David, and Carol Dweck. "Mindsets That Promote Resilience: When Students Believe That Personal Characteristics Can Be Developed." *Educational Psychologist* 47, no. 4 (2012), 302–314.

APPENDIX A

Resources

For Advocates of Gifted Students

Dumbing Down America: The War on Our Nation's Brightest Young Minds (And What We Can Do to Fight Back) by James Delisle (Prufrock Press, 2014). Delisle shares many specific examples of how gifted students are shortchanged by our educational system and a society that buys into all the myths about giftedness. He concludes with multiple suggestions for ways we can improve our public schools to better meet gifted students' needs.

A Nation Empowered: Evidence Trumps the Excuses Holding Back America's Brightest Students, volume 2 edited by Susan Assouline, Nicholas Colangelo, Joyce VanTassel-Baska, and Ann Lupkowski-Shoplik (Belin-Blank, 2015). This compendium includes much of the current research on the successful subject and grade acceleration of gifted students that will help educators make decisions for the brightest learners in their own districts.

The Davidson Institute for Talent Development: www.davidsongifted.org.

Hoagies' Gifted Education Page: hoagiesgifted.org.

The National Association for Gifted Children: nagc.org.

SENG (Supporting Emotional Needs of the Gifted): sengifted.org/resources.

These three publishers offer a wide variety of books on giftedness:
- Free Spirit Publishing: freespirit.com/gifted-and-special-education
- Great Potential Press: greatpotentialpress.com
- Prufrock Press: prufrock.com

For Coordinator Advocates

Beyond Gifted Education: Designing and Implementing Advanced Academic Programs by Scott J. Peters, Michael Matthews, Matthew T. McBee, and D. Betsy McCoach (Prufrock Press, 2014). Specifically for gifted program coordinators or school administrators, this book guides readers in identifying student needs, exploring programming possibilities, and recognizing students who would benefit from advanced academic opportunities.

The Challenges of Educating the Gifted in Rural Areas by Joan D. Lewis (Prufrock Press, 2009). Lewis discusses the benefits and challenges that exist for gifted students in rural areas and recommends multiple ways to provide quality programming even when numbers are small and funding is limited.

Education of the Gifted and Talented by Gary A. Davis, Sylvia B. Rimm, and Del B. Siegle (Pearson, 2010). This textbook on gifted education is valuable for anyone who wants to see the big picture as well as all the details. It includes the characteristics of gifted students, identification, considerations for program planning, program models, differentiated curriculum models, and specifics on underrepresented groups.

Growing Up Gifted: Developing the Potential of Children at School and at Home by Barbara Clark (Pearson, 2012). A classic text that explores who gifted learners are, how they become gifted, and methods used to support their learning and development.

Programs and Services for Gifted Secondary Students: A Guide to Recommended Practices edited by Felicia A. Dixon (Prufrock Press, 2009). This is one of the few references devoted to the concerns of gifted students in middle and high school. It's a valuable reference for service and program options for this age group.

Council for Exceptional Children, The Association for the Gifted (TAG): cectag.com.

NAGC Gifted by State: nagc.org/resources-publications/gifted-state.

NAGC Gifted Education Practices: nagc.org/resources-publications/gifted-education-practices.

NAGC PreK to Grade 12 Gifted Programming Standards: nagc.org/resources-publications/resources/national-standards-gifed-and-talented-education/pre-k-grade-12.

For Parent Advocates

Bright, Talented & Black: A Guide for Families of African American Gifted Learners by Joy Lawson Davis (Great Potential Press, 2010). Davis highlights the vital role that adult advocates play in the lives of gifted black children. She includes valuable tools that help us better understand, nurture, and challenge these students.

A Parent's Guide to Gifted Teens: Living with Intense and Creative Adolescents by Lisa Rivero (Great Potential Press, 2010). One of the few resources specifically addressing the concerns of gifted teens, this guide helps parents understand their adolescent's intensity and excitability. Rivero also provides tips for nurturing self-discipline and being supportive without being controlling.

Parenting Gifted Children: The Authoritative Guide from the National Association for Gifted Children edited by Jennifer Jolly, Donald Treffinger, Tracy Ford Inman, and Joan Franklin Smutny (Prufrock Press, 2011). This edited volume includes some of the best articles published in NAGC's journal, *Parenting for High Potential*, over the last several years.

Parenting Gifted Kids: Tips for Raising Happy and Successful Children by James Delisle (Prufrock Press, 2006). Similar to his other helpful lists for students, here Delisle gives ten tips to parents of gifted children that encourage introspection and change, rather than quick-fix solutions.

A Parent's Guide to Gifted Children by James Webb, Janet Gore, Edward Amend, and Arlene DeVries (Great Potential Press, 2007). This book is the foundation of discussions during SENG Model Parent Groups. It presents a comprehensive and accessible overview of giftedness, including gifted characteristics, peer and sibling issues, motivation and underachievement, educational planning, and finding professional help.

Peak Performance for Smart Kids: Strategies and Tips for Ensuring School Success by Maureen Neihart (Prufrock Press, 2008). Neihart has created activities for gifted children and their parents that will help kids learn to manage stress and anxiety, set and achieve goals, improve performance, manage moods, and resolve many of their frustrations.

Re-Forming Gifted Education: Matching the Program to the Child by Karen Rogers (Great Potential Press, 2002). I've referenced this book frequently throughout these chapters. It is an important, complete guide to understanding how the education system could address the needs of gifted children. It provides a template for positive collaboration between parents and educators that leads to necessary changes.

For Teacher Advocates

Advancing Differentiation: Thinking and Learning for the 21st Century by Richard M. Cash (Free Spirit Publishing, 2017). This practical handbook guides teachers in developing a rigorous, concept-based curriculum across content areas and differentiated for all learners.

Autonomous Learner Model Resource Book by George T. Betts, Robin J. Carey, and Blanche M. Kapushion (Prufrock Press, 2017). More than 40 activities—all geared to the emotional, social, cognitive, and physical development of students—support the development of autonomous learners.

Differentiation for Gifted Learners: Going Beyond the Basics by Diane Heacox and Richard M. Cash (Free Spirit Publishing, 2014). For teachers who already practice the basics of differentiation, this book connects gifted students' unique learning differences to the teaching methods that will best meet their educational needs.

Teaching Gifted Kids in Today's Classroom: Strategies and Techniques Every Teacher Can Use by Susan Winebrenner, with Dina Brulles (Free Spirit Publishing, 2012). This book has been a key resource over the years for all teachers struggling to meet the learning needs of gifted students in their mixed-ability classrooms. It includes practical, time-saving strategies and templates, as well as clear instructions on how to use them.

When Gifted Kids Don't Have All the Answers: How to Support Their Social and Emotional Needs by Judy Galbraith and Jim Delisle (Free Spirit Publishing, 2015). Although this book has important information for all advocates, it's the perfect introduction to all things gifted for classroom teachers. It explores definitions, identification, emotional dimensions, and the differences between an underachiever and a selective consumer, and offers suggestions for creating and maintaining a gifted-friendly classroom.

Hoagies' Gifted Education Page: hoagiesgifted.org/educators.htm. Includes a wide range of curriculum enrichment resources.

NAGC Resources for Educators: nagc.org/resources-publications /resources-educators. Plus, the NAGC publication, *Teaching for High Potential*, is filled with practical guidance and classroom-based materials.

For School Counselor Advocates

The Essential Guide to Talking with Gifted Teens: Ready-to-Use Discussions About Identity, Stress, Relationships, and More by Jean Sunde Peterson (Free Spirit Publishing, 2008). Peterson created these guided discussions to reach out to gifted children. The focused questions make it easy for a trained counselor to lead students in sharing and reflecting on their social and emotional concerns.

Living with Intensity: Understanding the Sensitivity, Excitability, and Emotional Development of Gifted Children, Adolescents, and Adults edited by Susan Daniels and Michael Piechowski (Great Potential Press, 2009). This book describes overexcitabilities and strategies for dealing with children and adults who are experiencing them. The authors share practical methods for nurturing perfectionism, intensities, and sensitivities.

Models of Counseling Gifted Children, Adolescents, and Young Adults edited by Sal Mendaglio and Jean Sunde Peterson (Prufrock Press, 2007). The editors and other experts in the field share their experiences, strategies, and wisdom. The various models described provide frameworks for those interested in counseling gifted and talented clients.

Social-Emotional Curriculum with Gifted and Talented Students edited by Joyce VanTassel-Baska, Joyce, Tracy Cross, and F. Richard Olenchak (Prufrock Press, 2009). Many leaders in affective education for gifted children contributed to this book, incorporating strategies, research, counseling and curricular ideas, and special considerations for children from underrepresented groups.

The Social and Emotional Development of Gifted Children: What Do We Know? edited by Maureen Neihart, Steven Pfeiffer, and Tracy Cross (Prufrock Press, 2015). This is a wonderfully comprehensive summary of the research on the social and emotional development of gifted children. Every page offers valuable insights into their needs, making it an engaging read for all advocates.

Understanding the Social and Emotional Lives of Gifted Students by Thomas Hébert (Prufrock Press, 2011). Hébert's textbook discusses the social and emotional characteristics and behaviors of gifted students, as well as the friendships and family relationships that support them. Although written for graduate coursework, his style is personal, with many examples from his work with young people over the years.

For Gifted Students

The Gifted Teen Survival Guide: Smart, Sharp, and Ready for (Almost) Anything by Judy Galbraith and James Delisle (Minneapolis: Free Spirit Publishing, 2011). This is *the* best book for gifted teens learning to self-advocate. It provides much of the information they need to feel comfortable in their own skins and to take charge of their own lives.

If I'm So Smart, Why Aren't the Answers Easy? by Robert Shultz and James Delisle (Waco, TX: Prufrock Press, 2012). In the second book by this author team, more gifted teens share their perceptions, including their struggles and successes in the educational system.

More Than a Test Score: Teens Talk About Being Gifted, Talented, or Otherwise Extra-Ordinary by Robert Shultz and James Delisle (Minneapolis: Free Spirit Publishing, 2007). There are lots of insightful quotes from gifted kids about their lives, school, and relationships. Includes biographies and activities.

Smart Teens' Guide to Living with Intensity: How to Get More Out of Life and Learning by Lisa Rivero (Scottsdale, AZ: Great Potential Press, 2010). This guide for teens looks at the intensities associated with giftedness and the joys and frustrations many experience. Topics include becoming a self-directed learner.

The Survival Guide for Gifted Kids (For Ages 10 & Under) by Judy Galbraith (Minneapolis: Free Spirit Publishing, 2013). Excellent information for younger gifted students about what it means to be gifted. Includes "8 Great Ways to Make Regular School More Cool."

The Davidson Institute for Talent Development: davidsongifted.org. The Davidson Young Scholar program provides many services to gifted students and their families, including consulting services, an online community, in-person connections, and summer programs. There is also information on the Davidson Academy, a free public day school in Reno, Nevada. for profoundly gifted middle and high school students.

Hoagies' Gifted Education Pages. Although this site primarily provides resources for parents and educators, there are some pages that are of special interest to gifted kids:

Kids' Fun! hoagiesgifted.org/hoagies_kids.htm.

Reading Lists for Your Gifted Child: hoagiesgifted.org /reading_lists.htm.

Talent Search Programs: hoagiesgifted.org/talent_search.htm. Talent searches identify, assess, and recognize students with exceptional abilities through out-of-level testing. Most also provide school year and/or summer enrichment and acceleration programs geared toward gifted students.

Jack Kent Cooke Foundation: jkcf.org. This foundation is dedicated to advancing the education of highly gifted students who have financial need. Its support extends from elementary school to graduate school through information-sharing, scholarships, grants, and direct service.

APPENDIX B
GT CARPE DIEM WORKSHOP FACILITATOR GUIDE

Introduction

The GT Carpe Diem Workshop is designed to jump-start gifted students' self-advocacy and provide them with information that will help them successfully take charge of their own educations and lives.

The workshop is a one-day event that brings together gifted students and their adult advocates to network, learn about themselves, and create personal plans for change.

The workshop is purposefully designed to introduce students to the ideas and understandings they need to self-advocate and to connect with like-ability peers and supportive adults. Students learn about their rights and responsibilities, coping strategies, and a variety of educational options that match their profiles, as well as tools and procedures for developing skills in self-advocating.

Each workshop activity includes:

◆ Learner outcomes
◆ Related NAGC Standards
◆ Links to background information
◆ Materials list
◆ Facilitator instructions
◆ Conclusion and transition to the next activity

Workshop Essential Understandings

This workshop is designed to guide all participants in understanding that:

◆ Gifted students vary in their talents and interests
◆ Gifted students need educational opportunities that match their unique needs
◆ Gifted students can and should play a major role in designing their paths to graduation and beyond

Workshop Learner Outcomes

Students will increase their willingness and comfort level in asking for what they need to take charge of their own educations.

◆ Students will better understand their unique traits as gifted individuals.
  • They will reflect on the varying definitions of giftedness.
  • They will identify their own cognitive abilities, learning strengths, learning preferences, personality traits, and interests.
  • They will recognize similarities and differences with gifted peers.
◆ They will better understand their rights to an appropriately challenging education.
◆ They will better understand their responsibilities as gifted individuals and as students in general.
◆ They will consider what they would like to change in school, at home, or in life in general.
  • They will reflect on any frustrations they have.
  • They will recognize common concerns among gifted individuals.
  • They will better understand ways to work within and outside of the education system.
  • They will identify options and alternatives that match their learner profiles.
◆ They will create an action plan for change.
  • They will select a specific goal.
  • They will identify the steps necessary to reach that goal.
  • They will identify the people needed to support that goal.
  • They will create a reasonable timeline and series of steps to achieve their goal.
◆ They will practice communicating effectively with the advocates who can support their plan.
  • They will learn how to ask for help.
  • They will be able to listen and respond appropriately.

Adult advocates will better understand their roles in supporting gifted students.

◆ Advocates will reflect on the rights and responsibilities of gifted students and their adult advocates.

◆ They will discover more about the characteristics of gifted learners.

◆ They will better understand each of their students' individual characteristics and needs.

◆ They will assess and reflect on their own learner profiles, gaining insights into their differences and similarities with students.

◆ They will network with other advocates and recognize the differences and similarities between district approaches to gifted education.

◆ They will assist students in writing action plans and support the plans back in the home school.

To achieve all these goals in just one day, each workshop activity is carefully crafted to contribute to student understanding and increase the likelihood that students will self-advocate after their time together.

GT Carpe Diem Workshop Basic Requirements

◆ 5–7 hours of workshop time (including breaks and lunch)

◆ Workshop facilitator

◆ 15–50 gifted students

◆ At least one adult advocate from each school represented

◆ Large room

◆ Moveable tables and chairs

◆ Student handouts

◆ Facilitator PDF presentation

◆ Projector and screen

◆ Wi-Fi (optional)

Typical Six-Hour GT Carpe Diem Workshop Agenda*	
Activity 1.1 Welcome, Introductions, and Arrangements for the Day	15 min.
Activity 1.2 Express Yourself Talent Search	15
Activity 1.3 Gripes of Wrath	20
Activity 2.1 Defining the "G" Word	20
Activity 2.2 Your Rights	20
Activity 2.3 Your Responsibilities	20
Activity 2.4 Letting Go	5
Break	15
Activity 3.1 Where Do I Soar?	10
Activity 3.2 What Do I Like?	20
Activity 3.3 Who Am I?	30
Lunch	30
Activity 4 The Match Game	20
Activity 5 Teacher Talk Improv	40
Activity 6.1 Diving In	60
Activity 6.2 Share the Vision: Closing, Sharing, and Reflecting	20
	6 hours

*Note: Although at least six hours are typically required to complete all the activities, the schedule can be modified to fit other time frames.

Workshop Advance Preparation

Selection of Students

◆ Students should be identified by their school or district as having intellectual and/or specific academic abilities that require services beyond the regular classroom.

◆ Homeschool students may self-identify or be identified by their parents as having needs beyond their age or grade level.

◆ Students may be from one or more grade levels, from one school or multiple schools across a district, or from multiple districts across a region, state, or province.

◆ The workshop is most appropriate for students ages ten to eighteen or in upper elementary, middle school, junior high, or high school.

◆ The age range or grade-level range of attending students ideally should be no greater than four years, for example, ages twelve to fifteen or fifth through eighth grade.

◆ Ideal group size is twenty-five to forty students plus their advocates. The workshop activities can be modified for larger or smaller groups, but it is recommended that there be no fewer than fifteen and no greater than fifty students.

Facilitator Materials

◆ "Sample Workshop Flyer for Adults" (see digital content)

◆ "Sample Workshop Flyer for Students and Registration Form" (see digital content)

◆ "Pre-Workshop Information and Instructions for Advocates" (see page 160)

◆ "Post-Workshop Suggestions for Advocates" (see page 161)

◆ PDF presentation (see digital content)

Student Materials

◆ "GT Carpe Diem Learner Profile Assessments" (see pages 162–178)

◆ "Express Yourself Talent Search" and "Great Gripes of Gifted Kids," printed back-to-back on five different paper colors (see pages 179–180)

◆ Character Trait Cards (see pages 181–186)
  • "Perfectionism"
  • "Extroverts and Introverts"
  • "Analytical Minds and Creative Minds"

◆ "Learner Profile Wall Charts" (see page 187)

◆ "Pre-Workshop Survey" and "Post-Workshop Survey," printed back-to-back (optional) (see pages 188–189)

◆ Nametags

◆ Markers

◆ Pencils

◆ Pencil sharpener

◆ Paper shredder

◆ Small see-through wastebasket or similar container

◆ Masking tape or poster putty

◆ Poster paper

◆ Small sticky note pads (1.5" x 2")

◆ Snacks for break

◆ Lunch

Venue Setup

◆ Moveable tables

◆ Chairs (6–8 at each table)

◆ Table for nametags

◆ Table for lunch buffet and snacks

◆ Table for other supplies

◆ Space around perimeter of room for activities

◆ Screen that is clearly visible to all attendees

◆ Projector for PDF presentation

Pre-Workshop Setup

◆ Arrange handout, "GT Carpe Diem Learner Profile Assessments," on table near door for students to pick up as they enter.

◆ If you are using the pre- and post-workshop surveys, place them with the handout.

◆ If possible, email attending advocates "Pre-Workshop Information and Instructions for Advocates." Otherwise have this handout available to distribute as they arrive.

◆ Arrange nametags and markers on a table near the door.

- Plug in paper shredder and pencil sharpener. Place on easily accessible supply table.
- Place extra pencils on supply table.
- Distribute sticky note pads in centers of student tables, enough for at least five notes per student.
- Hang "Learner Profile Wall Charts" around the room.
- Place the Character Trait Cards in a convenient location for use during workshop.

Other Suggestions for Facilitator

- Check the website links listed on the last page of the "GT Carpe Diem Learner Profile Assessments" to make sure they are still valid.

- Select a means of gaining attention at the end of noisy activities. For instance, rhythmic hand clapping works well with teens. Start clapping a pattern followed by, "If you hear my voice, stop talking and clap with me."
- Follow the plan for grouping and regrouping students to ensure they interact with a wide range of students.
- Throughout the day, remind adults to participate in activities, mingle with students, listen to student discussions, and co-facilitate as needed.

Workshop Part One: Introduction

Activity 1.1 Welcome, Introductions, Arrangements for the Day (15 minutes)

Learner Outcomes:
1. Attendees understand the purpose of the workshop.
2. Attendees understand the arrangements for the day.
3. Students understand that they are in attendance because their teachers recognize that their intellectual or academic abilities indicate they may need accommodations in addition to the regular classroom.

Related NAGC Standards: 1.2, 1.4, 5.1, 5.5, 6.1, 6.2

Background Information: *The Power of Self-Advocacy for Gifted Learners* Chapters 1, 2, and 8

Materials:
- Tables for groups of 6–8 students
- PDF presentation slides:
  1: GT Carpe Diem Workshop
  2: Why *Carpe Diem*?
  3: The G Word

Facilitator Instructions

As attendees arrive:
- Show **slide 1: GT Carpe Diem Workshop**.
- Ask everyone to create and wear nametags.
- Ask attendees to pick up the handout.
- Ask attendees to pick up pencils, if they need them.
- Allow attendees to sit wherever they like.
- If you are using the pre- and post-workshop surveys, ask attendees to complete the "Pre-Workshop Survey" while they wait for others to arrive.
- Confirm that advocates received and have read the pre-workshop instructions.

After all attendees are present:
1. Welcome participants.
2. Show **slide 2: Why *Carpe Diem*?**
3. Ask for a volunteer to translate *carpe diem.* Tell students that by "seizing today" they may be changing their lives forever.

4. Show **slide 3: The G Word**. Explain the G word. Some people are uncomfortable with the word *gifted*. They may use lots of other terms like *able learner, talented, high achieving, highly capable,* and so on. But using the word *gifted* is fine. As the day progresses, students will discover more about what giftedness means and doesn't mean. Assure students that they were invited to the workshop because they are gifted and that the term refers to them.
5. Explain informal objectives for the day.
   - Get to know others who are like you.
   - Spend time thinking about yourself as a learner.
   - Recognize the similarities and differences you have with other gifted kids.
   - Think about what you'd like to change about school or your education.
6. Ask students to look at the sizes and styles of their shoes and the shoes of those around them. What do they see? Explain that just as one size or style of shoe doesn't fit all, one educational path doesn't fit everyone. The goal today is to help students select and wear the "size and style of education" that is right for them.
7. Remind adult advocates of their roles:
   - Guide table discussions.
   - Encourage participation.
   - Participate in all activities.
   - Vary sitting with your own student(s) and at other tables.
   - Assist in discussing and writing action plans with your student(s).
8. Share arrangements for the day.
   - Location of restrooms
   - Overview of schedule
     - Break time
     - Lunch time
     - Departure time
   - Signal for quieting down

Conclusion and Transition: "Any questions? If you have any personal concerns at any time, you can speak to any of the advocates privately. And now it's time to get going!"

Activity 1.2 Express Yourself Talent Search (15 minutes)

Learner Outcomes:

1. Attendees assess their interests, abilities and talents, and comfort level while interacting casually with peers and adult advocates.

2. Attendees understand that gifted students vary in all the above.

Related NAGC Standards: 1.1, 1.2, 1.4, 4.2

Background Information: *The Power of Self-Advocacy for Gifted Learners* Chapters 1 and 2

Materials:

- Handout: "Express Yourself Talent Search" and "Great Gripes of Gifted Kids" (printed on five different paper colors)
- PDF presentation slides:
  4: Are Gifted Kids All Alike?
  5: Express Yourself Talent Search
  6: Multiple Intelligences
  7: As Gifted Kids . . .
  8: Self-Advocacy
  9: Four Steps to Self-Advocacy

Facilitator Instructions

1. Show **slide 4: Are Gifted Kids All Alike?** One of the common myths about gifted kids is that they are all the same. Ask students for examples of the stereotype. In the first activity, students will explore some of the ways in which gifted people are very different from each other.

2. Show **slide 5: Express Yourself Talent Search**. Distribute "Express Yourself Talent Search" and "Great Gripes of Gifted Kids." Explain the Talent Search activity.

   - Both students and advocates are participants.
   - Participants should read each of the squares and decide which tasks they are comfortable doing.
   - Participants are to find people who can help them fill in their grids.

   - Participants have five minutes to walk around the room and ask others to do one of the Talent Search tasks and then initial that square.
   - Participants are to find twenty different people who are comfortable doing the twenty different tasks.
   - Participants do not have to do a task that is difficult for them or that makes them uncomfortable.
   - Remind advocates to join the Talent Search.

3. Ask students to stand up, move around the room, and begin approaching other students.

4. After five minutes, get the attention of the group and ask participants to stand where they are. Based on the color of their Talent Search papers, they are to rotate to new tables so no more than two of the same colored papers are at each table.

   - Briefly allow participants to settle into their new tables.
   - Show **slide 6: Multiple Intelligences**. Explain that the talent search squares represent different abilities and interests related to Howard Gardner's theory of multiple intelligences: linguistic, logical/mathematical, interpersonal, intrapersonal, naturalistic, musical/rhythmic, visual/spatial, and psychomotor/kinesthetic. We all have strengths in some areas and less ability in others.
   - Quickly determine which students have the most squares signed by asking, "Who has all 20 squares signed?" and "19?" "18?" and so on. Congratulate all the participants.

5. Ask students to introduce themselves to everyone at their table by stating their names and schools and sharing which talent search task they did *not* want to do. Advocates participate and assist as needed at each table.

6. Show **slide 7: As Gifted Kids . . .** Explain the enduring understandings for the day:

   - Gifted students vary in their talents and interests.
   - Gifted students need educational opportunities that match their unique needs.

◆ Gifted students can and should have a major role in designing their paths to graduation and beyond.

7. Show **slide 8: Self-Advocacy**. Tell students that the best way to have a major role is to self-advocate. Ask for a volunteer to read the definition. Ask how someone's dignity could be compromised. Your own? Another student's? A teacher's? A parent's? Explain that self-advocacy relies on relationships and is reflected in concern for everyone's dignity.

8. Show **slide 9: Four Steps to Self-Advocacy**. Explain that throughout the workshop students will begin work on each of the four steps:

1) Understanding their rights and responsibilities as gifted individuals

2) Assessing and reflecting on their learner profiles

3) Matching their profiles to appropriate opportunities

4) Learning to communicate clearly to the adult advocates who can support their self-advocacy

But the real work on self-advocacy begins when they get back to school.

Conclusion and Transition: "While some people might think that having exceptional abilities makes your life a breeze, every day you'll face frustrations that you'll want to address as you self-advocate."

Activity 1.3 Gripes of Wrath (20 minutes)

Learner Outcome:

1. Attendees acknowledge and affirm the frustrations inherent in being gifted and having unique needs.

Related NAGC Standards: 1.1, 1.2, 1.3, 1.4

Background Information: *The Power of Self-Advocacy for Gifted Learners* Chapters 1 and 2

Materials:

◆ Handouts: "Great Gripes of Gifted Kids" (printed on back of "Express Yourself Talent Search") and "GT Carpe Diem Learner Profile Assessments"

◆ Pencils

◆ PDF presentation slides:
   10: Great Gripes of Gifted Kids
   11: Gripes of Wrath

Facilitator Instructions

1. Show **slide 10: Great Gripes of Gifted Kids**.
   ◆ Have students turn to the backside of the "Express Yourself Talent Search" handout.
   ◆ Explain that a survey of several thousand gifted students revealed that these are the top gripes about being gifted.

2. Show **slide 11: Gripes of Wrath**.
   ◆ Ask students to check the gripes that affect them and to cross out the ones that are not an issue for them. Then ask students to write a few sentences about the gripes they checked, noting things that specifically bug them. Assure students that no one else will be reading their comments, so they can be as honest as they like.
   ◆ Ask students to get into pairs at their tables to discuss which gripes they agree and disagree on. They can give examples from their experiences. Allow two minutes for discussion.
   ◆ Ask students to go around the table and take turns commenting on their gripes, with advocates assisting as needed.
   ◆ After allowing a few minutes for discussion, ask a volunteer from each table to share the table's most common gripe.
   ◆ Encourage students to add additional thoughts to their list of gripes, then ask them to set aside the papers for later.

3. On their "GT Carpe Diem Learner Profile Assessments," ask students to record their greatest gripes in the space provided on the last page and to list two to three things they would like to change about their education to make it better.

4. Ensure that students have put their names on their "GT Carpe Diem Learner Profile Assessments" handouts and instruct them to keep the handouts handy for upcoming activities.

Conclusion and Transition: "Throughout the workshop, you'll find ways to eliminate some of your gripes by understanding the four steps of self-advocacy. So, let's get started with the first step."

Workshop Part Two:
Self-Advocacy Step #1: Understand Your Rights and Responsibilities

Activity 2.1 Defining the "G" Word (20 minutes)

Learner Outcomes:

1. Attendees deepen their understanding of what giftedness means and doesn't mean.
2. Attendees recognize the various profiles of gifted students.
3. Attendees recognize their status within the six profiles.

Key Concepts:

◆ Definitions, descriptions, and profiles of giftedness vary greatly.

Related NAGC Standards: 1.1, 1.2, 1.3, 1.4

Background Information: *The Power of Self-Advocacy for Gifted Learners* Chapter 3

Materials:

◆ Handout: "GT Carpe Diem Learner Profile Assessments"
◆ PDF presentation slides:
   12: Do I Have the Right?
   13: Two Rights
   14: Federal Definition of Gifted
   15: Giftedness Is . . .
   16: Whatcha Thinkin' About?
   17: Six Profiles
   18: On the Road to Autonomy

Facilitator Instructions

1. Show **slide 12: Do I Have the Right?** The first step in self-advocacy is to understand your rights and responsibilities.
   ◆ Ask if anyone included "No one explains what being gifted is all about" in their gripes.
   ◆ Tell participants that since so many kids say that no one has ever explained to them what it means

to be gifted, you will now spend a few minutes talking about it. They have a right to know.

2. Show **slide 13: Two Rights**.
   ◆ Ask a volunteer to read the slide. (You will use this volunteer reading technique several times throughout the day. Encourage students to simply begin reading rather than raising their hands when you ask for volunteers. Remind eager readers to give others an opportunity to read.)
   ◆ Tell students that they will be looking at each right individually.

3. Show **slide 14: Federal Definition of Gifted**.
   ◆ Read the heading and then ask for volunteers to read each bullet.
   ◆ Ask students to point out key phrases, for example, outstanding ability, achievement and/or potential, services beyond those normally provided.

4. Show **slide 15: Giftedness Is . . .** Ask a volunteer to read the quote. Tell students that this is a simpler way of looking at this complicated issue.

5. Show **slide 16: Whatcha Thinkin' About?** Say, "And this is how it might feel to be gifted!"

6. Show **slide 17: Six Profiles**. State that not all gifted teens fit the successful student stereotype. Then briefly describe the six-profile concept in this way:
   ◆ The Successful Learners do well in school because they have figured out how to adapt to the education system.
   ◆ The Creative Learners choose not to conform to an overly rigid system.
   ◆ The Underground Learners feel their social milieu is at odds with the system.
   ◆ The At-Risk Learners find the system hostile and irrelevant.
   ◆ The Twice/Multi-Exceptional (2E) Learners spend more time within the system focusing on their disabilities than their strengths.
   ◆ The Autonomous Learners have figured out how to use the system to create their own unique educational path.

7. Ask students to complete the Six Profiles Self-Assessment in the "GT Carpe Diem Learner Profile Assessments."

8. Do not discuss their results, but ask them to record their type(s) in their handouts.

9. Show **slide 18: On the Road to Autonomy**. Assure students that regardless of which profile or profiles describe them at this moment, they are all on the road to greater autonomy and to taking charge of their own educations.

Conclusion and Transition: "Not only do you have the right to know what giftedness is and how that term applies to you, you also have the right to an education that matches your unique needs."

Activity 2.2 Your Rights (20 minutes)

Learner Outcome:

1. Attendees recognize their rights as gifted individuals.

Key Concepts:

◆ School districts' mission statements include gifted children and their needs.

◆ Gifted students have a right to an appropriately challenging education.

◆ As outliers, gifted children may need different educational experiences.

Related NAGC Standards: 1.1, 1.2, 1.3, 1.4

Background Information: *The Power of Self-Advocacy for Gifted Learners* Chapter 3

Materials:

◆ PDF presentation slides:

19: State Statues, Rules, and Regulations

20: School District of Anytown (see alternatives at right)

21: The Gifted Children's Bill of Rights

Facilitator Instructions

1. Show **slide 19: State Statues, Rules, and Regulations**. Share the specific legal requirements for gifted education in your state or province.

2. Show **slide 20: School District of Anytown**. Tell students that schools *want* to make sure they have an appropriate education. Ask students to read the statement and identify wording that indicates the schools intend to meet the needs of gifted students.

3. Assure students they *do* have the right to an appropriately challenging education.

4. Show **slide 21: The Gifted Children's Bill of Rights**. Share the NAGC Bill of Rights and ask for student volunteers to read each right aloud. Ask for comments and discussion.

Alternatives to Activity 2.2:

◆ Modify slide 20: School District of Anytown to show the district mission statements of students in attendance.

◆ Or ask students to use their smart phones or tablets to find, read aloud, and reflect on their own district's mission statement.

Conclusion and Transition: "Yes, you have rights, but you also have responsibilities and we'll talk about those now."

Activity 2.3 Your Responsibilities (20 minutes)

Learner Outcome:

1. Attendees recognize their responsibilities as gifted individuals.

Key Concepts:

- Gifted students have the responsibility to take charge of their own educations.
- The attributes of giftedness should not be confused with the attributes of good character.
- Gifted students have the responsibility to develop the personal characteristics that will support their success.

Related NAGC Standards: 1.1, 1.2, 1.3, 1.4

Background Information: *The Power of Self-Advocacy for Gifted Learners* Chapter 3

Materials:

- Handout: "GT Carpe Diem Learner Profile Assessments"
- PDF presentation slides:
  22: Two Responsibilities
  23: Attributes
  24: Good Character/Giftedness
  25: The System
  26: Every Student's Right and Responsibility

Facilitator Instructions

1. Show **slide 22: Two Responsibilities**. Ask for volunteers to read the slide.
2. Show **slide 23: Attributes**. Make sure students have their "GT Carpe Diem Learner Profile Assessments" handout. Point out the Attributes section. Inform students that in addition to rights, gifted people also have responsibilities, including working to develop their attributes of good character. Sometimes people assume that if someone is gifted, he or she should naturally be the perfect student. But some attributes are generally true of all people of good character and some attributes research has shown are generally true of gifted individuals.

3. Show **slide 24: Good Character/Giftedness**. Ask students to work with a partner. Pairs read through each phrase and draw an arrow indicating whether an attribute is one of giftedness or one of good character.

4. Discuss. Allow students to defend their decisions. Remind them that being gifted means "better at, not better than." One of their responsibilities (and of all people) is working to develop the attributes of good character. For instance, being bored is no excuse for turning in poorly done homework.

5. If a student comments that "keen observer" is on the list twice, jokingly tell them they are indeed a keen observer.

6. Ask students to record their strongest attributes and areas for growth in their "GT Carpe Diem Learner Profile Assessments."

7. Show **slide 25: The System**. Explain that all students must deal with the educational system as we know it. At times, it might feel like the goal of the educational system is to force everyone into the same mold: the stereotypical successful student. But students can change that.

Conclusion and Transition: Show **slide 26: Every Student's Right and Responsibility**. "If you want to take charge of your own education, you have the responsibility to understand the educational system and the right to adapt it to meet your needs."

Activity 2.4 Letting Go (5 minutes)

Learner Outcome:

1. Students symbolize turning their frustrations into positive actions through self-advocacy.

Related NAGC Standards: 1.1, 1.4

Background Information: *The Power of Self-Advocacy for Gifted Learners* Chapters 1 and 2

Materials:

◆ Handouts: "Express Yourself Talent Search" and "Great Gripes of Gifted Kids"

◆ Paper shredder

◆ Large clear wastebasket, fishbowl, or other container to hold shredded gripes

◆ PDF presentation slide 27: Letting Go

Facilitator Instructions

1. Show **slide 27: Letting Go**. Ask students to reflect for a moment on everything they've been discussing. Can they think of other gripes they have regarding being a gifted kid? If so, they should add the gripes to the last page of their "GT Carpe Diem Learner Profile Assessments."

2. Assure students that their gripes are legitimate and that they have a right to be frustrated, but now is the time to let go of their gripes. Tell them that they will spend the rest of the day figuring out how to make things better.

3. Ask students to "release" their gripes by putting their greatest gripes sheets through the paper shredder during the break. (During the break, empty the paper from the shredder into a clear wastebasket, fish bowl, or other container and leave it in sight at the front of the room.)

4. Tell students that when they return from the break they may sit at any table they wish, but they should have their "GT Carpe Diem Learner Profile Assessments" with them.

Alternatives to Activity 2.4: Instead of shredding gripes, students could 1) wad their papers into balls and shoot them at the wastebasket, or 2) fold their papers into airplanes and fly them into the wastebasket.

Break (15 minutes)

Conclusion and Transition: After students return from the break, review what has been looked at so far: better understanding of giftedness, rights, and responsibilities. Point out the container full of shredded gripes and state the gripes will remain at the front of the room as a reminder of things students are going to be able to change.

Workshop Part Three:
Self-Advocacy Step #2: Assess and Reflect on Your Learner Profile

Activity 3.1 Where Do I Soar?
Cognitive Functioning, Learning Strengths, and Interests (10 minutes)

Learner Outcome:

1. Attendees briefly assess and reflect on their cognitive functioning, learning strengths, and interests.

Key Concepts:

◆ While similar in intellectual ability, gifted kids can be very different from each other.

◆ These assessments are not absolute. They're intended to get students thinking about various aspects of their learner profiles.

◆ Cognitive ability, learning strengths, and interests can change as one grows and has new experiences.

Related NAGC Standards: 1.1, 1.2, 1.3, 1.4, 1.7, 4.1, 4.2

Background Information: *The Power of Self-Advocacy for Gifted Learners* Chapter 4

Materials:

◆ Handout: "GT Carpe Diem Learner Profile Assessments"

◆ PDF presentation slides:
   28: Who Am I?
   29: Five Areas of Your Learner Profile
   30: Cognitive Functioning
   31: IQ (Intelligence Quotient)
   32: The Bell Curve
   33: Things Not Measured by Most Tests
   34: Learning Strengths
   35: Personal Interests

Facilitator Instructions

1. Confirm that students have their "GT Carpe Diem Learner Profile Assessments."

2. Show **slide 28: Who Am I?**
   ◆ Inform participants that because gifted kids are very different from each other, to create their own unique educational paths, they need to do some self-assessment and understand their own learner profiles. This is the second step in self-advocacy.

3. Show **slide 29: Five Areas of Your Learner Profile**. Share the five areas students should consider when they're putting together their personal learner profiles. They won't have time to assess all areas today, but they will sample a few.

4. Show **slide 30: Cognitive Functioning**. Inform participants that cognitive functioning is how well or how quickly one learns. It is generally referred to in terms of IQ. IQ tests are designed to measure a person's general ability to solve problems and understand concepts. The tests may include assessments of spatial, mathematical, language, and memory abilities.

5. Show **slide 31: IQ (Intelligence Quotient)**. Describe briefly IQ as one way of measuring cognitive ability. It is simply an equation: one's mental age divided by life age, multiplied by 100.

6. Show **slide 32: The Bell Curve**.
   ◆ Describe the bell curve first in terms of 100 runners with most people running somewhere in the middle of the pack, someone way ahead, and someone bringing up the rear.

   ◆ Then relate the bell curve to intellectual ability. If your life age and mental age are the same, then your IQ is 100, at the center of the bell curve.

   ◆ Explain that gifted students might need something different in school because much of what is done in classrooms is aimed at the center of the bell curve to meet most students' needs.

   ◆ Outliers need something different. Refer to the line in the federal definition of gifted: "require differentiated educational programs beyond those normally provided by the regular school program."

   ◆ Students are attending this workshop because they are "above average." The more "above average" they are academically and intellectually, the more they may need a differentiated educational program. Assure students that later today they will be reflecting on which experiences may be personally right for them.

◆ Mention that all the "attributes of giftedness" discussed in Activity 2.3 could also be placed along a continuum depending on individual student's abilities.

7. Show **slide 33: Things Not Measured by Most Tests**. Ask for two volunteers to each read one of the columns. Ask students to consider what other range of abilities or traits might be described by the bell curve or a continuum of some sort.

8. Repeat **slide 30: Cognitive Functioning**. Ask participants to use the My Attributes chart on their "GT Carpe Diem Learner Profile Assessments" to record any additional attributes of giftedness that describe them.

9. Show **slide 34: Learning Strengths**. Allow students to read the slide and react to the pun, a little joke for both math and language lovers.

◆ Tell students that *learning strengths* refers to high performance in specific academic areas, subjects, and talents.

◆ Ask students to list in their "GT Carpe Diem Learner Profile Assessments" the areas that they believe they excel in, based on grades and test scores and compared to others they know.

10. Show **slide 35: Personal Interests**. Personal interests could mean school subjects but also hobbies, extracurricular activities, ideas, and causes.

◆ Tell students that tying their learning experiences to their interests/passions helps them find appropriate *and* interesting challenges. For students to feel like they're learning, it's important that their challenge level is balanced with their skill level.

◆ In their "GT Carpe Diem Learner Profile Assessments," have students list those things—school subjects, hobbies, extracurricular activities, artistic pursuits—about which they are truly passionate.

Conclusion and Transition: "We've started to zero in on the first three parts of your learner profile, which include the things you are good at and interested in. Now we'll look at another part: the things you prefer when it comes to school and studying."

Activity 3.2 What Do I Like?
Learning Preferences (20 minutes)

Learner Outcome:

1. Attendees briefly assess and reflect on their learning preferences.

Key Concepts:

◆ While similar in intellectual ability, gifted kids can be very different from each other.

◆ Learning preferences can change as one grows and has new experiences.

Related NAGC Standards: 1.1, 1.2, 1.3, 1.4, 1.7, 4.1, 4.2

Background Information: *The Power of Self-Advocacy for Gifted Learners* Chapter 4

Materials:

◆ Handout: "GT Carpe Diem Learner Profile Assessments"

◆ PDF presentation slides:
36: Learning Preferences
37: Learning Modes

Facilitator Instructions

1. Show **slide 36: Learning Preferences**. Explain that learning preferences refer to ways people prefer to acquire information and demonstrate knowledge.

2. Conduct the following activity.

   ◆ Explain that in this activity participants will move to one of the four corners of the room indicated by you to visually demonstrate their differences and similarities.

   ◆ Students are to listen to each prompt and directions for where they will move.

   ◆ They are to be aware of what they observe regarding other students and the generalizations they can make.

   Instructions: Ask students to go to corners of the room to indicate their preferences in terms of each area. Tell them to go quietly without talking so you can quickly move from one preference to another. Point to the corner as you announce each option, as in the first example below.

"When it comes to classroom instructional techniques, do you prefer . . ."

◆ Lecture and discussion? (point to one corner)

◆ Individual projects? (point to another corner)

◆ Experiments and simulations? (point to third corner)

◆ Games and competitions? (point to fourth corner)

"When it comes to learning environment, do you prefer to study . . ." (continue pointing to corners as you call out options)

◆ In the morning, afternoon, evening, or late at night?

◆ At home, at school, or somewhere else?

◆ In silence? Or while listening to the TV, conversation, or music? If music, what kind?

"When preparing for a test, do you prefer to study . . ."

◆ With a partner?

◆ In a small group?

◆ In a large group?

◆ Alone?

"When it comes to learning assessments, do you prefer . . ."

◆ Essays, term papers, and written compositions?

◆ Performance tasks, such as exhibitions, presentations, and demonstrations?

◆ Portfolios and journals?

◆ Independent research projects with a rubric?

3. Ask students to take their seats.

4. Show **slide 37: Learning Modes**. Tell students that there are many ways to think about learning modes or styles, but that this trio is one of the most common models. Emphasize to students that most people generally use a combination of the three modes but usually have strengths in some.

5. Conduct the Phone # Game.

   ◆ Say "Remember this phone number: 273-5253."

   ◆ After five seconds say, "Stop. What are you doing to remember the number?"

- Relate each student response to one of the three modes.
- Ask "What is your go-to learning mode: auditory, visual, or kinesthetic? Other?"

6. In their "GT Carpe Diem Learner Profile Assessments," have students rank their learning modes and record some of the things they just learned about their learning preferences.

Conclusion and Transition: "Now we'll spend a little time assessing and reflecting on the final part of your learner profile: your personality character traits."

Activity 3.3 Who Am I?
Personality Character Traits (30 minutes)

Learner Outcome:

1. Attendees briefly assess and reflect on their personality traits and how those traits might affect self-advocacy.

Key Concepts:

◆ While similar in intellectual ability, gifted kids can be very different from each other.

◆ Personality traits can change as one grows and has new experiences.

Related NAGC Standards: 1.1, 1.2, 1.3, 1.4, 1.7, 4.1, 4.2

Background Information: *The Power of Self-Advocacy for Gifted Learners* Chapter 4

Materials:

◆ Handout: "GT Carpe Diem Learner Profile Assessments"

◆ Create "Learner Profile Wall Charts"

◆ Copies of the Character Trait Cards (pages 181–186)
  • "Perfectionism"
  • "Extroverts and Introverts"
  • "Analytical Minds and Creative Minds"

◆ PDF presentation slides:

  38: Personality Character Traits

  39–45: Optimism/Pessimism (7 slides)

  46: Motivation

  47: To Become an Independent Learner

  48: Three Things Motivated, Independent, Self-Directed Learners Know

  49: More Character Traits

  50: Perfectionism

  51: Introvert/Extrovert/Ambivert

  52: Analytical/Creative

  53: Overexcitabilities

Facilitator Instructions

1. Show **slide 38: Personality Character Traits**. State that personality character traits (behaviors and attitudes) may affect students' abilities to successfully self-advocate.

2. Inform participants that while there are numerous personality character traits, they will look at only six areas at this time. Remind them that the assessments are not definitive or black and white; but they do help people reflect on themselves and where they are on a continuum. When students are finished with the character trait assessments, they will write their scores on sticky notes and post the notes on the "Learner Profile Wall Charts" hung around the room, comparing where they all fall on the continuum.

3. Show **slides 39–45: Optimism/Pessimism**.

   ◆ Instruct students to look at each slide and choose either answer A or B.

   ◆ In the "GT Carpe Diem Learner Profile Assessments," they are to make slash marks in the boxes to keep track of their answers.

   ◆ Click through the slides quickly, reading each phrase, pausing, and then reading both responses.

   ◆ After students have tallied their responses, ask them to record their results on a sticky note. They should write O/P on the top of the note (lengthwise) and their score underneath it. They should save the note on the table in front of them.

4. Show **slide 46: Motivation**. Relate the differences between intrinsic and extrinsic motivation. Extrinsic motivation occurs when we are motivated to perform a behavior or engage in an activity to earn a reward or avoid a punishment. Intrinsic motivation involves engaging in a behavior because it is personally rewarding.

   ◆ Explain to students that both types of motivation are needed at one time or another.

   ◆ Ask which type of learner, Successful or Autonomous, is more likely to be intrinsically motivated.

5. Show **slide 47: To Become an Independent Learner**. Explain that an independent learner is someone who

can manage his or her own learning to achieve a goal and who is not wholly dependent on a teacher.

- ◆ Give a personal example of a time when you were an independent learner: learning a new skill or concept, studying in college, planning an event, and so on.

- ◆ Ask students to share one or two sentences about a time when they were independent learners. Depending on time, you can call on a few students to share with the whole group or ask them to share with others at their table.

6. Show **slide 48: Three Things Motivated, Independent, Self-Directed Learners Know.**

- ◆ Ask students to rate their motivation, independence, and self-direction in their "GT Carpe Diem Learner Profile Assessments."

- ◆ Ask them to record their rating on a sticky note. They should write "Motiv" on the top of the note (lengthwise) and their score underneath it.

- ◆ Then ask students to go to the "Learner Profile Wall Charts" and place both their "O/P" and "Motiv" sticky notes on the appropriate continuums.

7. Show **slide 49: More Character Traits.**

- ◆ Have students count off by threes to form groups for the next activity.

- ◆ Each of the three groups will report on one of the three character traits as follows.

- ◆ Students are to read one of the three Character Trait Cards, do the related assessments in the "GT Carpe Diem Learner Profile Assessments," and discuss their results as a group.

- ◆ The group also should discuss "How might this trait affect my ability or willingness to self-advocate?"

- ◆ Groups are to prepare a short 2- to 3-minute presentation to share their concept and results with the other groups.

- ◆ Advocates should rotate through the groups, listening and helping as needed. They should do the assessments with the students.

- ◆ Bring the whole group back together and call on each small group to report their findings.

8. Show **slide 50: Perfectionism** as students present on the topic.

9. Show **slide 51: Introvert/Extrovert/Ambivert** as students present on the topic.

10. Show **slide 52: Analytical/Creative** as students present on the topic.

11. Show **slide 53: Overexcitabilities.**

- ◆ Explain how Dabrowski's theory of overexcitabilities (OE) relates to gifted individuals. Intensities/overexcitabilities are common in gifted individuals expressed as high energy, greater awareness of their surroundings, deeply felt emotions, vivid imaginations, and constant questioning of ideas and theories.

- ◆ Give examples of each of the five OE.

  - **Intellectual intensity** may lead you to seek answers to difficult questions like "What is the meaning of life?"

  - If you have **psychomotor overexcitability**, you may have surplus bodily energy that causes you to move, speak rapidly, or use your hands when talking.

  - **Sensual intensity** can involve any or all of the five senses. For example, colors may seem more vivid, sounds may be more annoying, mosquito bites might feel itchier, or chocolate may taste more delectable.

  - If you have **emotional overexcitability** you may experience a very wide range of both positive and negative feelings, sometimes many feelings at the same time.

  - **Imagination intensity** could result in vivid dreams or a fascination with fantasy, and might be expressed through involvement in the arts or other creative outlets.

12. Ask students to complete the OE assessment in the "GT Carpe Diem Learner Profile Assessments" and to record their results in the appropriate box.

13. Encourage students to try the assessments they haven't yet done before the afternoon session begins. They are to record their results in their "GT Carpe Diem Learner Profile Assessments" and on sticky notes. They should write "Perf" and "E/I" and "A/C" on the top of the notes (lengthwise) and their scores underneath it.

14. Before and during lunch, students can place their sticky notes on the appropriate continuums of the "Learner Profile Wall Charts."

Conclusion and Transition: "That's all the time we have to spend on your learner profiles today, but we've only scratched the surface. If you're interested in learning more about yourself, there are links in your handouts and your advocate can help you find additional resources."

Lunch (30 minutes)
Give instructions for lunch.

Workshop Part Four: Self-Advocacy Step #3: Match Attributes to Options and Opportunities

Activity 4 The Match Game (20 minutes)

Learner Outcomes:

1. Attendees understand that not all options are right for all students.

2. Students understand they have the greatest chance of succeeding if educational alternatives are matched to their learner profiles.

3. Students identify educational options that are appropriate for them.

Related NAGC Standards: 1.1, 1.7, 4.1, 5.5, 5.7, 6.2

Background Information: *The Power of Self-Advocacy for Gifted Learners* Chapter 5

Materials:

◆ Handout: "GT Carpe Diem Learner Profile Assessments"

◆ PDF presentation slide 54: What Could I Do Differently?

Facilitator Instructions

1. Transition: Review what you accomplished in the morning: defining giftedness, rights, responsibilities, and learner profiles. Look at the "Learner Profile Wall Charts." What patterns do students see? Are all gifted students alike? What generalizations can they make?

2. Show **slide 54: What Could I Do Differently?** Tell participants that the next activity will help them match their learner profiles with appropriate educational options and opportunities, the third step in self-advocacy.

3. Have students turn to the page in their "GT Carpe Diem Learner Profile Assessments," "Which Options Are Right for Me?" which describes possible academic options. Allow students time to peruse the chart, putting a check mark next to the options that sound interesting.

4. Ask students to share stories of any educational alternatives they have already experienced and if they would recommend the option to others.

5. Ask if there are questions about any of the options or if any options need more of an explanation.

6. Ask if there are options not on the list that students have done or heard about.

7. Allow students to spend a few minutes reviewing what they have recorded on their learner profiles.

8. Then have students compare the option requirements with their learner profiles.

9. Inform students that success in each of the options listed requires that a person have the attributes checked in that column.

10. Ask students to go back through the list and circle two or three options that fit their learner profiles and that they would like to try.

Conclusion and Transition: "In addition to addressing your academic needs, you may be able to change other things at school or home to make your life better. And the good news is, a lot of people are available to help you do it."

Workshop Part Five: Self-Advocacy Step #4: Connect with Advocates Who Can Support Your Goals

Activity 5 Teacher Talk Improv (40 minutes)

Learner Outcomes:

1. Students identify the adults in their lives who understand their needs and can help them self-advocate.
2. Students identify and practice constructive ways to talk with the adults who can help them successfully self-advocate.

Key Concepts:

◆ Parents, teachers, counselors, and gifted education coordinators are the primary advocates for students who are learning to self-advocate.

◆ Other adults, especially administrators, also play a role in advocacy.

Related NAGC Standards: 1.4, 4.1, 4.2, 6.1, 6.2

Background Information: *The Power of Self-Advocacy for Gifted Learners* Chapter 6

Materials:

◆ Handout: "GT Carpe Diem Learner Profile Assessments"

◆ PDF presentation slides:
55: Who Can Help?
56: Talking to Teachers Improv

◆ Large, open space in meeting room for presentations

Facilitator Instructions

1. Show **slide 55: Who Can Help?** Reassure students that they are not alone in this endeavor and that the fourth step in self-advocacy is connecting with advocates who can support their goals.
2. In their "GT Carpe Diem Learner Profile Assessments," ask students to list the names of people they know who can help them get what they need and want. Students should include people who can vouch for their self-direction, motivation, and independence; who have witnessed their successes in various learning situations; and who understand their need for accommodations. Allow two to three minutes to write.
3. Remind students that it's not just about knowing *who* to talk to, it's also important to know *how* to talk to possible advocates. Have students turn to the "Ten Tips for Talking to Teachers" in their "GT Carpe Diem Learner Profile Assessments." Ask for volunteers to read each of the ten tips aloud.
4. Show **slide 56: Talking to Teachers Improv**.
   ◆ Divide students into groups.
   ◆ Each group will create and perform two short improvised sketches in which students approach a teacher regarding their concerns: in one, students don't use the ten tips and fail, and in the other, students use the ten tips and succeed.
   ◆ Allow ten minutes for work.
   ◆ Move to the open area of the room and make sure that everyone can see the performance area.
   ◆ Depending on the number of groups, allow ten to fifteen minutes for all sketches.
   ◆ Assign one student as the timer who will call out "scene" when one minute has passed in each sketch. Actors must freeze where they are and the scene is over. Applaud each one.
   ◆ Move quickly to the next group's performance.
   ◆ When all sketches are finished, ask students to sit at tables with others from their school.

Alternatives to Activity 5:

If your day allows for more time for this activity, students may choose one of these options instead of the improvisation:

◆ **Rap and Slam.** Students will prepare and perform some of the ten tips using rap and/or poetry slam techniques.

◆ **Warhol, Picasso, or Rembrandt.** Using chart paper and markers, students will create a visual representation of the ten tips. Digital media may be used if available.

- **The Office.** Using chart paper and markers, students will create a flowchart of the ten tips. Digital media may be used if available.
- **Tips for Talking to Gifted Teens.** Using the Ten Tips for Talking to Teachers as an example, students will write ten tips that teachers should use when talking with gifted teens. They will share the tips with the group.

Conclusion and Transition: "So there you have it. You've experienced the four steps of self-advocacy. You've thought about what giftedness means (and doesn't mean), you've recognized your rights and responsibilities, you've begun to reflect on your own unique learner profile and the options that are best for you, and you've identified the advocates who can support you. Now it's time to figure out the first thing that you'd like to self-advocate for. What do you want to change?"

Workshop Part Six:
Action Plans for Change

Activity 6.1 Diving In (60 minutes)

Learner Outcomes:

1. Students choose an educational goal.
2. Students create an action plan for that goal.

Related NAGC Standards: 1.1, 1.7, 4.1, 5.5, 5.7, 6.2

Background Information: *The Power of Self-Advocacy for Gifted Learners* Chapter 7

Materials:

◆ Handout: "GT Carpe Diem Learner Profile Assessments"
◆ PDF presentation slides:
   57: What Do You Need or Want?
   58: More Challenging Work
   59: Explore an Interest
   60: More Time with Kids Like You
   61: Changes to Match Your Profile
   62: Sample Self-Advocacy Action Plan

Facilitator Instructions

1. If students are not already at tables with others from their school, ask them to move there now.

2. Tell students that they have experienced the four steps of self-advocacy and it is time for them to determine what changes they'd like to make. "If never before, this is the time to begin to make school what *you* want it to be." Ask them to reflect:
   ◆ How happy are you with the way things are going right now?
   ◆ Is there something big or little that you'd like to change?

3. Show **slide 57: What Do You Need or Want?** Explain that most students' desire for change falls into one of these four categories.
   ◆ Give a few examples. Use those on the slides or substitute some from your personal experience.

4. Show **slide 58: More Challenging Work**. "Some kids wanted to do more challenging work and these are the goals they chose."

5. Show **slide 59: Explore an Interest**. "Some kids wanted to explore an interest and selected these goals."

6. Show **slide 60: More Time with Kids Like You**. "Some kids wanted more time with other gifted kids and set these goals."

7. Show **slide 61: Changes to Match Your Profile**. "Some kids wanted changes to meet their personal character traits and these are their goals."

8. Show **slide 62: Sample Self-Advocacy Action Plan**.
   ◆ Share the example of how a student named Mandy began her plan. Read the statement goal aloud and point out the three columns.
   ◆ Refer students to "Questions to Consider When Creating a Self-Advocacy Action Plan" in the "GT Carpe Diem Learner Profile Assessments," and remind them to find answers to these questions as they craft their plan.
   ◆ Remind students that self-advocacy means getting what they want and need without compromising the dignity of themselves or others.
   ◆ Emphasize the importance of creating a workable plan: "Failing to plan is planning to fail!"

9. Provide writing time (advocates assist students from their schools).
   ◆ Allow as much time as possible for students to work on their plans, leaving fifteen minutes at the end of the day for concluding the workshop.
   ◆ After five minutes of thinking and writing, ask students to share their goals. Those who are still considering a goal will benefit from hearing others.
   ◆ Announce the amount of time left to work on the plans and allow students and advocates to continue working.
   ◆ Encourage advocates to meet briefly with every student from their school during the work time so they have a sense of what will need to be done back in the school to help students follow through with their self-advocacy.

Conclusion and Transition: "We've had limited time to work this afternoon, so you may have just begun your plan. Please set a time when you're back in school to meet with your advocate and finalize your plan together."

Activity 6.2 Share the Vision (20 min)

Learner Outcome:

1. Attendees share and compare the goals they have set for themselves.

Related NAGC Standards: 1.1, 1.4, 1.7, 4.1, 5.7

Background Information: *The Power of Self-Advocacy for Gifted Learners*

Materials:

◆ Handout: "Post-Workshop Survey" (optional)

◆ PDF presentation slide 63: *Carpe Diem! Carpe Vitam! Carpe Omnia!*

Facilitator Instructions

1. If you are using the workshop evaluation, ask students to complete the "Post-Workshop Survey" on the back of the "Pre-Workshop Survey." Collect the surveys before you begin sharing.

2. Share action plans. Ask students to read their goals and the first action in their plans. Do not take time to discuss each, but point out similarities. Congratulate everyone on taking the first step.

3. Review the day. Ask students:

   ◆ Who met someone new today?

   ◆ Who talked to someone today they'd never talked to before?

   ◆ What was one important thing you discovered about yourself today?

4. Show **slide 63:** *Carpe Diem! Carpe Vitam! Carpe Omnia!* Tell students that because they have chosen to seize this day, they have also chosen to *Carpe Vitam* (seize life). And it is your hope that this day will help them to *Carpe Omnia* (seize it all)!

Pre-Workshop Information and Instructions for Advocates

Thank you for bringing your students to the GT Carpe Diem Workshop and for agreeing to help them self-advocate both during the workshop and back in their schools. By doing so, you are indeed their advocate!

What Is the GT Carpe Diem Workshop?

The workshop will introduce your students (and you) to the ideas and understandings they need to self-advocate and begin to take charge of their own educations.

Through the workshop, students will

- network with like-ability peers and supportive adults
- study the theories and definitions of intelligence
- use those concepts to analyze their own strengths
- review their rights and responsibilities as gifted individuals
- discover a variety of educational options that match their learning profiles
- select a self-advocacy goal and create an action plan for change

What Is the Advocate's Role?

During the day, you will be actively engaged, interacting with students and assisting the facilitator. You will:

- be the guide-on-the-side during small-group discussions
- encourage participation by all students
- help ensure that all students feel included
- join in all student activities
- keep an eye out for students who are struggling with the day for one reason or another
- vary sitting with your own student(s) and at tables with other students
- assist in discussing goals and writing action plans with your student(s)

In the morning, you and the other advocates will work with students from all attending schools. In the afternoon, you'll focus specifically on the students from your own school(s) while they discuss and write their individual goals and action plans. Ideally, you'll be able to meet with every student from your school during the work time so you have a sense of what will need to be done back in school to ensure the students will follow through with their self-advocacy.

What Will My Students and I Learn?

Ideally, both you and your students will leave the workshop with these essential understandings:

1. Gifted students vary in their talents and interests.
2. Gifted students need educational opportunities that match their unique needs.
3. Gifted students can and should play a major role in designing their own paths through the educational system and beyond.

Post-Workshop Suggestions for Advocates

As an advocate, you have a critical role in supporting your students' plans when they are back at their school. Most students leave the workshop feeling empowered and energized. However, one day at a workshop will not insure that they self-advocate. It may be the initial step that opens the door, but it is what happens at school and home after the workshop that leads students from understanding to action.

As the advocates who attended the workshop with your students, you are privy to all they have learned. You are their primary partner in moving ahead with their action plans for change. Some students may be ready to move forward on their own, but some will need more nurturing.

To help them succeed, you will need to:

◆ Set appointments to meet with students within a week or two following the workshop to help them finalize their plans.

◆ Introduce them to the adults whose support and permission they will need.

◆ Fulfill whichever step(s) of their action plan lists you as the "responsible person."

◆ Meet with students periodically to provide ongoing feedback and encouragement.

◆ Communicate with parents and other educators about what self-advocacy is and their roles in helping students accomplish it.

  • Immediately following the workshop, send parents, teachers, and school counselors a brief overview of what you and your students experienced.

  • Provide teachers with a copy of "Ten Tips for Talking to Teachers" (see page 173 or digital content) and prepare them for the possibility that students will be making appointments with them and asking for accommodations. Teachers may want to post the ten tips in their classrooms so all students will feel comfortable asking for what they need.

  • Ask school counselors to provide students with access to their cumulative records as well as additional learner profile assessments.

  • Notify principals of students' plans to self-advocate.

◆ Make sure that your school and district provide access to options students want and need.

◆ Inform students of new opportunities or alternatives that arise during the year and fit their learner profiles.

◆ And finally, continue to remind students to self-advocate whenever you can throughout their school years. Their need to speak up for themselves will fluctuate as they experience changes in teachers, classes, grade levels, subjects, interests, motivation, and movement toward independence.

GT Carpe Diem Workshop Learner Profile Assessments

Name:

School:

Date:

Six Profiles of Gifted and Talented Students

Circle those that are true for you.

TYPE I: THE SUCCESSFUL LEARNER

◆ I've learned to fit into "the system" by listening closely to my parents and teachers.

◆ I feel good about myself as a student.

◆ Adults are pleased with me and my achievements.

◆ I've figured out what appropriate behavior is and I demonstrate it at home and school.

◆ I usually score high on achievement tests.

◆ I'm sometimes bored with school and there are times I can get by with very little effort.

Definitely Not Me			Maybe Me				Definitely Me		
1	2	3	4	5	6	7	8	9	10

TYPE II: THE CREATIVE LEARNER

◆ I don't conform to "the system."

◆ My sense of humor and creativity are enjoyed by peers but are not always appreciated in school.

◆ I'm sometimes frustrated because teachers don't seem to recognize my talents and abilities.

◆ Adults often think I'm sarcastic, obstinate, or tactless.

◆ I've been known to question authority and may even challenge the teacher in front of the class.

◆ The things I'm most interested in usually aren't part of my school day.

Definitely Not Me			Maybe Me				Definitely Me		
1	2	3	4	5	6	7	8	9	10

TYPE III: THE UNDERGROUND LEARNER

◆ I feel "the system" is pushing me to take academic challenges that make me uncomfortable.

◆ Fitting in with my friends is more important than being thought of as gifted.

◆ I sometimes feel anxious about other people understanding the real me.

◆ Adults often expect too much of me academically.

◆ I wish more of my close friends were in gifted or accelerated classes.

◆ Some of the people in my life make fun of me for being smart and liking school.

Definitely Not Me			Maybe Me				Definitely Me		
1	2	3	4	5	6	7	8	9	10

TYPE IV: THE AT-RISK LEARNER

- ◆ I feel angry because "the system" doesn't understand my needs.
- ◆ My family doesn't really understand my needs either.
- ◆ I sometimes feel depressed, withdrawn, or defensive.
- ◆ My real interests lie outside the regular school curriculum so I seldom receive support or praise for my efforts in those areas.
- ◆ School seems irrelevant and sometimes hostile.
- ◆ I wish there were an adult who understood me and could help me get where I want to go.

Definitely Not Me			Maybe Me				Definitely Me		
1	2	3	4	5	6	7	8	9	10

TYPE V: THE TWICE/MULTI-EXCEPTIONAL (2E) LEARNER

- ◆ I have a physical, learning, or other disability.
- ◆ I feel "the system" usually focuses on my disability rather than on my strengths or talents.
- ◆ I sometimes feel stressed, discouraged, frustrated, or isolated.
- ◆ My district's gifted programming doesn't address my special needs.
- ◆ Some of the people around me don't think a person with a disability can also be gifted.
- ◆ I sometimes have difficulty completing work in traditional ways because of my disability.

Definitely Not Me			Maybe Me				Definitely Me		
1	2	3	4	5	6	7	8	9	10

TYPE VI: THE AUTONOMOUS LEARNER

- ◆ I've figured out how to use "the system" to create new opportunities for myself.
- ◆ I feel my school is meeting my needs.
- ◆ I am independent and self-directed, and I don't mind taking risks.
- ◆ I'm comfortable expressing my own feelings, goals, and needs freely and appropriately.
- ◆ I create change in my own life and don't wait for others to facilitate change for me.
- ◆ I choose my own educational and personal goals and make "the system" work for me.

Definitely Not Me			Maybe Me				Definitely Me		
1	2	3	4	5	6	7	8	9	10

My Learner Profile(s)

I'm best described as: (choose all that apply)

___ Successful	___ Creative	___ Underground
___ At-Risk	___ Twice/Multi-Exceptional (2E)	___ Autonomous

Draw an arrow indicating whether the attribute represents good character or giftedness.

Attribute of Good Character   Attribute of Giftedness

Attentive

Turns in work on time

Learns rapidly

Works hard

Listens with interest

Excellent memory

Enjoys peers

Prefers older companions/adults

Keen observer

Works well in a group

Intense

Completes assignments

Early or avid reader

Organized

Copies neatly and accurately

Strong curiosity

Enjoys school

Keen observer

Perfectionistic

Fascinated by puzzles

Alert

Vivid imagination

Considerate of others

Enjoys learning

My Attributes

Good Character	Giftedness
Strengths:	Strengths:
Needs work:	Needs work:

Five Aspects of My Learner Profile

1. **Cognitive Functioning.** I have achievement capability well beyond grade level.
   - Consider your attributes of giftedness.
   - Consider your achievement test scores if you know them.
   - Consider your ability test scores if you know them.

2. **Learning Strengths.** Circle subject areas where you excel based on grades, test scores, and compared with others you know.
   - The Arts
   - Language Arts
   - Math
   - Science
   - Social Sciences
   - Technology
   - World Languages
   - Other:

3. **Interests.** I'm passionate about:
   - Subjects, hobbies, activities:

4. **Learning Preferences.**
   - Favorite classroom instruction technique(s):

   - Best learning/studying environment:

   - Favorite way(s) for me to show what I've learned:

   - My preferred learning mode is (rank 1 through 3, with 1 being most preferred)
     ___ visual   ___auditory   ___kinesthetic

5. **Personality Characteristics: A–F.**

A. Optimist or Pessimist?	
A answers	B answers

B. Motivation, Independence, Self-Direction

What are you doing when you're highly motivated?

Rate your motivation/independence/self-direction in planning your own educational route.

0	1	2	3
Haven't a clue	Still thinking about it	On my way	Highly focused

C. Analytical Minds and Creative Minds

Circle the number from either column that best describes you.

Analytical

1. I like to think through options before choosing.
2. I like true/false and multiple-choice tests.
3. I like to follow numbered written directions.
4. I ask many questions before deciding.
5. I like to read and compute.
6. I like things to be on time.
7. I'm no good at thinking up funny things to say or do.
8. I like to organize things neatly.
9. I can concentrate for a long time.
10. I'm good at remembering names.

_____ total

Creative

1. I like to jump right into things.
2. I like essay and short-answer tests.
3. I tend not to follow written directions.
4. I use simple intuition when problem solving.
5. I like to draw, doodle, and daydream.
6. I have my own concept of time and may show up late.
7. I'm always thinking up funny things to say or do.
8. I look disorganized, but I know where things are.
9. My mind wanders a lot.
10. I'm good at remembering faces.

_____ total

Analytical Minds and Creative Minds																			
10	9	8	7	6	5	4	3	2	1	1	2	3	4	5	6	7	8	9	10
Analytical										Creative									

D. How Much of a Perfectionist Are You?*

Rate each statement.

5 = Exactly like me

4 = Sometimes like me

3 = Can't decide

2 = Not often like me

1 = Not at all like me

1. _____ I'm critical of people who don't live up to my expectations.
2. _____ I get upset if I don't finish something I start.
3. _____ I do things precisely down to the very last detail.
4. _____ I argue about test scores I don't agree with, even when they won't affect my grade.
5. _____ After I finish something, I often feel dissatisfied.
6. _____ I feel guilty when I don't achieve something I set out to do.
7. _____ When a teacher hands back a paper, I look for mistakes before looking for right answers or positive comments.

continued

8. _____ I compare my test scores with those of other good students in my class.

9. _____ It is hard for me to laugh at my own mistakes.

10. _____ If I don't like the way I've done something, I start over and keep at it until I get it right.

_____ total

Perfectionism								
10	15	20	25	30	35	40	45	50
Low			Average			High		

*From *Perfectionism: What's Bad About Being Too Good?* by Miriam Adderholt and Jan Goldberg (Free Spirit Publishing, 1992). Adapted with permission.

E. Extroverts and Introverts

Circle the number from either column that best describes you.

Extroverts

1. I like being the center of attention.
2. I'm comfortable in new situations.
3. I'm a risk taker in groups.
4. I think out loud.
5. I make lots of friends easily.
6. I feel energized around people.
7. I have the same personality in public and private.
8. I'm open and trusting.
9. I learn by doing.
10. I'm distractible.
11. I'm impulsive.
12. My energy comes from interacting with others.

_____ total comments circled

Introverts

1. I hate being the center of attention.
2. I'm uncomfortable in new situations.
3. I'm quiet in groups.
4. I mentally rehearse before speaking.
5. I'm loyal to a few close friends.
6. I feel exhausted around people.
7. I have private and public selves.
8. I need privacy.
9. I learn by watching.
10. I can concentrate intensely.
11. I'm reflective.
12. My energy comes from within.

_____ total comments circled

Extroverts and Introverts																							
12	11	10	9	8	7	6	5	4	3	2	1	1	2	3	4	5	6	7	8	9	10	11	12
Extrovert												Introvert											

F. Overexcitabilities (OE) Checklist

Check the responses that most accurately describe you.

Psychomotor Intensity	Strongly Disagree	Disagree	Neutral	Agree	Strongly Agree
like physically exhausting activities					
have a lot of energy					
gesture a lot, speak quickly					
when stressed, must do something physical					

continued ➤

Overexcitabilities (OE) Checklist (continued)

Sensual Intensity	Strongly Disagree	Disagree	Neutral	Agree	Strongly Agree
respond to music with my whole body					
delight in shape, feel, color, sound, and texture of things					
notice differences in aromas, odors, and tastes					
deeply moved by beauty in nature					
Imaginational Intensity	**Strongly Disagree**	**Disagree**	**Neutral**	**Agree**	**Strongly Agree**
like to daydream					
can vividly picture things in my mind					
tell long, detailed stories with vibrant imagery					
clearly recall dreams and nightmares					
Intellectual Intensity	**Strongly Disagree**	**Disagree**	**Neutral**	**Agree**	**Strongly Agree**
question why things are the way they are					
thrive on theories and facts					
love to solve problems and develop new ideas					
try to analyze my thoughts and actions					
Emotional Intensity	**Strongly Disagree**	**Disagree**	**Neutral**	**Agree**	**Strongly Agree**
worry a lot					
strong feelings of joy, anger, excitement, and/or despair					
deeply concerned about other people					
strong emotions that often lead to tears					

Do you have overexcitabilities? If so, which are strongest?

____ psychomotor

____ sensual

____ imaginational

____ intellectual

____ emotional

Which Options Are Right for Me? Program Options and Requirements

Program Options	Requirements									
	Achieves well above grade level	Has strong interest in subject	Can spend time outside school	Is ready to leave school or home	Likes in-depth study	Enjoys great challenge	Works at fast pace	Works alone or at own pace	Works with ability peers	Is motivated and self-directed
Alternative Assignment. If some of the work you are assigned does not challenge your thinking, your teacher may be willing to allow an alternative. Think about the assignment's purpose. Brainstorm ideas to fulfill that purpose in a different way. Alternative assignments should be more intellectually challenging and something that interests you and allows you to use a special talent or skill.	X	X			X			X		X
Independent Study. In place of regular classwork, you research a topic on your own, developing a product to demonstrate the learning acquired. Independent study is also sometimes used to complete an entire course on your own, often working with a tutor.	X	X	X		X			X		X
Curriculum Compacting/Pretesting. Pretesting demonstrates your prior knowledge of what is about to be taught. In compacting, you skip what you already know and follow a study plan that allows you to work at a faster pace or more in-depth than the rest of the class.	X	X			X	X	X	X	X	X
Within-Class Grouping. The teacher may create a cluster group of high-ability students within the classroom who will work together for a particular assignment or unit. The group will do alternative work at a faster pace or in greater depth than the rest of the class.	X	X			X		X		X	X
Online Learning. Many online programs allow you to study subjects not offered by your school, including AP and honors courses. Be sure to check each website carefully since the quality of programs varies. Some are purely for enrichment while others grant high school or college credit. Not all colleges and universities allow you to transfer credits.	X	X	X	X	X			X		X

continued

Which Options Are Right for Me? Program Options and Requirements (continued)

Program Options	Requirements									
	Achieves well above grade level	Has strong interest in subject	Can spend time outside school	Is ready to leave school or home	Likes in-depth study	Enjoys great challenge	Works at fast pace	Works alone or at own pace	Works with ability peers	Is motivated and self-directed
Subject Acceleration. If you can handle much more difficult work in a subject, then you may need to accelerate in that subject into a higher grade level. You will need test or performance information to indicate your readiness to accelerate.	X	X				X	X	X	X	X
Concurrent/Dual Enrollment. You attend classes in more than one level during the same year. For example, you take classes at both the middle school and the high school.	X	X		X		X		X	X	X
Mentorship. You work with an adult who has specific expertise in your area of interest. Mentorships must be carefully planned with input from parents, the mentor, and school personnel. Generally, you work on a project and meet with the mentor once a week to discuss your progress.	X	X	X		X			X		X
Summer Program, Semester Schools, Other Specialization Schools. These options are typically residential, where you live away from home. Some grant high school or college credit. Semester schools offer a variety of semester-long educational opportunities, usually with an academic focus such as the environment (see Conserve School in northern Wisconsin). Programs may provide scholarships.	X	X		X	X				X	X
Grade Acceleration. Students who score extremely high on out-of-level exams such as the ACT or SAT may be able to skip a grade level. You need to be highly motivated to do this. Use of a thorough assessment process like the Iowa Acceleration Scale and ongoing support is recommended.	X In all subjects		X			X			X	X In all subjects
AP, IB, Honors, College in High School. Advanced, accelerated, or college-level courses may be offered in your school district (or sometimes online) and can allow you to "test out of" or earn credit for college courses while still in high school.	X	X	X		X	X			X	X

continued

Which Options Are Right for Me? Program Options and Requirements (continued)

Program Options	Requirements									
	Achieves well above grade level	Has strong interest in subject	Can spend time outside school	Is ready to leave school or home	Likes in-depth study	Enjoys great challenge	Works at fast pace	Works alone or at own pace	Works with ability peers	Is motivated and self-directed
Post-Secondary Youth Options. About half of U.S. states allow high school juniors and seniors who meet certain requirements to take courses at state universities or other institutions, earning credits that count toward both high school graduation and college credit. You do not pay the college fees if a similar course is unavailable in your district.	X	X	X	X	X	X		X	X	X
Study Abroad. You can gain life experience and increase your independence and cultural awareness by spending a summer, semester, or year living and studying in another country.	X		X	X						X
Early College Admission. You may be able to take extra classes during the year or in the summer to earn enough credits to graduate early. Sometimes credit can be awarded through examination rather than completing a course. You usually need approval from your high school principal and school board.	X In all subjects			X	X	X			X	X In all subjects
Gap Year. Some colleges allow you to defer admission and spend a year or semester exploring faraway places, getting involved in community service, or digging deeper into a career that interests you.	X			X						X

My Advocates

List four or more people you know who can help you create your own unique educational path.

Name (for example, Mr. Jones)	Relationship (for example, math teacher)

Ten Tips for Talking to Teachers*

Are you having a problem with a class or an assignment? Can you see room for improvement in how a subject is taught? Do you have a better idea for a special project or term paper? Don't just tell your friends. Talk to the teacher! Many students don't know how to go about doing this. The following suggestions are meant to make it easier for everyone—students *and* teachers.

1. **Make an appointment to meet and talk.** This shows the teacher that you're serious and you have some understanding of his or her busy schedule. Tell the teacher about how much time you'll need, be flexible, and don't be late.

2. **If you know other students who feel the way you do, consider approaching the teacher together.** There's strength in numbers. If a teacher hears the same thing from four or five people, he or she is more likely to do something about it.

3. **Think through what you want to say before you go into your meeting with the teacher.** Write down your questions or concerns. Make a list of the items you want to cover. You may even want to copy your list for the teacher so both of you can consult it during your meeting. (Or consider giving it to the teacher ahead of time.)

4. **Choose your words carefully.** *Example:* Instead of saying, "I hate doing reports; they're boring and a waste of time," try, "Is there some other way I could satisfy this requirement? Could I do a video instead?" Strike the word *boring* from your vocabulary. It's a negative and meaningless buzzword for teachers.

5. **Don't expect the teacher to do all the work or propose all the answers.** Be prepared to make suggestions, offer solutions, even recommend resources. The teacher will appreciate that you took the initiative.

6. **Be diplomatic, tactful, and respectful.** Teachers have feelings, too. And they're more likely to be responsive if you remember that the purpose of your meeting is conversation, not confrontation.

7. **Focus on what you need, not on what you think the teacher is doing wrong.** The more the teacher learns about you, the more he or she will be able to help. The more defensive the teacher feels, the less he or she will want to help.

8. **Don't forget to listen.** Strange but true, many students need practice in this essential skill. The purpose of your meeting isn't just to hear yourself talk.

9. **Bring your sense of humor.** Not necessarily the joke-telling sense of humor, but the one that lets you laugh at yourself and your own misunderstandings and mistakes.

10. **If your meeting isn't successful, get help from another adult.** "Successful" doesn't necessarily mean that you emerged victorious. Even if the teacher denies your request, your meeting can still be judged successful. If you had a real conversation— if you communicated openly, listened carefully, and respected each other's points of view—then congratulate yourself on a great meeting. If the air crackled with tension, the meeting fell apart, and you felt disrespected (or acted disrespectful), then it's time to bring in another adult. *Suggestions:* a guidance counselor, the gifted program coordinator, or another teacher you know and trust who seems likely to support you and advocate for you. Once you've found help, approach your teacher and try again.

*From *When Gifted Kids Don't Have All the Answers: How to Meet Their Social and Emotional Needs* by Judy Galbraith, M.A., and Jim Delisle, Ph.D. (Free Spirit Publishing, 2015). Used with permission.

Questions to Consider When Creating a Self-Advocacy Action Plan

Your Goal Statement:

Discussion Questions for Students and Advocates to Consider

As you set your goals and create your plan, think through the following questions. If you don't know the answer to a question, name a person who might help you find out. *Note: Not all questions will pertain to all students' situations.*

1. **Self-Advocacy Step #1: Understand My Rights and Responsibilities**
   - Are there district policies I need to consider regarding this plan?

   - Are there state (or provincial) laws that impact the plan?

   - How will this plan affect my graduation?

   - How will this plan affect my college admission?

   - What are the consequences if I don't follow through on my plan?

2. **Self-Advocacy Step #2: Develop My Learner Profile**
   - How does this plan address my unique needs?

   - Am I truly interested in following this plan?

   - How will the plan improve my life in general?

   - What skills do I need to work on to be successful with my plan?

continued ➤

Questions to Consider When Creating a Self-Advocacy Action Plan (continued)

3. **Self-Advocacy Step #3: Investigate My Options**
   - ◆ What options are already available in my community related to this plan?

   - ◆ What would I have to create or find on my own?

   - ◆ How do I check for quality in these options?

   - ◆ Is there a precedent in my school that will help my chances of success? Any that will hinder it?

   - ◆ Is there a cost involved with this plan? If so, who pays it?

   - ◆ Do I want credit for following my plan?

4. **Self-Advocacy Step #4: Connect with Advocates**
   - ◆ Who must approve this plan?
     - ○ Parent
     - ○ Teacher
     - ○ Department Chair
     - ○ Gifted Program Coordinator
     - ○ Counselor
     - ○ Principal
     - ○ Superintendent
     - ○ School Board
     - ○ State Department of Education
     - ○ Other _____
   - ◆ What will I do if someone says no?

   - ◆ Who is apt to be supportive?

   - ◆ Who else might benefit from my plan?

   - ◆ Who can help keep me on track?

Action Plan		
Goal Statement:		
Implementation: Action Steps	**Person(s) Responsible**	**Date to Be Completed**
1.		

Resources

The Gifted Teen Survival Guide: Smart, Sharp, and Ready for (Almost) Anything. Judy Galbraith and Jim Delisle. Minneapolis: Free Spirit Publishing, 2011.

Smart Teens' Guide to Living with Intensity: How to Get More Out of Life and Learning. Lisa Rivero. Scottsdale, AZ: Great Potential Press, 2010.

What to Do When Good Enough Isn't Good Enough: The Real Deal on Perfectionism: A Guide for Kids. Thomas Greenspon. Minneapolis: Free Spirit Publishing, 2007.

Davidson Institute for Talent Development (davidsongifted.org).

Hoagies' Gifted Education Page (hoagiesgifted.org). Lots and lots of great resources on all things gifted.

Jack Kent Cooke Foundation (jkcf.org). Dedicated to advancing the education of highly gifted students who have financial need.

Websites for Learner Profile Information

Cognitive Ability

- Mensa International (mensa.org/workout)
- Hoagies' Talent Search Programs Page (hoagiesgifted.org/talent_search.htm)

Learning Strengths

- Purdue Academic and Vocational Rating Scales (iu19giftednetwork.wikispaces.com/file/view /Purdue_scales.doc)

- Renzulli Scales for Rating the Behavioral Characteristics of Superior Students (prufrock.com/assets/clientpages/pdfs /Renzulli_Scales_Sample_Copyright_Prufrock _Press_2013.pdf)

Interests

- The Interest-A-Lyzer (www.researchgate.net/publication/267373715)
- The Secondary Interest-A-Lyzer (www.prufrock.com/Assets/ClientPages/pdfs/SEM _Web_Resources/Secondary%20Interest-A-Lyzer .pdf)

Learning Preferences

- Learning Styles Assessment (how-to-study.com/learning-style-assessment)
- Visual-Spatial Resource (visualspatial.org)

Personality Traits

- Ten Item Personality Measure (The Big Five) (gosling.psy.utexas.edu/scales-weve-developed)
- Authentic Happiness (optimism questionnaire, plus more interesting assessments) (authentichappiness.sas.upenn.edu)
- *Psychology Today* Extroversion/Introversion Test (www.psychologytoday.com/tests/personality /extroversion-introversion-test)
- 10 Myths About Introverts (carlkingdom.com/10-myths-about-introverts)

My Greatest Gripes and Things I'd Love to Change:

Express Yourself Talent Search

Name:

Name 3 words that rhyme with *cast*.	Draw an elephant.	Sing the last line of your country's national anthem.	Draw an oak leaf.	Solve this equation: 3y + 10 = 2y + 20	Describe the route from here to the vehicle you rode in today.
Pantomime pitching a softball or baseball.	Give your own definition of *love*.	**EXPRESS YOURSELF TALENT SEARCH**		Name a favorite author.	Name a great philosopher.
Balance on one foot.	Draw the outline of Wisconsin.			Do your favorite dance move. (Ballet? Tap? Waltz? Salsa? Hip Hop?)	Name a scientific theory.
Hum or sing a TV theme song.	Give the chemical formula for salt.	Name your best friend's favorite color.	Name 3 dog breeds or types of fish.	Name 3 organizations you belong to.	Recite a line of poetry.

Great Gripes of Gifted Kids

Put a check mark next to any gripes you have. Cross out any that don't apply to you. Write a comment or two about your personal experience.

_____ **1.** No one explains what being gifted is all about—it's kept a big secret.

_____ **2.** Our friends and classmates don't always understand us, and they don't see all of our different sides.

_____ **3.** Parents, teachers, and even our friends expect too much of us.

_____ **4.** Kids often tease us about being smart.

_____ **5.** The stuff we do in school is too easy and it's boring.

_____ **6.** We miss out on activities other kids get to do while we're in gifted class.

_____ **7.** We have to do extra work in school.

_____ **8.** When we finish our schoolwork early, we often aren't allowed to work ahead.

_____ **9.** Other kids ask us for too much help.

_____ **10.** Tests, tests, and more tests!

_____ **11.** We feel overwhelmed by the number of things we can do in life.

_____ **12.** We worry about world problems and feel helpless to do anything about them.

Character Trait Card: Perfectionism

From *The Power of Self-Advocacy for Gifted Learners* by Deb Douglas, copyright © 2018. Free Spirit Publishing Inc.; freespirit.com.

Suppose on the first day of school, your language arts teacher announces this assignment:

"Write a five-paragraph essay on the theme: *The greatest lesson I learned over the summer.* Please do your best on this assignment, because I will be using your essay to determine your writing workshop goals for the first quarter."

Which of these scenarios comes closest to your response?

a. In study hall that afternoon, you write one paragraph about each of the five video games you mastered over the summer. You show it to your friend who thinks it's pretty cool. You print it and put it in your notebook for the next day. It seems good enough.

b. You choose the topic of personal independence and expand on three experiences you had during the summer that made you more independent: a part-time job, going to camp, and learning to ride a moped. Next, you write a clear introduction and conclusion. Then you use spell and grammar check, ask your friend to proof it, and make revisions. You read it again in the morning before printing it out just in case you missed something. You feel you've done a good job in demonstrating your writing skills, which was the teacher's goal for this assignment.

c. Since you were really immersed in political news over the summer, you decide to write on the importance of democracy. You stop at the library after school and bring home several books that provide expert opinions and associated research. At home, you Google "value of democracy" and get almost a million hits. You spend the rest of the day (and night) reading, writing, rereading, and rewriting. Around midnight, your parents say you must go to bed, but you can't because your essay "isn't good enough yet." The next day you hand in a *ten-page* essay, telling the teacher, "This isn't really my best work, but if I have a few more days, I can revise it some more."

If the third scenario sounds familiar, you may be a *perfectionist*. You set high standards for everything you do, worry about disappointing others, and do whatever you can to avoid what feels like failure. Gifted people tend to exhibit perfectionism at higher levels than the general population. When used adaptively, as in striving for excellence, perfectionism can motivate you to reach your goals. On the other hand, unhealthy, maladaptive perfectionism could drive you to pursue an unattainable ideal.

continued

Character Trait Card: Perfectionism (continued)

Problematic Perfectionism in the Classroom

What it looks like:

◆ You hesitate to start homework because you feel you're not going to do it "right."

◆ You procrastinate because doing it "right" takes a lot of time and focus.

◆ You obsess over errors when your homework is returned.

◆ You repeatedly start over to make your work perfect.

◆ You are excessively neat.

◆ You are distressed if you make mistakes or get a low grade.

◆ You are more focused on grades than on learning something new and challenging.

◆ You are dissatisfied with a quality of work that others find acceptable.

◆ You are slow to participate in discussions so you don't answer inaccurately or incompletely.

What you can do:

◆ Begin by changing your thinking.

◆ Make a list: "Why it's okay for me to make mistakes!"

◆ Refer to your list often.

◆ Match your time commitment to the goals of your assignments.

◆ Know when "good enough is good enough," even if it isn't perfect.

◆ Remind yourself to place greater value on your *effort* than on your grade.

◆ Set your own assignment goals that reflect your personal need for growth and challenge.

◆ Enlist your teachers in helping you combat perfectionism. (They may not realize that they are partially responsible for it!)

◆ Ask your school counselor to start a book study on combating perfectionism.

What do you think? Does this trait fit your own learner profile?

ASSIGNMENT

❖ Individually, complete the Perfectionism portion of your "GT Carpe Diem Learner Profile Assessments" handout.

❖ As a group, prepare a three- to five-minute presentation that covers the most important aspects of these characteristics and summarizes your group members' assessment scores.

❖ Place a sticky note on the continuum of the Perfectionism wall chart to indicate your assessed trait.

Character Trait Card: Extroverts and Introverts

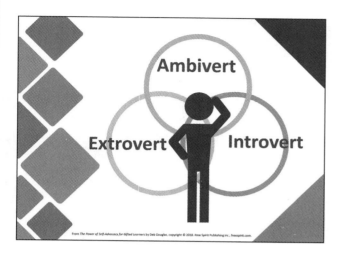

Suppose you are considering joining the cross-country team. At the informational meeting, which scenario *best* describes how you act?

a. You walk in chattering with a group of friends and sit in the front of the room. As you listen to the coach describe the season, you imagine the fun bus rides to the meets and the excitement of running with dozens of other athletes. When the coach asks for questions, you eagerly raise your hand and make a witty remark that gets everyone laughing. At the end of the meeting, you quickly fill out the sign-up form, thinking, "This is going to be great!"

b. You walk into the meeting with a close friend and you both sit off to the side toward the back of the room. As you listen to the coach describe the season, you imagine yourself running swiftly and quietly along the course, concentrating on your pace, your breathing, your heartbeat. The coach asks for questions, but you wait until after the meeting to talk with her privately. As you are leaving you think, "This sounds like something I'd like to do." But you take the sign-up form home to give it more serious thought before committing.

The first scenario illustrates common traits of *extroversion*, the second one *introversion*.

Reflecting on this trait may be especially important to helping you understand yourself. In the general population, extroverts outnumber introverts three to one. However, among gifted individuals it's the opposite: introverts outnumber extroverts three to one.

Extroverted people often:

◆ gain energy from external sources, such as people, activities, and objects

◆ are very social and make a lot of friends easily

◆ are comfortable joining groups, speaking up, and being the center of attention

◆ make decisions quickly, take risks, and learn by doing

◆ develop their thoughts from bits of information in short-term memory

Introverted people often:

◆ gain energy from their inner world of ideas, opinions, and emotions

◆ have only a few close friends or prefer to be alone

◆ are quiet in groups and feel drained by interactions with people

◆ concentrate intensely, need time to make decisions, and learn by observing

◆ recall their thoughts from long-term memory to build more complex connections

There is no right or wrong, better or worse. We all fall somewhere along the continuum between introversion and extroversion. People who seem to bounce between the two are sometimes called ambiverts. Recognizing your natural inclination and the tendencies of those around you may help you make better sense of social situations. Are you the life of the party? Or would you rather sit quietly and watch what's going on? (Or maybe not go to the party at all!) Introverts aren't necessarily shy, but they often prefer to be in their own inner world.

continued ➤

Character Trait Card: Extroverts and Introverts (continued)

Introverts and Extroverts in the Classroom

In the regular classroom, when students work in groups and actively participate in lively discussions, there's a lot of social interaction that energizes extroverts. Introverts, however, may feel increasingly drained. Alternately, when a lesson involves quiet individual research and reflection, introverts may thrive. But extroverts may lose interest, becoming inattentive, and possibly disruptive.

So, what can you do to increase your comfort level in the classroom?

◆ Recognize that you don't need fixing. Diversity of personality traits is natural.

◆ Reflect on how teachers and peers may perceive your tendencies.

◆ Make an appointment and privately talk with your teacher about your introversion/extroversion and how it affects your participation in class.

◆ Ask your teacher to allow choices in how students work and demonstrate what they have learned: independently, with chosen partners, or in small groups.

◆ Challenge yourself to go against your type once in a while. For example, as an extrovert, make one comment during a group discussion and then wait to contribute again until you've listened to several other students speak. As an introvert, ask the teacher for the discussion questions in advance, formulate your responses, and be the first to raise your hand.

What do you think? Do either of these traits fit your learner profile?

ASSIGNMENT

❖ Individually, complete the Extroverts/Introverts portion of your "GT Carpe Diem Learner Profile Assessments" handout.

❖ As a group, prepare a three- to five-minute presentation that covers the most important aspects of these characteristics and summarizes your group members' assessment scores.

❖ Place a sticky note on the continuum of the Extroverts/Introverts wall chart to indicate your assessed trait.

Character Trait Card: Analytical Minds and Creative Minds

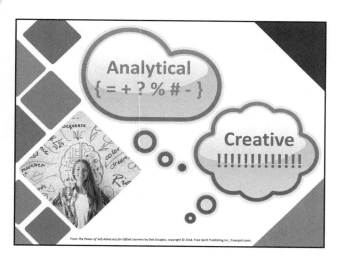

From *The Power of Self-Advocacy for Gifted Learners* by Deb Douglas, copyright © 2018. Free Spirit Publishing Inc.; freespirit.com.

Suppose you are walking down the street when someone asks you for directions to the library. Which of these sounds more like the way you would respond?

a. "The most efficient route is to go south for two blocks and then turn east onto King Avenue. Go five blocks on King and then turn north onto Main Street. The library will be on your right."

b. "It's not that far away. Keep going straight until you get to the post office (pointing ahead), which is just after the railroad tracks. Then you turn left (pointing left). You've gone too far if you get to Costco. So, keep going straight and at the first light, there's a Starbucks on your right and a Pizza Hut across from it. Turn left and you'll see the big Public Library sign."

People are said to prefer one type of thinking over the other. The directions in the first example might be given by a person with a preference for *analytical thinking* (logic and objectivity) while the second set of directions sound more like a person with a preference for *creative thinking* (intuition and subjectivity).

It's important to remember, however, that while we might have a natural tendency toward one way of thinking or the other, the various parts of our brain work together in complex ways.

The **analytical** parts of our brains:
◆ focus on the verbal
◆ process information more sequentially
◆ look first at the pieces, then put them together to get the whole
◆ process what we hear
◆ handle most of the duties of speaking
◆ carry out logic and exact mathematical computations
◆ retrieve facts from our memory

The **creative** parts of our brains:
◆ process information intuitively and simultaneously
◆ look first at the whole picture, then the details
◆ control spatial abilities, facial recognition, and music processing
◆ make rough mathematical estimations and comparisons
◆ comprehend visual imagery and make sense of what we see
◆ play a role in language, particularly in interpreting context and a person's tone

There is no right or wrong, better or worse tendency for analytical or creative thinking. We all fall somewhere along the continuum. What is important is to be aware that there are different ways of thinking, and by knowing what your natural inclination is, you can also pay attention to your less dominant trait and find areas for improvement.

continued ➤

Character Trait Card: Analytical Minds and Creative Minds (continued)

Analytical and Creative Minds in the Classroom

If your mind is more **analytical**, you might prefer to work alone, read independently, and incorporate research into your papers. You also may dislike distraction and prefer learning in a quiet classroom.

For example, if your science class is beginning a unit on the human brain, these are some of the instructional strategies you might prefer:

◆ The teacher writes outlines of the unit and of the daily lessons on the board.

◆ The teacher delivers a lecture (especially if she/he is an expert on the subject and passionate about it).

◆ Class makes a list of vocabulary words and discusses them.

◆ Students work alone on independent research, focusing on the big concepts relating to the brain (for example, cognition, sensory input, emotions, diseases).

◆ Students write a research paper on the brain that includes both scientific details and conceptual analysis.

If your mind is more **creative**, you might prefer to work in groups, see concepts as well as hear them, and show what you've learned through art projects, drama, creative writing, and graphic design.

Using the brain unit as an example, these are some of the instructional strategies you might prefer:

◆ During a lecture, students have study guide outlines to fill in as the teacher talks.

◆ Students draw illustrations, arrows, and other symbols in the margins of the study guide.

◆ Students participate in group activities.

◆ Students create a project (such as a play/poem/song/story or a poster/chart/map of the brain and its functions) in lieu of writing a paper.

◆ Students research and then write a paper focusing on the big concepts related to the brain (for example, cognition, sensory input, emotions, diseases) using the real-life story of an individual with either exceptional or diminished mental capabilities.

What do you think? Do any of these traits fit your own learner profile?

ASSIGNMENT

❖ Individually, complete the Analytical Minds and Creative Minds portion of your "GT Carpe Diem Learner Profile Assessments."

❖ As a group, prepare a three- to five-minute presentation that covers the most important aspects of these characteristics and summarizes your group members' assessment scores.

❖ Place a sticky note on the continuum of Analytical/Creative wall chart to indicate your assessed trait.

Learner Profile Wall Charts

These charts are used in Activity 3.3.

Instructions:

- Using poster paper, create wall charts (like the graphic below) for each of the following character traits:
  - Introvert/Extrovert
  - Optimist/Pessimist
  - Perfectionist
  - Motivated/Unmotivated
  - Analytical/Creative
- The charts should be approximately 18" x 36".
- Students will place their sticky notes in the appropriate place on each continuum to indicate the results of their assessments.

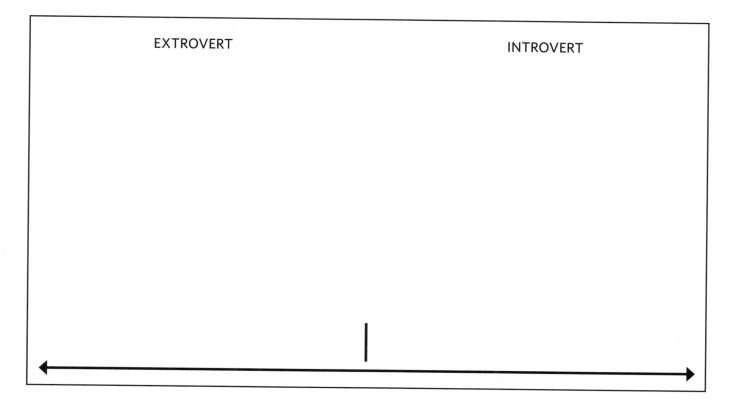

Pre-Workshop Student Survey

Name _____ Age ___ Grade ___ Gender ___ School District _____

Please complete this side **before** the GT Carpe Diem Workshop.

1. How comfortable are you asking a teacher to modify something to make your work more challenging or interesting?

0	1	2	3	4	5	6	7	8	9	10
very uncomfortable				okay			very comfortable			

2. How comfortable are you having your parent ask a teacher to modify something for you?

0	1	2	3	4	5	6	7	8	9	10
very uncomfortable				okay			very comfortable			

3. How often have teachers asked you to do something different from the rest of the class to make your work more challenging or interesting?

0	1	2	3	4	5	6	7	8	9	10
never				occasionally			always			

4. How often have you **wished** a teacher would modify something for you?

0	1	2	3	4	5	6	7	8	9	10
never				occasionally			always			

5. How often have you **asked** a teacher to modify something for you?

0	1	2	3	4	5	6	7	8	9	10
never				occasionally			always			

6. How likely are you to talk with someone soon at your school about better meeting your needs?

0	1	2	3	4	5	6	7	8	9	10
not likely				likely			very likely			

7. Has anyone talked with you about what it means to be gifted? ___ yes ___ no If yes, who was it?
___ parent ___ teacher ___ gifted coordinator ___ school counselor ___ other: _____

8. Has anyone talked with you about programming for gifted students in your district? ___ yes ___ no
___ parent ___ teacher ___ gifted coordinator ___ school counselor ___ other: _____

9. Has anyone encouraged you to talk with your school about better meeting your needs? ___ yes ___no
___ parent ___ teacher ___ gifted coordinator ___ school counselor ___ other: _____

10. Have you created your own individual route to graduation that may be different from the norm?
___ yes ___no   If yes, please describe what you are doing differently.

11. During this school year, are you in any of these settings?
___ gifted school   ___ gifted classroom   ___ gifted group within a classroom

12. So far this year, how often have you been grouped to work with other students at your ability level?

0	1	2	3	4	5	6	7	8	9	10
never				occasionally			always			

STOP! Do not complete the other side until after the workshop.

Post-Workshop Student Survey

Please complete this side **after** the GT Carpe Diem Workshop.

After participating in today's workshop:

1. How comfortable are you asking a teacher to modify something for you?

0	1	2	3	4	5	6	7	8	9	10
very uncomfortable				okay			very comfortable			

2. How comfortable are you having your parent ask a teacher to modify something for you?

0	1	2	3	4	5	6	7	8	9	10
very uncomfortable				okay			very comfortable			

3. How likely are you to talk with someone soon at your school about better meeting your needs?

0	1	2	3	4	5	6	7	8	9	10
not likely				likely			very likely			

4. Do you have a greater understanding of what it means to be gifted? ___ yes ___ no Comments?

5. Do you have a greater understanding of your own learner profile? ___ yes ___ no Comments?

6. Which of these learner profile assessments helped you discover more about yourself?

__ Analytic/Creative __ Perfectionism __ Introvert/Extrovert

__ Overexcitabilities __ Optimist/Pessimist __ Learning Preferences

7. What is the most important thing you have learned about yourself today?

8. Do you want to create a unique route to graduation? ___ yes ___ no
If yes, what things would you like to do differently?

9. Do you feel better prepared to self-advocate? ___ yes ___ no Comments?

10. What is your action plan goal?

11. Would you recommend this workshop to other gifted students? ___ yes ___ no Comments?

12. How could this workshop be improved to better address your needs?

13. Please rate your overall experience today:

0	1	2	3	4	5	6	7	8	9	10
poor				okay			great			

Comments:

INDEX

To download the GT Carpe Diem Workshop materials and other digital content for this book, visit **freespirit.com/self-advocacy-forms**. Use the password **2empower**.

ABOUT THE AUTHOR

Deb Douglas consults and advocates for gifted kids in the Upper Midwest and beyond, specializing in workshops that help kids take charge of their own educations. Her original research on empowering gifted students to self-advocate was published in *The Roeper Review* and *Parenting for High Potential* more than a dozen years ago. She is a frequent presenter at national and state conferences. Previously she was the gifted education coordinator for the Manitowoc (WI) Public School District for fifteen years and developed their International Baccalaureate Diploma Program. She began her career teaching high school English, speech, and theater, and then served as a gifted resource teacher  for seven years. She was president of the Wisconsin Association for Talented and Gifted from 2011 to 2013 and a board member for nine years.

Deb's guilty pleasures include travel, British murder mysteries, kayaking, gardening, morning coffee, and *The New York Times* crossword. She is the mother, stepmother, and mother-in-law of five uniquely talented adults, and grandmother to the magnificent Miles and awesome Anthony. She lives in Madison, Wisconsin, with her husband, Ramon Aldag—professor of business at the University of Wisconsin, Madison—and their wickedly gifted Bichon, Lily. She can be reached via her website www.gtcarpediem.com, Twitter @debdouglas52, and facebook.com/GTCarpeDiem.

Other Great Resources from Free Spirit

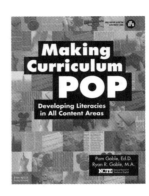
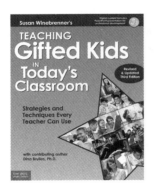